The Filmmaker's Philosopher

The Filmmaker's Philosopher

Merab Mamardashvili and Russian Cinema

Alyssa DeBlasio

EDINBURGH
University Press

Edinburgh University Press is one of the leading university presses in the UK. We publish academic books and journals in our selected subject areas across the humanities and social sciences, combining cutting-edge scholarship with high editorial and production values to produce academic works of lasting importance. For more information visit our website: edinburghuniversitypress.com

© Alyssa DeBlasio, 2019, 2021

Edinburgh University Press Ltd
The Tun—Holyrood Road
12 (2f) Jackson's Entry
Edinburgh EH8 8PJ

First published in hardback by Edinburgh University Press 2019

Typeset in Monotype Ehrhardt by
Servis Filmsetting Ltd, Stockport, Cheshire

A CIP record for this book is available from the British Library

ISBN 978 1 4744 4448 4 (hardback)
ISBN 978 1 4744 4449 1 (paperback)
ISBN 978 1 4744 4450 7 (webready PDF)
ISBN 978 1 4744 4451 4 (epub)

The right of Alyssa DeBlasio to be identified as author of this work has been asserted in accordance with the Copyright, Designs and Patents Act 1988 and the Copyright and Related Rights Regulations 2003 (SI No. 2498).

Contents

List of Figures	vi
Acknowledgments	vii
Note on Transliteration and Translation	ix
Introduction: The Freest Man in the USSR	1
1. Alexander Sokurov's *Demoted* (1980): Consciousness as Celebration	30
2. Ivan Dykhovichnyi's *The Black Monk* (1988): Madness, Chekhov, and the Chimera of Idleness	57
3. Dmitry Mamuliya's *Another Sky* (2010): The Language of Consciousness	78
4. Alexei Balabanov's *The Castle* (1994) and *Me Too* (2012): Kafka, the Absurd, and the Death of Form	100
5. Alexander Zeldovich's *Target* (2011): Tolstoy and Mamardashvili on the Infinite and the Earthly	124
6. Vadim Abdrashitov and Alexander Mindadze's *The Train Stopped* (1982): Film as a Metaphor for Consciousness	147
Conclusion: Andrey Zvyagintsev's *Loveless* (2017): The Philosophical Image and the Possibilities of Film	160
Appendix	177
Bibliography	181
Index	196

Figures

I.1	Merab Mamardashvili, early 1970s	10
I.2	Mamardashvili as a student of philosophy, early 1950s	14
1.1	The demoted taxi driver in the early morning light	47
1.2	Water imagery in *Demoted*	51
2.1	Tania seems to address Kovrin by addressing the camera	60
2.2–2.3	Two monks: Dykhovichnyi's Andrei Kovrin and Tarkovsky's Andrei Rublev	72
2.4–2.5	Kovrin speaks to the camera when he speaks with the monk	73
3.1	Mamardashvili in *Should the Sighted Lead the Blind?*	85
4.1–4.2	Remote winter landscapes and religious symbolism in Balabanov's *Me Too* and *The Castle*	105
5.1	Zoia is measured by Viktor at 27 percent evil and 73 percent good	140
C.1	Zhenia runs on the treadmill in the snow	166

Acknowledgments

As with all large projects, the publication of this book calls for expressions of gratitude to friends and colleagues near and far, all of whom have generously offered their support in some way.

At the earliest stage of this project, as a fellow with the American Council of Learned Societies, I benefited from the generosity of Sergei Kapterev and Nikolai Izvolov (Institute of Cinematic Art, Moscow), who helped me locate important primary source material. I am grateful to the many film directors, especially Alexander Zeldovich, Olesia Fokina, and Dmitry Mamuliya, who shared their experiences in Mamardashvili's classroom. Alexander Kolbovsky, Olga Shervud, and Vsevolod Korshunov assisted in making important connections, while Anastasiya Khlopina was extremely valuable as my research assistant during the summer of 2017.

My work benefited from conversations with students and colleagues at the Slavic departments of the University of Virginia and Princeton University, where I was invited to talk about this project; thank you to Edith Clowes and Victoria Juharyan for making these visits possible. Conversations with the participants of the 20th Annual Russian Film Symposium, too many to name here, were instrumental as I completed the final chapter on Zvyagintsev.

Irina Anisimova, Andrew Chapman, Mikhail Epstein, Viktoriia Faibyshenko, Margaret Frohlich, Diana Gasparyan, Phil Grier, and Chauncey Maher provided valuable feedback on this work at various stages. I also extend thanks to my editors at Edinburgh University Press and the two peer reviewers, who captured the role of "anonymous reader" perfectly—by providing careful commentary that encouraged me to clarify my thinking at critical moments in the text, but in a way that was always in the spirit of the project I had set out to undertake. My friends and mentors, Nancy Condee, Phil Grier, Volodia Padunov, and Jim Scanlan, have been models for my work on the intersections of philosophy, literature, and film.

I am grateful for the support of Dickinson College Research and Development funds, which supported this project in several forms. My colleague, Elena, has created a departmental environment that is conducive to both vigorous research and rewarding teaching. My irreplaceable friends—Claire, Peggy, and Sarah—have since 2010 been encouraging faces across the table for many hours of writing and non-writing in the small town of Carlisle, PA.

My sincere gratitude goes out to Alena Mamardashvili and the Merab Mamardashvili Foundation for their permission to use the archival photographs included within.

It is commonplace to thank one's family, but indeed mine—Chris and Nina—has made me a more efficient writer and a more empathetic reader. They are always eager to join me on adventures and not only afforded me the extra time to do this work when the project hit critical moments, but are the reason for the work in the first place.

Note on Transliteration and Translation

All citations to Russian-language sources follow the Library of Congress system, i.e. in the notes, the bibliography, and the appendix.

Russian proper names pose particular challenges when writing in English. While there are several established systems for transliterating Russian into English, ranging from technical to reader-friendly, contemporary authors, critics, and filmmakers often have preferred English spellings of their own names, few of which conform to any of the accepted transliteration systems. In this book, I have tried to balance two things: readability (for non-specialists) and consistency (both within the text and with the way people spell their own names in English).

For these reasons, Russian proper names have been transliterated according to the Library of Congress system, with some important and widespread modifications. I have spelled well-known names according to their established English spellings: e.g. Tarkovsky instead of Tarkovskii and Tolstoy instead of Tolstoi. For prominent filmmakers and authors, I use the spellings that appear most frequently at international festivals and in English-language promotional materials and/or their preferred spelling of their own name: e.g. Andrey Zvyagintsev instead of Andrei Zviagintsev and Dmitry Mamuliya instead of Dmitrii Mamuliia. To facilitate reading, I have also removed diacritical marks from proper names even within the Library of Congress system, resulting in, for instance, Ilia instead of Il'ia and Evald instead of Eval'd.

These adjustments might initially be unfamiliar to scholars used to working with scholarly systems of Russian transliteration. It also means that certain common names appear in multiple ways in the text, depending on which spelling the name holder uses. My goal was to bring my transliteration choices in line with existing international film promotional materials and with the wishes of authors and filmmakers themselves, while also making the manuscript as accessible as possible to readers in other fields, especially those who do not read Russian.

All translations are my own unless otherwise noted.

INTRODUCTION

The Freest Man in the USSR

> The kind of freedom that Pushkin possessed is not something he could, say, pass on to his pupils. It is no coincidence that he didn't have a school of followers.
> Merab Mamardashvili, *Cartesian Meditations* (1981)[1]

> Why do you consider Tarkovsky a good director?
> It's because he died, and even Pushkin said that this country loves only the dead.
> Merab Mamardashvili, interview (1991)[2]

Merab Mamardashvili has been called many things: the Georgian Socrates of Soviet philosophy, a lighthouse of the late-Soviet intelligentsia, a pioneer in using cognition as a form of resistance against state authority, a gifted orator in the classical tradition, and even a "preeminent theologian."[3] He was Merab Konstantinovich within the conventions of Russian formality, he was Merab to his friends, and to Marxist philosopher Louis Althusser he was "my dearest Merab," a confidant abroad, and a "sympathetic brother."[4] Between 1966 and his death in 1990 at age sixty, philosopher Merab Mamardashvili taught and worked at some of the most prestigious institutions in Moscow and Tbilisi, including Moscow State University, the institutes of the Russian Academy of Sciences, the Academy of Pedagogical Sciences, and Tbilisi State University.[5] He was one of only a handful of Soviet-born practitioners of a European, French-influenced style of philosophical discourse that, in Mamardashvili's case, bordered at times on a form of Marxist existentialism, given both his methodological foundation in Marxist analysis and his commitment to investigating the human experience. Though his name was nearly unknown outside the communist bloc, his lectures drew crowds of listeners from across the social strata of Soviet society—"from intellectuals to hairdressers," as one attendee summarized the make-up of his audiences.[6] His presence behind the podium came to represent liberal ideals of freedom and cosmopolitanism that had no place within the official discourse of Soviet academia of the era. As one of his students remarked: "Like many of my peers, I went to his lectures the way people go to church."[7]

Important for my purposes in this book is the little-known fact that between 1977 and 1990, Mamardashvili taught the required courses in philosophy at the country's two leading film schools: the All-Union State Institute of Cinematography (VGIK) and the Higher Courses for Scriptwriters and Directors, both in Moscow. This means that any director, screenwriter, cinematographer, or film professional of any kind who passed through one of these two film schools during those years, as many did, would have encountered Mamardashvili in some way. In Moscow in the 1970s and 1980s, Mamardashvili taught and worked alongside a long list of internationally recognized directors, including Alexander Sokurov (Cannes Festival regular and winner of the Golden Lion at Venice), Pavel Lungin (Best Director at Cannes and Golden Eagle for Best Motion Picture), Alexei Balabanov, Ivan Dykhovichnyi, Vladimir Khotinenko, and Alexander Zeldovich. His influence also extends to film professionals in other spheres, most notably to Sergei Shumakov (director of the Russia-K/Kultura TV channel), to journalist and TV host Alexander Arkhangelsky, and to producer-mogul Sergei Selianov, who attended Mamardashvili's courses in philosophy at VGIK in the late 1970s.[8]

Mamardashvili's status among the Moscow intelligentsia also meant that he mingled with leading figures of the older generation of film professionals. Among them were screenwriter Nataliia Riazantseva and director Larisa Shepitko, the latter of whom reportedly sought his opinion on her script for the ill-fated *Farewell to Matyora* (*Proshchanie s Materoi*, 1983).[9] He worked alongside the country's most talented animators, including Fedor Khitruk, Andrei Khrzhanovskii, and Yuri Norshtein. There was also actor Aleksandr Kaidanovskii, who played the role of "stalker" in Andrei Tarkovsky's film of the same name, and who in the early 1980s studied simultaneously under Tarkovsky and Mamardashvili at the Higher Courses for Scriptwriters and Directors. Even directors who did not pass through one of Russia's two main film schools have claimed intellectual affinity to Mamardashvili. One such "outsider" is two-time Academy Award nominee Andrey Zvyagintsev, who did not study film in Moscow but has quoted Mamardashvili in interviews, to the extent that critics have interpreted Zvyagintsev's paraphrases of Mamardashvili's ideas as among the director's original aphorisms. Mamardashvili's legacy in the film industry is also apparent in the more than ten films that have been made about him posthumously.

The task of this book is to investigate Mamardashvili's role in the Russian cinematic imagination, keeping in mind that there is no single formula to describe or capture his influence. Dykhovichnyi and Mamuliya speak of the philosopher's direct influence on their creative work, while for Zeldovich, "Mamardashvili stayed in [his] mind more as an image than as a thought."[10] Sokurov describes the importance of his study under Mamardashvili in the 1970s, though he admits that at the time he did not attach to those lectures the profound significance they would have for him later.[11] At the other end of the spectrum of influence resides Norshtein, who reports that the two never had a single intellectual conversation, though they spent six years as colleagues at the Higher Courses.[12] Balabanov's classmates have described how they listened with "open mouths" while Alexei Oktiabrinovich, the misanthropic prodigy of post-Soviet cinema, sat in the back of the auditorium and "did not find the lectures of legendary philosopher Merab Mamardashvili particularly interesting."[13] When Khotinenko was asked about Mamardashvili, however, he recalled "the smell of tobacco . . . and an unhurried tempo of speech. He was a true philosopher. I know only one true philosopher: Merab Mamardashvili."[14]

In his 2016 study of contemporary Russian cinema, Vlad Strukov distills the majority of criticism on recent Russian film into several categories of inquiry: thematic studies (e.g. war and patriotism), Cultural Studies (e.g. power, ideology, identity), and studies of individual directors and personalities who are often taken to represent parts of the broader Russian cinema market and aesthetic canon.[15] My book takes the very different approach of intellectual legacy and generation, offering a new way to engage philosophically with filmmakers that appear to share nothing except their expressed connections—some more direct, and some less direct—to the intellectual phenomenon that was Merab Mamardashvili at the twilight of the Soviet century. One significant difference between the approach I engage here and much of the existing work on film-philosophy in the Russian Studies context is that I do not propose we use philosophical ideas as an interpretive lens, but instead propose that we start at the moments where we already find historical affinities between philosophical and cinematic texts. When we consider the Russian film industry in the context of its own rich intellectual history, we open up the possibility for individual films to engage philosophically with viewers on their own terms.

To be clear, I am not arguing that we try to identify Mamardashvili with any "school" of filmmaking, or that we draw artificial links, aesthetic or conceptual, among the directors of his generation. Neither am I arguing in this study for a vision of Soviet continuity, which might attempt to position the films of Mamardashvili's students as sharing some common cinematic grammar that we could trace from the late-Soviet period to the present. Alexei Yurchak argues that the concept of generation has less to do with birthdate or chronology as it does "a certain shared experience or events shared by all."[16] Generational markers can be strong or tenuous, absent or present, and are often expressed in dramatically different ways among individuals sharing similar experiences. In Karl Mannheim's 1923 essay "The Problem of Generations," he emphasizes the importance of the "identity of location" to shared modes of thought, or what he calls the "mental climate" of a generation.[17] What I argue in this book is not that these directors see themselves as an artistic unit (they do not) or that we should try to force such a category upon them (we should not), but that we can view them as a cinematic *generation*—that many of them have expressed the presence of Mamardashvili's influence in some way, that many carry with them a memory of Mamardashvili as embodying an important cultural turn of late Socialism, and that their work often lends itself to dialogue with Mamardashvili's philosophy insofar as many of them came of age in that very intellectual climate that Mamardashvili's voice and presence came to define.[18]

The philosophical concern that permeated nearly all Mamardashvili's work was a broadly construed understanding of human consciousness—the epistemological, sometimes metaphysical, and (in his later work) moral dimensions of the nature of thought. He saw himself as engaged in the "inner archeology" of the complex web of human consciousness, which reveals itself only incompletely, and only through rigorous self-contemplation; we must "search *in* ourselves and transcribe and grasp *through* ourselves," as Mamardashvili explained.[19] Though Mamardashvili developed the same themes for more or less his entire career, and despite the celebrity that he enjoyed among the Soviet intelligentsia, a school of thought never crystalized around him. Just as we cannot speak of a Mamardashvili school of filmmaking, neither is there a Mamardashvili school of philosophy, in the way that Mamardashvili himself argued that Alexander Pushkin had no disciples. As Mamardashvili put it, Russia's great poet possessed the "Pushkinian phenomenon of freedom," understood as "freedom and power over oneself," but also a freedom from both the restrictions and supports of convention.[20]

Beginning in the late 1950s, philosophy became a graduation requirement for all undergraduate degrees in the Soviet Union, as it remains in Russia today. Thus, between 1966 and his death in 1990, Mamardashvili taught introductory courses in philosophy to students of all professions and vocations, at universities all over Moscow and in Tbilisi, as well as elsewhere in the Soviet Union, educating future politicians, psychologists, artists, film professionals, and engineers of the communist bloc. The nomadic element of Mamardashvili's career, during which he moved around Moscow's universities until he was repatriated to his native Georgia by Soviet authorities in 1980, meant that it was impossible for a centralized school of thought to form around his work in any one institution or location. The precariousness of his position was, in a direct way, his punishment for speaking so openly on topics that were not allowed within the official discourse of Soviet academia.

At the same time, his institutional mobility opened up new possibilities for interdisciplinary freedom and challenged the historical rigidity of the Soviet academic structure. The fact that Mamardashvili was not tethered to any single institution, or even a single profession, explains how his influence extends well beyond the borders of the discipline of philosophy. What is more, the expansive and poetic architecture of his work easily lends itself to comparison and dialogue with films of practically all dates and genres, as the themes and tropes to which Mamardashvili consistently returned raise the most fundamental questions of human reflection. At the same time, he was committed to the unique philosophical potential of film, in the way that Stanley Cavell argued in *The World Viewed* (1969) that there was a special affinity between the discipline of philosophy and the art of film.

In keeping with the spirit of Mamardashvili's philosophical style, my investigation into his influence on cinema is informed by the role of dialogue and ambiguity in his own work, without presuming to offer an exhaustive summary or explication of his views. I have compiled and summarized some of his main thoughts and positions as he expressed them in lectures, publications, interviews, documentary footage, and personal papers, keeping in mind the unavoidable shortcomings that go along with creating a single, unified narrative from a large body of work that spans significant temporal, geographical, and methodological distances. My research also included synthesizing the many interpretations of Mamardashvili's life and career circulated by his friends, contemporaries, and the filmmakers he influenced. I have taken great care to weed out rumor and speculation from these accounts, but also to include those details that consistently reoccurred across multiple sources. If the films and directors I discuss in this book share anything in common in their conceptual output, it is that they all engage the philosophical potential of the image in defining the borders of the human mind, be it the nature of consciousness, the limits of language, the borders between the private and the public, or the absurdity of the human condition altogether—all topics to which Mamardashvili was deeply committed.

The Georgian Socrates

What does it mean to be the Socrates of Soviet philosophy, as Georgian-born philosopher Merab Mamardashvili has been called?[21] Like Socrates, Mamardashvili was known primarily as an orator. In the 1970s and 1980s, he appeared behind the podium at the most prestigious institutions in the Soviet Union, often lecturing to standing-room-only crowds. One philosopher recalls how, as a first-year philosophy major, she attended one such event in the southeast Russian city of Rostov-on-Don:

> Mamardashvili was at the peak of his popularity, and listeners treated him accordingly. The 400-seat lecture hall was overcrowded: people were sitting on the floor and standing between rows. Many took notes, but some tape-recorded the talk. I found that lecture intellectually thrilling; I had understood only some of it, but was excited by his very thought process and knew it was something fantastic.[22]

VGIK professor Paola Volkova and others have described how Mamardashvili's lectures were pitched not at professional philosophers, or even professionals in general.[23] As a directing student at VGIK in the mid-1970s, Sokurov recalled how Mamardashvili's lectures attracted more members of the public than they did film students, even though they were intended for the latter.[24]

Mamardashvili's oratory had its own distinctive content, which marked a radical departure from the available subjects of investigation in the typical Soviet classroom of the day. Tamara Dularidze, for instance, remembers him beginning a lecture at VGIK by telling the audience that "each of us answers only to our own immortal soul."[25] Mamardashvili described how Socrates "symbolized the arrival at consciousness," and for many of his students and colleagues, Mamardashvili played this same Socratic role: he exposed his audiences to a freedom of thought that was inaccessible, in the sense of its intellectual range and engagement with non-canonical texts.[26] As filmmaker Valerii Balaian put it, "In front of our very eyes this man demonstrated true philosophical thought, in the ancient Greek sense of the term."[27] The comparisons of Mamardashvili to Socrates were only helped by the fact that the former, like his Athenian namesake, began balding early, exposing by his thirtieth birthday a wide forehead and pronounced Socratic brow. Screenwriter Nataliia Riazantseva, with whom Mamardashvili would have a romantic relationship that lasted over a decade, recalled him frequently reminding himself and others of the Socratic maxim: "All I know is that I know nothing."[28] The role of Socrates in the philosophical canon, for Mamardashvili, was not only mental but metaphysical—"for the pupil to assume a new mode of being."[29]

Mamardashvili did not publish significantly less than his Soviet colleagues and had a rich editorial career at two leading scholarly journals, yet it was his public presence and not his scholarly output that earned him a name among the Soviet intelligentsia. Those who attended his lectures knew him primarily as an orator and an intellectual celebrity and were unlikely to read his dense and technical scholarly work. The Socratic metaphor that has in many ways defined his legacy is not descriptive of his academic persona so much as it describes his public side: his role as a well-known public figure in Moscow and Tbilisi, and perhaps his role as a teacher, although there was rarely any extended dialogue between orator and students during his university lectures. If in his professional life Mamardashvili was a respected and accomplished philosopher, no more or less prolific than the average Soviet researcher of his day, in his public life he was, as philosopher and journalist Boris Mezhuev has called him, a "lighthouse" of the era.[30] The Socratic link has worked to popularize his name among non-Russian speakers and taps into his deep interest in Socrates as a philosophical problem, but it is not especially representative of his philosophical views or the trajectory of his career.

Mamardashvili's collected works, if published in their entirety, would comprise more than twenty volumes of material. In his lifetime he published only four books: his doctoral dissertation, *Forms and Content of Thought* (*Formy i soderzhanie myshleniia*, 1968); *Symbol and Consciousness* (*Simvol i soznanie*, 1982), which he co-authored with philosopher Alexander Piatigorsky in the early 1970s; *Classical and Nonclassical Ideals of Rationality* (*Klassicheskii i neklassicheskii idealy ratsional'nosti*, 1984), based on a series of lectures he gave at the University of Latvia in 1980; and a collection of previously published essays and interviews, *How I Understand Philosophy* (*Kak ia ponimaiu filosofiiu*, 1990).

His other publications number around forty works in a variety of genres, including academic articles, book reviews, conference presentations, encyclopedia entries, and essays, as well as a number of interviews given for print and television. Most of his publications in the latter two categories come to us primarily from the late 1980s, when his work took a turn toward contemporary social and political thought. His best-known academic articles were published in the short period between 1968 and 1970 and earned him a following among a younger generation of mostly Moscow-based philosophers working in the philosophy of mind and Marxist analysis. These articles include "An Analysis of Consciousness in the Work of Marx" ("Analiz soznaniia v rabotakh Marksa," 1968), "The Inverted Form" ("Forma prevrashchennaia," 1970), and an article he co-authored with Erik Solovyov and Vladimir Shvyrev entitled "Classical and Contemporary Bourgeois Philosophy. An Attempt at Epistemological Juxtaposition" ("Klassicheskaia i sovremennaia burzhuaznaia filosofiia. Opyt epistemologicheskogo sopostavleniia," 1970).

The majority of the work we have under Mamardashvili's name has made its way to us today not as written documents that were penned, edited, and approved by the philosopher himself, but as transcriptions of his university lectures, which he preferred to call "conversations" (*besedy*) or "variations" (*variatsii*). These are the philosophical achievements for which he is most known today, and which earned him near-celebrity status among the Soviet intelligentsia in the 1970s and 1980s. He recorded his own lectures on a foreign-bought Dictaphone that he would bring with him to class, often taping new lectures over the old, as cassettes were hard to come by in the Soviet Union. The transcriptions of his lectures as we have them today were sourced either from his tapes or the tapes and lecture notes of his students. In 2012 his only child, Alena Mamardashvili, established the Mamardashvili Foundation to republish her father's lectures in official editions and to weed out errors that were introduced during the process of transcription, some of which have led to significant distortions in the transmission of his ideas. In some cases, the foundation has also restored and digitized extant audio tapes of his lectures and made portions available to the public.

That Mamardashvili was primarily an orator was perhaps as much by political design as it was by choice. True, those who knew him have described how he wrote with difficulty, and that the apparent spontaneity of his lectures was a performative move that he constructed through a great deal of preparation.[31] Publication in those years also came with weighty consequences for Soviet scholars. Of the philosophers of Mamardashvili's generation, Georgii Shchedrovitskii was excluded from the Party in 1968; Alexander Piatigorsky and Alexander Zinoviev fled the Soviet Union altogether in 1974 and 1978 respectively; Evald Ilenkov committed suicide in 1979; and Mamardashvili was banned from travelling outside the Soviet Union for two decades after an unsanctioned trip to France in 1967. One can imagine how Mamardashvili might have attempted to avoid the attention of censors by sidestepping the official genre of scholarly publication altogether, favoring instead the ephemeral, and thus freer, form of the spoken lecture. One might equally wonder why he chose to record his own lectures, as audio tapes possessed a power that was both subversive and dangerous. In his memoirs about Mamardashvili's 1981 Vilnius Lectures (*Vil'niusskie lektsii*), philosopher Algirdas Degutis recalls how the KGB confiscated the cassette recordings of the event immediately after Mamardashvili's departure from Lithuania.[32]

Mamardashvili's friends and colleagues repeatedly highlight the extraordinary freedom he enjoyed. Not only did he lecture on topics one would not be able to hear in any other lecture hall in Moscow—justice, freedom, the good, and social responsibility—but his lectures were always open to interpretation, and rarely ended with concrete conclusions. According to Volkova:

> Merab Konstantinovich didn't teach anything—not how to live nor what to do, and he didn't really even teach philosophy. But talking with him, either in private or during a lecture, would simply change how you thought about the world, about culture, and about yourself . . . He taught people freedom of choice and the freedom to understand the world around them.[33]

Oleg Aronson points out how the topics of Mamardashvili's lectures are dually shocking to the contemporary reader: first, they shock in the freedom of their language, when we consider them in the context of the intellectual restrictions of the late-Soviet period; at the same time, Mamardashvili's reliance on abstract examples and a romantic attachment to the history of philosophy appear archaic to the contemporary reader, "as if [Mamardashvili] is ignoring an entire field of social inquiry, one that was so critical for Western philosophy of the twentieth century."[34] Mamardashvili's style of doing philosophy was both open and closed: it was open in the range of topics he addressed, his playful use of language, and the way his work lent itself to interpretation by the audience; it was closed in the fact that he only occasionally referenced other thinkers directly and rarely connected his ideas to the philosophical context outside his own thought process.

The importance of the idea of freedom extended not just to the topics that Mamardashvili discussed in his work, but to his presence among the Moscow intelligentsia of the era. The Socratic paradox was founded in Socrates' very physiognomy, that primordial philosophical antinomy of the beautiful mind in the ugly body. In this way Mamardashvili was profoundly un-Socratic, since the allure of physical and sartorial pleasures was a defining component of his persona in the late-Soviet period. His friends and colleagues often mention his refined sense of fashion and taste, which bore the marks of sojourns to the unreachable oases of the bourgeois world, like Italy and Paris.[35] An attendee at his Vilnius Lectures remembers how "his appearance made an impression: a large, balding head, relaxed, amiable, confident, well-mannered, and fashionably dressed."[36] Another account describes how Mamardashvili was reported to the Moscow authorities in the 1970s for the cultural dissonance of his bourgeois daily uniform: corduroy jeans that could not be found in Soviet

Figure I.1 Merab Mamardashvili in the early 1970s.
© Merab Mamardashvili Foundation.

stores, beautiful sweaters purchased abroad, and a pipe.[37] In a description of her first meeting with Mamardashvili, Riazantseva confirms that "he really did look like a guest from abroad."[38]

Sokurov summarized the perception of Mamardashvili's cosmopolitanism when he wrote that "it was unlikely that there was anybody else [in Russia] who possessed Mamardashvili's level of freedom."[39] Yet, this perception has also led to rumors about the source of that freedom. Mamardashvili reported never feeling like he was under surveillance, or that he needed to "write for the drawer" rather than for the public, though we know that his letters abroad were read by the censors and some were even returned to their senders, unopened.[40] In their most extreme form, speculations about Mamardashvili's freedom insist that he must have worked for the government in some way, although no evidence exists to support this view. Philosopher and publisher Iurii Senokosov describes Mamardashvili's meeting with the KGB in the early 1980s, when the philosopher was summoned to the secret police headquarters on Lubianka Square and accused of "considering [himself] the freest man in the country."[41]

Senokosov's decades of labor are responsible for a great deal of the early transcriptions and publications of Mamardashvili's lectures. They are also the source of yet another story about the source of Mamardashvili's freedom. According to this story, Senokosov was assigned by the KGB to keep tabs on Mamardashvili and to record all his lectures, but upon hearing him speak, Senokosov became enthralled by the philosopher's ideas, went on to complete a PhD in philosophy, and, as the story continues, over the course of several decades abandoned the role of informant in order to become the chronicler and keeper of Mamardashvili's legacy. These and other tales about the sustaining sources of Mamardashvili's intellectual freedom are part of the broader genre of Soviet apocrypha, which blends fact and fiction in its efforts to explain the "black box" of the Soviet political system—a system known for blurring the lines between truth and myth in its denunciations, and whose force rarely expressed itself on any two individuals in one and the same way. Mamardashvili's own concept of "Pushkinian freedom" comes forward here as an apt metaphor for his own experience: his intellectual freedom (though never entirely, and only temporarily) was only made possible by his exclusion from Soviet academia, and therefore his freedom always occurred at the expense of his integration into that very profession.

In 1987 Mamardashvili was again permitted to travel abroad, in conjunction with the new freedoms and reforms of Gorbachev's policies of glasnost and perestroika. It was in these last few years of his life that his work also became explicitly political, although questions of social consciousness had always been present in his writing, albeit articulated in forms that were either highly technical (in the language of Marxism) or historical (analyses of Kant and Descartes). Mamardashvili was still a regular in Moscow in the 1980s, returning frequently to the metropole to give lectures and, most notably, to teach at the Higher Courses, one of the few places that was willing to risk employing him in Moscow at that point.

In Georgia in the 1980s, however, Mamardashvili was a cultural, intellectual, and political icon—a leading opinion-maker in the home country to which he had been driven back. Not only did the Gorbachev reforms open up a discursive space for public dissent as part of the new values of the era, but in Georgia, as in the other republics of the Soviet Union, questions of national identity, language, and independence were surrounded by significant political interest and unrest, as citizens in the republics took to the streets to protest Soviet rule and demand independence. This was especially the case in Georgia, which had an unusually vibrant intellectual and civil life, even as early as the immediate post-Stalin period.[42]

In Tbilisi, Mamardashvili's lectures were more explicitly political. He travelled abroad regularly, published essays on the impending dissolution of the Soviet Union, and gave print and television interviews on shortcomings in the political systems of Russia and Georgia. Although Mamardashvili had been interested in the social and political dimensions of consciousness since his early work on Marx, his political turn in the 1980s is remarkable in the context of his own biography. We can trace the political development of this "Georgian who had never been a Georgian," as he called himself—a philosopher who had tried to be cosmopolitan like his beloved Kant but was forced into politics when he was forced out of Russia.[43] Even as late as 1988, Mamardashvili claimed to watch politics from a distance, at a time when rumors were circulating that he was a potential candidate for the 1990 Georgian presidential election.[44]

At a philosophical level, Mamardashvili's work is equal parts captivating and maddening. While his intellectual range is impressive and he at times appears to have had a nearly encyclopedic knowledge of the history of philosophy and literature, from Descartes to Proust, he rarely included direct quotations or citations in his work. His texts are rich with implicit influence, overflowing with private references to the history of philosophy, contemporary European philosophy, the classic canon of Russian literature, the European phenomenological tradition, and contemporary French thought. The act of philosophizing, for Mamardashvili, was an act of inertia with no beginning and no end, and was also profoundly individual; to engage in philosophical thinking was "an aesthetic act," as Elisa Pontini puts it.[45]

When Mamardashvili did make direct references, it was often to novels, poems, and films, or the lesser-known works of great philosophers, for instance Kant's psychological essay "On Illnesses of the Head" ("Versuch über die Krankheiten des Kopfes," 1764). He rarely referenced the work of his Soviet contemporaries and instead appealed to metaphor, poetic language, and paradox, especially when reflecting on the topics that permeated all his philosophical work—the epistemological, metaphysical, and (in his later work) moral nature of human consciousness. Moreover, his philosophical analyses often contained creative readings of classical philosophical ideas. Philosopher Anatolii Akhutin writes that "at times it seems that even classical concepts (cogito, a priori, reduction) are merely metaphors for him, just like gospel stories, verses, or physical theories."[46] Mamardashvili himself described his philosophy of investigating the self as a process of obscuring the concrete—from the physical to the abstract, and from the individual mind and body to human consciousness broadly construed—so that "any geographical concepts become nothing more than metaphors."[47]

We might easily attribute the challenging style of Mamardashvili's prose to the influence of twentieth-century French postmodernism, to his efforts to evade the censors, or to the disorienting style of the art that he favored, be it Czech new wave cinema or the novels of Marcel Proust. We would misunderstand Mamardashvili's poetics of paradox, however, if we also failed to recognize the essentially civic dimension to his project. Especially in his later work, he was committed to a version of social-political agency that demanded of his Soviet compatriots that they fight barbarism, xenophobia, and other "sicknesses of consciousness," as he called these vices, in order to join "European society."[48] In order to see this coming-of-age project out to full term, Mamardashvili first had to demonstrate what it looked like to think for oneself—something that could be achieved in Russia, to his mind, only through the creation of a civil society, which would require the (impossible in the Soviet context) decoupling of the state with the civil sphere.[49] Critical to his conception of "thinking for oneself" was that every person come to their own conclusions and not accept or repeat readymade platitudes, as Soviet philosophical rhetoric was accustomed to doing.

In *Sketch of the History of European Philosophy* (*Ocherk sovremennoi evropeiskoi filosofii*, 1979–80), for instance, Mamardashvili admitted that his method is not explanatory or argument-based. He described his rhetorical style in his Vilnius Lectures as "following a thread through debris."[50] "I am not going to discuss or summarize the content of philosophical scholarship," he admitted. "You can read that on your own . . . I am going to try and help you feel what philosophy is, be it European or non-European, old or new, censured by us or not."[51] This presence of *feeling* as an essential component of thought may have been the reason Mamardashvili was so popular among the intelligentsia of his day. It also may be the reason why scholarship on his work is still, to this day, burdened by the task of explication. His stylistic and methodological choices add a richness and mystery to his work, but they do not make the scholar's task an easy one.

From Marx to Marx

Mamardashvili was born in 1930 to a military family in Gori, the birthplace of Stalin. He spent his childhood in Russia, Ukraine, and Lithuania, but with the outbreak of the Second World War his father, a career military man and colonel in the Soviet Army, left for the front. The rest of the family was evacuated back to Tbilisi, where Mamardashvili finished high school with high honors. He graduated with a diploma from the Department of Philosophy at Moscow State University in 1954, just over a year after Stalin's death. He continued on at Moscow State University for graduate work, completing his Candidate's Degree (the first of two

Figure I.2 Mamardashvili as a student of philosophy in the early 1950s.
© Merab Mamardashvili Foundation.

postgraduate degrees in the Soviet higher education system) with a dissertation on forms of perception in Hegel.

Mamardashvili was part of an exceptional generation of philosophers trained in the Soviet-Marxist orthodoxy of dialectical materialism in the 1940s and 1950s, but who entered the profession in the years immediately following Stalin's death seeking to breathe new life into Marx, logic, and the philosophy of science. Many of these young philosophers came of intellectual age at Moscow State University, including Georgii Shchedrovitskii, Alexander Zinoviev, and Boris Grushin. Stalin's death in 1953 opened up in Soviet philosophy a space for new working groups, relatively more freedom from the dogmatism and oscillation of ideological prophylaxis, and more controversial hires, for instance Teodor Oizerman's recruitment of Hegel scholar Evald Ilenkov to the Philosophy Department at Moscow State University and, later, the Institute of Philosophy.

This period also saw the formation of two new schools of Marxist interpretation in Russia, the school of Hegelian Marxism (Ilenkov) and that of Soviet structural Marxism (Mamardashvili, Shchedrovitskii, Zinoviev, and Valerii Podoroga), which looked to liberate Marxism from its dogmatism through the influence of critical theory, structuralism, semiotics, and existentialism from Western Europe and elsewhere. In 1953 Mamardashvili and his classmates organized an informal discussion group they called the Moscow Logic Circle. This group of young men would wander the back alleys of Moscow from mid-afternoon to evening, exchanging ideas on logic, dialectics, and philosophy of mind, often stopping in at pubs along the way.[52]

The post-war effects must have been at least partially responsible for the boldness of this 1950s generation. Many university instructors and even students (e.g. Ilenkov and Zinoviev) had served the war effort, including in combat roles, and were now back at the university as Russia reeled from the devastation of the war. Erik Solovyov describes the experience of the Second World War as a rift around which generational lines were formed, and where the age gap between those who went to war and those who stayed behind was often only a few years, a difference defined not in terms of "fathers and sons" but "older and younger brothers."[53] All the same, the new freedoms of the era were tempered by very real ideological restrictions on philosophical work in the 1950s, including little to no direct contact with non-Soviet scholars, sources, and debates.

Like many of his contemporaries at Moscow State University and elsewhere, Mamardashvili's earliest work from the 1950s comprised studies of logic and epistemology in Marx's *Capital* and "Hegel's dialectic as secularized by Marx," which Viktoriia Faibyshenko aptly captures as "the common language of Soviet philosophy."[54] On the one hand, Faibyshenko describes how Mamardashvili worked to erase those heavy-handed traces of Soviet rhetoric from his writing style, a move that may have resulted, as she argues, in the challenging nature of his prose.[55] On the other hand, his philosophical methodology from that decade was still mired in the "Soviet gnoseology" (theory and metaphysics of knowledge) of his training as a Marxist-Soviet critic of Hegel, as it was in the broader rituals and habits of Soviet scholarship. We can see Mamardashvili battling the vestiges of his Soviet training in his first book, *Forms and Content of Thought*, where his reading of Hegel makes some standard Marxist-Leninist accusations, while at the same time offering an interpretation of Hegel that was innovative among the Soviet reception of Hegel of the day.[56] All this occurred in the context of a younger generation of philosophers, mainly working at the Institute of Philosophy in Moscow in the 1960s and early 1970s, who were all committed to reinvigorating the Soviet study of Marx through less dogmatic, original readings of canonical texts of Marxism.

It was really only in the 1970s that Mamardashvili began to fill out the methodological foundations of his early written work with the historical-philosophical content and idiosyncratic approach to philosophical biography that has become associated with his name today. This middle period of work included lectures on the history of philosophy (primarily on Descartes and Kant), exercises in phenomenology (e.g. Husserl and Sartre), a monograph on the role of symbol (in co-authorship with Alexander Piatigorsky), and literary analysis (e.g. his cycles on Proust). The result is a broad, complex study of consciousness from ancient philosophy through the present, with a particular focus on the structure of perception and the mind's relationship to itself. If Mamardashvili rejected the formulas of Soviet thought and habitus, however, he never did reject Marx. And though he truthfully insisted until the end of his career that he had never been a Marxist, we can trace Mamardashvili's polemics on Marxist-inspired topics, for instance the concept of the inverted form (*verwandelte Form*), through the trajectory of his philosophical development, from his early, dense analytical work through interviews he gave toward the end of his life.

To put it another way, Marx remained for Mamardashvili the methodological starting point of philosophical inquiry, from which he then branched out into philosophy of mind, social theory, phenomenology, and literary-cultural interpretation, often in forms that bore little relation to Marxism proper. In his later work, for instance, the inverted form became a social metaphor for an entire realm of logical possibility—a regressive world in which everything looks like our human world, but in which zombie-inhabitants "can do nothing but imitate death."[57] In his later work he was more explicit about his philosophical departures from Marx, including, for instance, his criticism of the way Marx neglected the concept of the private, both in terms of private property and in terms of the interiority of the living, thinking, human being—a peculiar mix of Marxism and existentialism that models the kind of intellectual blending Mamardashvili often undertook.[58]

Alongside Marx, the philosophical works and biographies of Kant and Descartes occupied pivotal roles for Mamardashvili's philosophical trajectory. He likened Descartes to a self-help guru, a ruthless self-actualizer who privileged freedom above all, and who provided the foundational *epoché* upon which Mamardashvili built his own philosophy of consciousness. Kant, on the other hand, was Mamardashvili's intellectual confidant—a metaphysician who occupied for him a "godly position," who first articulated the paradox of human experience, and who embodied the highest form of civility in his life and action.[59] Giorgi Nodia writes about how Georgian philosophers of the mid-twentieth century, who had not seen a surge of philosophical interest in their country since the twelfth century, went in search of a "new starting point" for their philosophical projects, one which often brought them to German philosophical trends like neo-Kantianism, neo-Hegelianism, and phenomenology.[60] Mamardashvili's work too turned to the history of philosophy for new beginnings, taking both Descartes and Kant as exemplars of philosophers who had, in their times, likewise thrown off the chains of established authority. Mamardashvili shaped his unlikely combination of Kant's transcendental apparatus with Descartes' cogito—philosophical positions that are at odds with one another in the history of philosophy—into complementary pillars of inquiry that shaped his distinctive philosophical approach.

Kant's Blue Eyes and Descartes' Wavy Hair

According to one account, over three hundred people attended the opening lecture of Mamardashvili's *Cartesian Meditations* (*Kartezianskie razmyshleniia*) cycle, which he delivered at the Institute of Psychology in Moscow in 1981. Mamardashvili was not alone in taking Descartes' *cogito ergo sum*, or *I think, therefore I am*, as the genesis point of the entire tradition of modern philosophy; as the "creator of that very apparatus of thought according to which we know," Descartes' work motivated many of the fundamental questions of Mamardashvili's thought.[61] Questions like: What is my place in the world? What is my role in truth, beauty, and order? Where does my consciousness begin and the world end?[62] Later, with the addition of Kant, these questions would take on a social dimension, as Mamardashvili asked not only what can I know about our world and how do I know it, but what social responsibilities do I have in this world? These philosophical concerns took place within Mamardashvili's desire to bring the history of philosophy to life again for his audiences—to connect the past and present through the timeless act of human thought, or *myshlenie*.[63]

It was not Descartes' process of radical doubt, whereby he dismissed all his accepted beliefs in order to prove them again philosophically, that intrigued Mamardashvili so much as it was what he saw as Descartes' emphasis on individual agency, self-affirmation, and freedom—all founded in Descartes' (according to Mamardashvili) lifelong disdain for "indecisive and melancholic conditions of the spirit."[64] Mamardashvili saw Descartes as a man searching for freedom, having moved twenty times in thirty years in his own "search for peace and free will," as Mamardashvili described in a quote from Pushkin.[65] Mamardashvili's comparisons to Pushkin paint an absolutely foreign portrait of Descartes; Descartes is no longer the skeptic in his dressing gown, doubting the existence of everything down to the self, but comes forth as a bold and Byronic embodiment of the "Pushkinian phenomenon of freedom," as a representative of the authority and responsibility of the individual "I" and the power of thought.[66] To his reading of Descartes, Mamardashvili extended his love of paradox, viewing the great philosopher's texts as simultaneously the most transparent and the most indecipherable in the history of modern thought.[67] Even the smallest details could become the starting point for philosophical analysis, down to the psychological implications of Descartes' "strange hair."[68]

From Descartes' intellectual biography and his search for certainty in *Meditations on First Philosophy* (1641), Mamardashvili crafted an entire conception of freedom on which he based his philosophical work. And though there remain significant disputes in the philosophical literature over the kind of human freedom to which Descartes was committed, Mamardashvili's task was not to present a philosophical explication of Descartes' philosophy of freedom, but to paint a picture of *freedom as possibility*. He relied on metaphor and poeticized the details of Descartes' biography, as he so often did, describing how "in a dark forest with many possible paths," Descartes would "choose one and never look back."[69] For Mamardashvili, and especially in the Soviet context, the abstract notion of freedom was as critical an element to Descartes' persona as it was his philosophical project. "If we remove the condition of human freedom," Mamardashvili learned from Descartes, "then we lose the capacity to think at all."[70] In his later work, Mamardashvili talked a great deal about the very act of thought as the primary way to exercise one's essential human freedom. He called on every person to realize their individual *cogito* in a social sense, as the principle on which agency and citizenship was possible.

Mamardashvili seized Descartes' claim that the "I think" was the one thing of which we could be sure, the foundation for any further philosophical inquiry. He also appreciated the way that in the *Meditations*, Descartes inserted himself into the philosophical process, so that Descartes the man became inextricable from Cartesianism the philosophy: "This man [Descartes] accepted from the world only that which he allowed through his own self, and only that which he had verified and tested in and on himself. Only that, which is 'the I'!"[71] This assertion of self-certainty, or the "locking in of the I," was foundational in Mamardashvili's reading of Descartes; by extension, the genesis moment of the modern "I," and the authority and certainty that it brings, would be just as foundational for Mamardashvili's more political philosophy in the 1980s.[72] The power of Descartes' "I" reverberated to the very top of the metaphysical chain, and put to the test the inherited Soviet truths of Marxism about the human mind, for instance the idea that individual consciousness is determined by "objective" external forces like economics. Just as Descartes' ontological argument hinged on the *cogito*, so did Mamardashvili emphasize that God did not create *man*, but created *this* man—this René Descartes, who had so compellingly filtered his argument for the existence of God through his own God-given "I."[73]

While Descartes' work provided Mamardashvili with a model for the importance and agency of the "I" in overcoming the hegemony of Soviet orthodoxy, it was Kant who filled in the content of what that "I" could achieve. Kant's transcendentalism added the verb "think" to the grammatical equation of the *cogito*, highlighting the importance of self-consciousness for epistemology and making possible what Mamardashvili called "the astringent power of self-knowledge."[74] Moreover, for Mamardashvili (as for Kant) the inclusion of the verb "to exist" was tautological, "for here it is simple—the fact or the act of 'I am' . . . means that I think. I think, I am!"[75] If for Descartes, that "I exist" was a necessary condition of the fact that "I think," for Kant, to know "I exist" I must first know something about the external world, where the "I think" extends to universal concepts of understanding. For Kant, in other words, to think at all requires thinking about the world beyond oneself. Mamardashvili was closer to the Kantian view in this regard, agreeing with Kant in the *Critique of Pure Reason* (1781) that the "I think must be able to accompany all my representations," though he seemed to want to also retain an idea of Ego as substance.[76] Perhaps the influence of Kant on Mamardashvili explains why, in *Cartesian Meditations*, Mamardashvili referred to *cogito ergo sum* in full only twice, preferring to use either *cogito* alone or, more often, the Russian *Ia mysliu* (I think).[77]

For Mamardashvili, Kant was a metaphysician, a social theorist, and the first philosopher to undertake the phenomenological reduction (before Husserl). However, Mamardashvili also wrote about Kant with a kind of intimacy, and even tenderness, that one rarely meets in works of philosophy.[78] In his *Kantian Variations* (*Kantianskie variatsii*) cycle, which he first delivered in 1982 at the Institute of General and Pedagogical Psychology at the Russian Academy of Sciences, he described *who Kant was*, as if he had personal knowledge of the philosopher's appearance, habits, and innermost thoughts and fears. He was a beacon of politeness and civility, and a model of the highest stage of human development. He was an honest, earnest, and polite man who doubted himself, struggled with vice, and desired for us to be good people in our interactions with ourselves and with others.[79] "In my consciousness," Mamardashvili continued, "Kant occupies a godly position."[80] Neither did Mamardashvili fail to describe

Kant's appearance: "Anybody who saw Kant's eyes thought that they were larger than they were in reality," Mamardashvili described, "since they were a strange ethereal blue color that one did not often see, and slightly watery, which only enhanced their shine and sharpness."[81]

People said the same about Mamardashvili's eyes: that he had "massive bulging blue eyes, just like Kant."[82] The inclusion of physiognomic details as material for philosophical analysis speaks to Mamardashvili's poetic approach to the history of philosophy. Descartes and Kant were characters in his story, and by offering up intimate details he invited his listeners to connect with these figures, both personally and philosophically. His own relationship to Kant rose above the expected rituals of scholarly discourse; his methodology, in his own words, was to "release" (*vysvobozhdat'*) meaning from Kant "like energy from an atom," where nothing is transferred but just moved/released to a different place.[83] He also frequently used the verb "to modulate" (*var'irovat'*) to describe his approach to Kant; in other words, Mamardashvili saw himself as modulating the ideas of Kant—adjusting the amplitude or varying the tone—without ever attempting to synthesize Kant's philosophical position. He filtered Kant's thoughts through his own, in such a way that his own voice blended with the historical text of Kant's philosophical "I." Though the subject was Kant, *Kantian Variations* always leads back to Mamardashvili.

A guiding concern for Mamardashvili was Kant's transcendental argument, which asserts that independently existing things are a necessary condition for the possibility of any experience, even though our innate concepts can never grasp those things as they are in themselves. Mamardashvili defined the transcendental as "the world in relation to first principles of knowledge about that world, or a world that was formed by, and presupposed, inner sources of knowledge about itself."[84] If Kant developed his transcendental deduction in the *Critique of Pure Reason* by arguing that there are certain a priori concepts that are universal and necessary to human experience, for Mamardashvili the transcendental question did not maintain the strict distinction between the unknowable transcendental and the phenomena of experience, but instead highlighted the paradox of human experience as split between the physical and metaphysical. This was the idea that "the human soul occupies space in this world, but this soul 'contains' (in quotations, because this is an empirical term) ideal constitutions, or essences, that are outside of space and time. The soul thinks by way of them."[85]

While Kant's transcendental argument attacks skepticism so as to demonstrate that we can indeed have knowledge about the physical world, even if only as organized by our concepts, for Mamardashvili the transcendental did not lead to certainty. It led to paradox: to the unbridgeable gap between "internal condition of the soul (thought and desire) and the external condition of the material of our body."[86] Mamardashvili's departure from a strict reading of Kant is perhaps best illustrated in his puzzling description of human life as the paradigm of this transcendental mystery, where "the human being is the walking example of the thing in itself."[87] Since Kant was quite clear that things in themselves are unknowable to the human mind, what does this statement say about the potential for self-knowledge or self-certainty for Mamardashvili?

Mamardashvili's philosophical roots in Descartes and Kant highlight two main tendencies in his philosophy. On the one hand, from his romanticized vision of Descartes he took the idea that everything begins with the "I" and the free act of thought, and that we can and must filter all experience, and test all conventions, through our own "I." On the other hand, from Kant he took the idea of the primacy of consciousness, which is the basis for a priori knowledge about the structure of the world and, by extension, the self. In both cases, Mamardashvili fed the history of philosophy through his own views and self, engaging in dialogue with philosophy rather than presenting a summary of thinkers or ideas, or even arguing any particular line of thought. Akhutin calls this "local meaning," in which the conceptual space that Mamardashvili's work opens up coincides with his personal, mental space.[88] This "local meaning" means that Mamardashvili's lectures on Descartes and Kant blend with his own philosophical views in a way that makes it almost impossible to ascertain the borderlines between philosophical interpretation and personal insertion. When Mamardashvili wrote that Kant "understood that the very existence of the human soul . . . in this world is a miracle," he very well could have been talking about himself.[89]

Nelli Motroshilova has suggested that Mamardashvili's personal maxim was not Descartes' "I think, therefore I am," but "I live, therefore I philosophize."[90] Mamardashvili himself proposed the following version of the Cartesian *cogito*: "I think, I exist, *I can*."[91] Just as Descartes and Kant understood their philosophical projects as throwing off the shackles of authority (Aristotle in the case of Descartes, tutelage in the case of Kant) to forge new philosophical beginnings, Mamardashvili inserts the *I can* as a statement that "everything needs to be done over, from the beginning."[92] And while Mamardashvili could never fully set aside his own ideological masters (Marx, Lenin, dialectical materialism), he could rely on the respective philosophical revolutions of Descartes and Kant as historical models of thinking in action and freedom in thought. He was not only "performing the Cartesian argument," as Evert van der Zweerde puts it, but in his life and work he was performing the Kantian argument too; to put it more broadly, he saw himself as performing the act of free thought in general.[93] His work in the history of philosophy, and elsewhere, was an attempt to retain freedom and agility of thought in a system dictated by external restraints and official teleology. "Our world is created," Mamardashvili argued in 1988, "but now the rest is up to you."[94]

Each of the seven chapters that follow investigates the work of a filmmaker who is connected to Mamardashvili in some way. At the same time, I will present the main themes of Mamardashvili's philosophy as illuminated by the work of the filmmakers he influenced. With regard to intellectual chronology, the book begins with Mamardashvili's tenure at VGIK in the 1970s (Chapter One: Sokurov) and moves through his time at the Higher Courses (Chapter Two: Dykhovichnyi) and Tbilisi State University (Chapter Three: Mamuliya) in the 1980s, the collapse of the Soviet empire in 1991 (Chapter Four: Balabanov), and the relevance of his philosophy on filmmaking in the twenty-first century (Chapter Five: Zeldovich). In Chapter Six, I have synthesized the comparatively little that Mamardashvili did write on film—around 6,000 words scattered among several lecture cycles—in order to present a picture of his own reflections on the discipline upon which he was so influential. In the Conclusion, I engage Zvyagintsev's work with approaches in the philosophy of the moving image, as one way of describing what the Mamardashvili generation of filmmakers can teach us about the movement of philosophical ideas from word to screen.

The tasks of this book are complicated not only by the trans-disciplinary challenges of analyzing film philosophically, but because Mamardashvili was not a systematic thinker. He saw philosophical texts as opportunities for dialogue. He engaged in those dialogues himself with Kant, Descartes, and others, speaking about their lives and thoughts with authority and maintaining "an intimate relationship with philosophers [of the past]."[95] My choice to place Mamardashvili's philosophical views in dialogue with cinematic texts is, thus, largely inspired by his own expressly dialogic approach to the very nature of philosophical inquiry. My approach is equally inspired by the field of intellectual history and its ability to cope with the transmission of ideas from philosophy to film and back, and within a lived historical context, in the way that Peter Gordon has pointed out that a defining characteristic of intellectual history is that its borderlines between disciplines remain highly flexible.[96] For some directors and films, the Mamardashvili influence is explicit, while for others, by influence I have in mind something akin to philosophical affinity, where

Mamardashvili's work can shed light on philosophical engagement with cinema in new ways. The structure of this book is meant to encourage a flexible approach to reading, where chapters can be read in or out of order, much in the same way that, as Andrei Paramonov suggests, one can start reading a text by Mamardashvili by opening to any page.[97]

Drawing out the Mamardashvili connection in Russian-Soviet cinema leads us to unexpected affinities among directors, films, and styles of filmmaking that, until now, have been assumed to share no common cinematic threads. Filmmakers like Abdrashitov, Balabanov, Dykhovichnyi, Mamuliya, and Sokurov, whom we might otherwise not place in dialogue with one another, are suddenly brought into a new relationship when we consider how they share the generational experience of Mamardashvili's legacy. Although I never assume influence where it has not been articulated directly by the directors themselves, the connections I draw between the philosopher and these films highlight how Mamardashvili's work and persona embodied the defining characteristics of the late-Soviet intelligentsia, both in reality and in image. It is only when we begin to trace the influence of Mamardashvili on his intellectual generation, and on filmmakers in particular, that we see, as filmmaker Olesia Fokina remarked in 1993, "We live in the time of Merab."[98]

Notes

1. Merab Mamardashvili, *Kartezianskie razmyshleniia*, ed. Iurii Senokosov (Moscow: Progress – Kul'tura, 1993), p. 20.
2. Qtd from interview footage with Olesia Fokina in her documentary *The Time of Merab* (*Vremia Meraba*). Fokina, *Vremia Meraba*, 1993, 47:40.
3. For Olga Sedakova's discussion of Mamardashvili's use of thought as a form of resistance, see: Sedakova, "Zhertvy veka ili samouchki 'predatel'stva sebia': k analizu 1970-x godov," Gefter.ru (Jan. 27, 2014), http://gefter.ru/archive/11164. For references to Mamardashvili as theologian, see: Anna Golubitskaia, "'Vnutrennii sad' Meraba Mamardashvili," *Otrok* 2, No. 80 (2017), http://otrok-ua.ru/ru/sections/art/show/vnutrennii_sad_meraba_mamardashvili.html; Andrei Paramonov, "Svobodnaia mysl' Meraba Mamardashvili: Interv'iu s issledovateliem filosofa," *Sputnik* (Sept. 15, 2017), https://sputnik-georgia.ru/interview/20170915/237345280/Svobodnaja-mysl-Meraba-Mamardashvili-intervju-s-issledovatelem-filosofa.html; Tamara Dularidze, "Merab Mamardashvili segodnia," Fond Meraba Mamardashvili (1997), https://www.mamardashvili.com/ru/merab-mamardashvili/pamyati-m.m/tamara-dularidze/merab-mamardashvili-segodnya. Susan Buck-Morss has called Mamardashvili the leading figure of "what might be called the Continental school of Soviet philosophy," emphasizing in particular his influence on the

philosopher-celebrity Slavoj Žižek: Buck-Morss, *Dreamworld and Catastrophe: The Passing of Mass Utopia in East and West* (Cambridge, MA: MIT Press, 2000), p. xii.
4. Elena Mamardashvili (ed.), *Vstrecha. Merab Mamardashvili – Lui Al'tiusser* (Fond Meraba Mamardashvili, 2016), pp. 37 and 45.
5. The Soviet Academy of Sciences was a system of research institutions, though some of its more than three hundred affiliated institutes offered undergraduate degree programs. This was not the case at the Institute of the History of Science and Technology, where Mamardashvili worked between 1974 and 1980, and where he did not have teaching responsibilities. Neither did he lecture as part of his position at the Institute of the International Workers Movement, another affiliate institute of the Academy of Sciences. It continues to be common for Russia-based scholars to hold multiple appointments simultaneously, splitting teaching and research among two or sometimes more institutions.
6. Uldis Tirons, "I Come to You from My Solitude," *Eurozine* (June 2006), http://www.eurozine.com/articles/2006-06-22-tirons-en.html.
7. Qtd ibid.
8. Aleksandr Arkhangel'skii, "Istoriia sil'nee vozhdia," Arzamas Academy. Course No. 9, https://arzamas.academy/materials/260; Sergei Sel'ianov, "Skazki, siuzhety i stsenarii sovremennoi Rossii," Polit.ru (May 1, 2004), http://polit.ru/article/2004/05/01/selianov/.
9. Nataliia Riazantseva, "Adresa i daty," *Znamia* 11 (2011), http://magazines.russ.ru/znamia/2011/11/ra4.html.
10. Aleksandr Zel'dovich, "Zel'dovich to DeBlasio," Sept. 8, 2014.
11. Aleksandr Sokurov, "Pamiati Meraba Mamardashvili," *Seans* 3 (July 1991), http://seance.ru/n/3/mamard_sokurov/. Sokurov also cites Mamardashvili in *V tsentre okeana* (St Petersburg, 2011), pp. 16–17.
12. Brian Phillips, interview with Iurii Norshtein, trans. Alyssa DeBlasio, May 2016.
13. Irina Balabanova, "Byvshaia zhena Balabanova rasskazala o schast'e i tragediiakh v zhizni rezhissera.," 7days.ru, http://7days.ru/caravan-collection/2013/9/byvshaya-zhena-balabanova-rasskazala-o-schaste-i-tragediyakh-v-zhizni-rezhissera.htm.
14. Vladimir Khotinenko, "Maksimal'no ispol'zovat' vremia, predostavlennoe sud'boi," in *Professiia – kinematografist*, ed. P. D. Volkova, A. N. Gerasimov, and V. I. Sumenova (Ekaterinburg: U-Faktoriia, 2004), p. 444.

Mamardashvili's name and ideas also appear in unexpected places in Russian film criticism, including in an interview with Konstantin Lopushansky and in a review of the *Six Degrees of Celebration* (*Elki*) series by Timur Bekmambetov. See: Elena Iakovleva, "Otkroi okno v ogon'. Rezhisser Konstantin Lopushanskii khochet byt' uslyshannym v svoei strane," *Rossiiskaia gazeta* (March 23, 2012), https://rg.ru/2012/03/23/lopushanskiy.html; Mariia Kuvshinova, "Nakrylis' elkami," Colta.ru (Dec. 20, 2010),

http://os.colta.ru/cinema/events/details/19391/. For a contemporary example of Mamardashvili's influence beyond the spheres of cinema and philosophy, we might turn to Pussy Riot member Maria Alekhina's report of reading Mamardashvili while incarcerated. See: Masha Gessen, *Words Will Break Cement: The Passion of Pussy Riot* (New York: Riverhead, 2014), p. 247.
15. Vlad Strukov, *Contemporary Russian Cinema. Symbols of a New Era* (Edinburgh: Edinburgh University Press, 2016), p. 12.
16. Aleksei Iurchak, "Rossiiskoe obshchestvo ne delitsia na bol'shuiu 'vatu' i malen'kuiu 'svobodu,'" *Gor'kii* (Nov. 30, 2016), https://gorky.media/intervyu/rossijskoe-obshhestvo-ne-delitsya-na-bolshuyu-vatu-i-malenkuyu-svobodu/. Lev Anninskii also includes in his description of generational affinity the idea of the defining moment or common event, which plays a conformational function. Anninskii, "The Sixties Generation, the Seventies Generation, the Eighties Generation . . . : Toward a Dialectic of Generations in Russian Literature," trans. Nancy Condee and Vladimir Padunov, *Soviet Studies in Literature* 27, No. 4 (1991): p. 13.
17. Karl Mannheim, "The Problem of Generations," in *Karl Mannheim: Essays*, ed. Paul Kecskemeti (New York: Routledge, 1972), pp. 291–2.
18. Erik Solovyov speaks of the shared "generational experience" of participating in lectures and seminars by Mamardashvili, Evald Ilenkov, and other philosophers of the 1950s–1960s generation in Moscow. See: Solov'ev, "Filosofiia kak kritika ideologii. Chast' II," *Filosofskii zhurnal* 10, No. 3 (n.d.): p. 6.
19. Merab Mamardashvili, "Odinochestvo – moia professiia. Interv'iu Uldisa Tironsa," Mamardashvili.com. https://mamardashvili.com/files/pdf/euro/28%20Одиночество%20-%20моя%20профессия....pdf. Emphasis mine.
20. *Kartezianskie razmyshleniia*, pp. 20 and 15.
21. The first reference to Mamardashvili as the Georgian Socrates appears in J. P. Vernant, "Georgian Socrates", translated by M. Kharbedia, *Arili*, 14 (2000): pp. 6–8.
22. Marina F. Bykova, "The Georgian Socrates," *Russian Studies in Philosophy* 49.1 (2010): p. 6.
23. Paola Volkova, "Paola Volkova o Merabe Mamardashvili," Youtube.com, March 18, 2015, 5:25, https://www.youtube.com/watch?v=vW-fEGo2b4k.
24. Sokurov, "Pamiati Meraba Mamardashvili." Journalist Mikhail Nenashev's account also describes how the audiences at Mamardashvili's lectures were made up almost entirely of members of the public. Nenashev, "O Merabe Mamardashvili," in *Binokl'*, http://binokl-vyatka.narod.ru/B12/nenash.htm.
25. Tamara Dularidze, "Stranstvuiushchii filosof, kotoryi liubil kino," 1991, https://www.mamardashvili.com/ru/merab-mamardashvili/pamyati-m.m/tamara-dularidze/my-vse-ego-tak-lyubili-vspominaya-meraba-mamardashvili.
26. Merab Mamardashvili and Aleksandr Piatigorskii, *Simvol i soznanie. Metafizicheskie rassuzhdeniia o soznanii, simvolike i iazyke* (Moscow: Shkola "Iazyki russkoi kul'tury," 1999), p. 95.

27. Valerii Balaian, "Fil'm o Merabe, sniatyi ego uchenikom," ed. Aleksandr Arkhangel'skii, Arzamas Academy, Course No. 9: Nesovetskaia filosofiia v SSSR (2015), http://arzamas.academy/materials/334.
28. Riazantseva.
29. Mamardashvili and Piatigorskii, p. 95.
30. Boris Mezhuev, "Dekart v mire Kafki," *Russkii zhurnal* (Nov. 24, 2010), http://www.russ.ru/layout/set/print/pole/Dekart-v-mire-Kafki.
31. On Mamardashvili's writing habits, see: Iurii Senokosov, "Vstupitel'noe slovo," in *Kongenial'nost' mysli. O filosofe Merabe Mamardashvili* (M: Progress – Kul'tura, 1994), p. 11; and Solov'ev, "Filosofiia kak kritika ideologii," p. 16. Mamardashvili's handwritten lecture notes indicate a significant amount of preparation; he also speaks about his worries over finding a "common language" with new audiences. Merab Mamardashvili, *Vil'niusskie lektsii po sotsial'noi filosofii (Opyt fizicheskoi metafiziki)* (St Petersburg: Azbuka, 2012), p. 9.
32. Algirdas Degutis, "Vospominaniia o vil'niusskikh lektsiiakh Meraba Mamardashvili," in *Vil'niusskie lektsii*, p. 306.
33. Volkova, "Paola Volkova o Merabe Mamardashvili."
34. Oleg Aronson, "Neumestnoe bytie," in *Vil'niusskie lektsii po sotsial'noi filosofii (Opyt fizicheskoi metafiziki)* (St Petersburg: Azbuka, 2012), pp. 291–2.
35. See, for instance: Fokina.
36. Degutis, p. 304.
37. Tirons and Degutis, p. 304.
38. Riazantseva. Pierre Bellefroid wrote about Mamardashvili's love for fine jewelry in "Prazhskie gody. Merab Mamardashvili," 2008, http://mamardashvili.com/about/bellefroid/1.html.
39. Sokurov, "Pamiati Meraba Mamardashvili."
40. Merab Mamardashvili, "Esli osmelit'sia byt'," in *Kak ia ponimaiu filosofiiu*, ed. Iu. P. Senokosov, 2nd edn (Moscow: Progress – Kul'tura, 1992), p. 178; Annie Epelboin, "The Crossed Destinies or Two Philosophers: Louis Althusser and Merab Mamardashvili," *Transcultural Studies*, No. 5 (2009): p. 4.
41. Iurii Senokosov, "Vstrecha Meraba Mamardashvili s otsom Aleksandrom Menem," *Vestnik moskovskoi shkoly grazhdanskogo prosveshcheniia* 68 (2015): p. 3.
42. Irakli Zurab Kakabadze and Ronald Grigor Suny have written about intellectual life in Georgia in the post-Stalin era. See: Irakli Zurab Kakabadze, "I Am with Chubik: Faces of Georgian AlterModernity, Modernity and Anti-Modernity," *Arcade* (Jan. 31, 2013), http://arcade.stanford.edu/blogs/i-am-chubik-faces-georgian-altermodernity-modernity-and-anti-modernity; Ronald Grigor Suny, *The Making of the Georgian Nation*, 2nd edn (Bloomington: Indiana University Press, 1994).
43. Merab Mamardashvili, *Lektsii o Pruste (Psikhologicheskaia topologiia puti)*, ed. E. B. Oznobkina, I. K. Mamardashvili, and Iu. P. Senokosov (Moscow: Ad Marginem, 1995), p. 8.

44. See: Merab Mamardashvili, "Moi opyt ne tipichen," in *Kak ia ponimaiu filosofiiu*, ed. Iu. P. Senokosov, 2nd edn (Moscow: Progress – Kul'tura, 1992), pp. 356–64.
45. Elisa Pontini, "The Aesthetic Import of the Act of Knowledge and Its European Roots in Merab Mamardašvili," *Studies in East European Thought* 58 (2006): p. 177.
46. Anatolii Akhutin, "In Mamardashvili's Country," *Russian Studies in Philosophy* 49, No. 1 (summer 2010): p. 21.
47. "Odinochestvo – moia professiia," p. 555.
48. Merab Mamardashvili, "Filosofiia – eto soznanie vslukh," in *Kak ia ponimaiu filosofiiu*, ed. Iu. P. Senokosov, 2nd edn (Moscow: Progress – Kul'tura, 1992), pp. 57–71.
49. Ibid., p. 63.
50. *Vil'niusskie lektsii*, p. 24.
51. Merab Mamardashvili, *Ocherk sovremennoi evropeiskoi filosofii* (Moscow: Azbuka-Attikus, 2012), p. 11.
52. Shchedrovitskii describes these meetings in *Ia vsegda byl idealistom* (Moscow: Put', 2001), p. 323.
53. Erik Solov'ev, "Prostornoe slovo avtoritetov. Beseda T. A. Umanskoi s E. Iu. Solov'ev," in *Kak eto bylo. Vosponinaniia i razmyshleniia*, ed. V. A. Lektorskii (Moscow: ROSSPEN, 2010), p. 308.
54. Viktoriia Faibyshenko, "Istoriia poznanie, ili poznanie kak istoriia," in *Formy i soderzhanie myshleniia* (St Petersburg: Azbuka, 2011), p. 267.
55. Faibyshenko analyzes the change in Mamardashvili's language, suggesting that his efforts to remove Soviet jargon from his work might account for the difficulty of his philosophical style. See: Faibyshenko, "Istoriia poznanie."
56. Merab Mamardashvili, *Formy i soderzhanie myshleniia* (St Petersburg: Azbuka, 2011), p. 180.
57. Merab Mamardashvili, "Soznanie i tsivilizatsiia," *Soznanie i tsivilizatsiia* (St Petersburg: Lenizdat, 2013), p. 17.
58. On Mamardashvili's critique of the lack of a notion of privacy in Marx, see: Merab Mamardashvili, "The Civil Society. A Conversation with Merab Mamardashvili," *The Civic Arts Review* (summer 1989), p. 8.
59. Merab Mamardashvili, *Kantianskie variatsii. Put' k ochevidnosti* (Moscow: Agraf, 2002), p. 65.
60. Giorgi Nodia, "'Back to the Man Himself': The Philosophical Inspiration of Zurab Kakabadze," ed. A. T. Tymieniecka, *Analecta Husserliana* XXVII (1989): p. 2.
61. Mamardashvili, *Kartezianskie razmyshleniia*, p. 8.
62. Ibid., p. 26.
63. Van der Zweerde discusses Mamardashvili's vision of philosophy as tasked with reviving and performing history in the here and now. Evert Van der Zweerde, "Philosophy in the Act: The Socio-Political Relevance of Mamardashvili's Philosophizing," *Studies in East European Thought* 58 (2006): p. 188.

64. *Kartezianskie razmyshleniia*, p. 18.
65. Ibid., pp. 14–15.
66. Ibid., p. 15.
67. Ibid., p. 8.
68. Ibid., p. 88.
69. Ibid., p. 18.
70. Ibid., p. 111.
71. Ibid.
72. Ibid., p. 63.
73. Ibid.
74. *Kantianskie variatsii*, p. 15.
75. *Kartezianskie razmyshleniia*, p. 50.
76. Immanuel Kant, *Critique of Pure Reason*, trans. Paul Guyer and Allen W. Wood (Cambridge: Cambridge University Press, 1998), B132.
77. On Descartes' "I think, therefore I am" in relation to Kant's "I think," see: Béatrice Longuenesse, "Kant's 'I Think' versus Descartes' 'I Am a Thing That Thinks,'" in *Kant and the Early Moderns*, ed. Daniel Garber and Béatrice Longuenesse (Princeton, NJ: Princeton University Press, 2008), pp. 9–31.
78. Merab Mamardashvili, "Byt' filosofom – eto sud'ba," in *Kak ia ponimaiu filosofiiu*, ed. Iu. P. Senokosov, 2nd edn (Moscow: Progress – Kul'tura, 1992), p. 36.
79. *Kantianskie variatsii*, pp. 53–4.
80. Ibid., p. 65.
81. Ibid., p. 16.
82. Golubitskaia.
83. *Kantianskie variatsii*, p. 8.
84. Ibid., p. 145.
85. Ibid., p. 130.
86. Ibid., p. 133.
87. Qtd Nelli Motroshilova, *Merab Mamardashvili. Filosofskoe razmyshlenie i lichnostnyi opyt* (Moscow: Kanon+, 2007), p. 98.
88. Akhutin, p. 21.
89. *Kantianskie variatsii*, pp. 27, 16, 47, and 8.
90. Motroshilova, *Merab Mamardashvili*, p. 195.
91. "Soznanie i tsivilizatsiia," p. 14.
92. *Kartezianskie razmyshleniia*, p. 49.
93. Van der Zweerde, p. 190.
94. "Soznanie i tsivilizatsiia," p. 14.
95. Paola Volkova, "Ob"iasnenie neob"iasnimogo," in *Professiia – kinematografist*, ed. P. D. Volkova, A. N. Gerasimov, and V. I. Sumenova (Ekaterinburg: U-Faktoriia, 2004), p. 212.
96. Peter E Gordon, "What Is Intellectual History? A Frankly Partisan Introduction to a Frequently Misunderstood Field," 2012, 4, http://pro

jects.iq.harvard.edu/files/history/files/what_is_intell_history_pgordon_mar2012.pdf.
97. Paramonov.
98. Fokina, 46:44.

CHAPTER 1

Alexander Sokurov's *Demoted* (1980): Consciousness as Celebration

Between 1976 and 1980, Merab Mamardashvili was a professor in the Department of Philosophy and Scientific Communism on the faculty of the All-Union State Institute of Cinematography, known in Russian abbreviation as VGIK. The topics of his courses there included Introduction to Philosophy, Ancient Philosophy, and Contemporary European Philosophy. But no matter the topic on which Mamardashvili was writing or lecturing, he was always—in one way or another—talking about the problem of consciousness. Here I refer to consciousness as a *problem* because the topic was for Mamardashvili, as it remains among scientists and philosophers today, ambiguous at best. "There is nothing we know more intimately than conscious experience, but there is nothing that is harder to explain," philosopher David Chalmers put it in 1995.[1] Although neuroscience, cognitive science, and other fields in the study of mind have uncovered a great deal about the role and structure of consciousness in the decades since Mamardashvili's death, there is still no consensus on a theory that fully explains how consciousness arises or, by extension, is lost. Consciousness structures our experience of the world and ourselves, yet we are unable to adequately explain the mysterious unity of emotions, impressions, sensations, and thoughts that comprises human conscious experience. "Consciousness is very difficult to explain not because there is no explanation," Mamardashvili wrote in co-authorship with Alexander Piatigorsky in the 1970s, "but because there are too many explanations."[2]

This chapter is the first of seven philosophical-cinematic dialogues in which I will place Mamardashvili's life and work in conversation with a director from the Mamardashvili generation—that very disparate group of directors who share the historical accident of beginning their careers at a time when Mamardashvili was a defining figure in Moscow's film schools and in Soviet intellectual culture more broadly.[3] The present chapter looks at Alexander Sokurov's short film *Demoted* (*Razzhalovannyi*) from 1980, which is the earliest cinematic nod to Mamardashvili, and which includes a lengthy recording of his voice at the film's halfway-point. Stanley Cavell argues in his extensive work on the philosophy of film that we can speak about film as a kind of thinking, as well as a new philosophical possibility in its own right, providing new ways for self-reflection and moral reasoning.[4] My hope is that the following side-by-side reading of Mamardashvili's work on consciousness and Sokurov's *Demoted* is generative in the same way; that such a reading can shed light on Mamardashvili's paradoxical, but ultimately celebratory, view of human consciousness experience, as well as draw out ways that markers of consciousness are embedded in the visual language of Sokurov's film.

Moscow–Prague–Moscow

Mamardashvili joined the Department of Philosophy and Scientific Communism at VGIK in the fall of 1976. He descended upon VGIK just as he had entered the Moscow philosophical scene a decade earlier: commandingly, captivatingly, and with a notably exquisite, decidedly European, style. His lectures were public events, and many accounts, including Sokurov's recollections as an undergraduate student at VGIK, describe auditoriums so full that attendees spilled onto the floors and into the aisles.[5] Philosopher Viktor Vizgin writes about how Mamardashvili's audience listened to him with undivided attention and animation, describing his lectures as currents of air that could lift the listener "into unfamiliar territory of Thought, Philosophy, and Spirit."[6] As filmmaker Valerii Balaian puts it, "In front of our very eyes this man demonstrated true philosophical thought, in the ancient Greek sense of the term."[7] For VGIK professor Paola Volkova, Mamardashvili "included his audience in the process of how thought is born."[8] By the end of his first year at VGIK, Mamardashvili was earning 370 rubles a month, a generous salary for the time and one possible indication of the notoriety he had achieved among Moscow's intellectual elite.[9]

Much of the scholarly work on Mamardashvili in the past two decades has emphasized his role as a guiding voice of Soviet philosophy of the 1960s, and also of the liberal values that have come to be associated with the immediate post-Stalin period.[10] Scriptwriter Valerii Zalotukha describes him as part of a small handful of people who could transcend time and space "not just through words, but through gestures, the intonation of his voice, and with a single look could convince us that human freedom is not given from birth, but must be secured and defended every day of one's life."[11] For Sokurov, "[Mamardashvili] was unabashedly engaged in a kind of thought that was inaccessible to the majority of us."[12] His intellectual presence—his manner of speech, the views he expressed, and even the way he dressed—came to represent the liberal fantasies of the Soviet intelligentsia in the late-Soviet period. For many, Mamardashvili was a living beacon of Western culture and of the short-lived freedoms of the Soviet sixties.

In the spirit of his philosophical idol Immanuel Kant, who constructed for himself a cosmopolitan lifestyle without ever leaving his hometown of Königsberg, Mamardashvili's intellectual and sartorial image stretched beyond the borders imposed by Soviet isolationism. Even during the two decades he was classified as *nevyezdnoi*, which meant he was forbidden from leaving the Soviet Union for any reason, Nataliia Riazantseva decribes how "he was able to live a foreign life even in Moscow."[13] Mamardashvili was a philosophical palindrome, at once a voice from an irretrievable past and an inconceivable future; a simultaneous holdover from the early 1960s and a window to the late 1980s, "as if Merab knew it all in advance," as Boris Grushin puts it.[14] In the words of a former student: "Merab Mamardashvili was free."[15]

The often hyperbolic tone present in these and other recollections of Mamardashvili, indicates nostalgia not just for the man, but for the era he represented. The twenty-first century in particular ushered in a period of revived enthusiasm for the generation of the 1960s (*shestidesiatniki*) and for the era of the Thaw, which began with Khrushchev's 1956 denunciation of Stalin's cult of personality to a closed session of congress and had ended definitively by the time the Soviet Union invaded Czechoslovakia in the summer of 1968. The creative period of the Thaw was characterized by "anti-monumentalism and a yearning for individual self-expression capable of restoring the revolutionary spirit lost under Stalin," as Alexander Prokhorov puts it.[16] Restrictions on freedom of expression and movement were temporarily relaxed, while widespread amnesties following Stalin's death led to the staggered release of some four million prisoners from the Gulag camp system by 1960.

In philosophy, the *shestidesiatniki* were the generation that had come of intellectual age during the immediate post-Stalin era. They are often celebrated for producing original and significant philosophical work in spite of the restrictions of dialectical materialism and Marxism-Leninism. Together with the many prevalent myths about the 1960s generation, Mamardashvili's life and work have come to comprise a kind of legend that, in the recollections of his former students and colleagues, represents the ideals of freedom, honesty, and refinement associated with nostalgia for the 1960s.

Mamardashvili was abroad for much of the Thaw. He lived and worked in Prague between 1961 and 1966, in the years leading up to the Prague Spring. Amid the backdrop of artistic and expressive freedom that Prague offered its Soviet residents, Mamardashvili worked as an editor of the "Criticism and Bibliography" section at one of the most widely distributed Russian-language communist periodicals: *Problems of Peace and Socialism* (*Problemy mira i sotsializma*), often known by the title of its English-language edition, *The World Marxist Review*. Although *Problems of Peace and Socialism* had the reputation of enjoying significantly more freedom than any of the other communist periodicals, it was still a Party periodical, and with that territory came "the linguistic squalor and conceptual parochialism of its content, with its overuse of revolutionary rhetoric," in the words of one of the journal's long-time editors.[17]

At the same time, the journal was disproportionately influential with government officials back home, influencing Soviet Marxism by refracting Party ideology through the filter of the Eastern Bloc. Mamardashvili recalled that there was a feeling among the staff of the journal that they could go on to "serve progress," and many of the writers indeed did.[18] *Problemy* was the birthplace for the formative ideas behind the reforms of perestroika, and many of its writers and editors, such as Anatolii Cherniaev and Evgenii Ambartsumov, went on to become high-ranking advisors to Mikhail Gorbachev in the 1980s.

While Mamardashvili explicitly avoided politics until much later in his career, the years he spent in Prague were an unparalleled period of freedom and edification. He read Nietzsche, Freud, Heidegger, and the novels of Proust. He listened to Dvořák and Smetana, and mingled with a wide circle of European intellectuals. He drank Sauternes, enjoyed French detective novels, and developed a taste for European fashion that would follow him back to the Soviet Union.

In film, the Czechoslovak New Wave was well underway, where directors like Věra Chytilová, Miloš Forman, and Štefan Uher were reacting against the dominant tropes of socialist art through inventive cinematography, circuitous and surreal narratives, and the use of unscripted dialogue and non-professional actors. Mamardashvili and fellow philosopher-abroad Boris Grushin organized a film club called "Prague Meetings," where they interviewed Czech directors and screened films that were impossible to see in the Soviet Union.

According to French writer Pierre Bellefroid, who also worked at *Problemy* and with whom Mamardashvili would share a lifelong friendship, Merab possessed "the Georgian zest for life, a joy for life without reason, an 'illicit' joy, as he used to say."[19] As part of this "illicit joy,"

Merab and Pierre would read and discuss Proust, on whom Mamardashvili later delivered two famous cycles of lectures at Tbilisi State University in the 1980s. In order to communicate with his colleagues at *Problemy*, Mamardashvili studied languages. He arrived in Prague knowing English, French, German, and Italian, and would later become proficient in Spanish and Portuguese.

His position at the journal also allowed him the opportunity to travel, and from Prague he made a number of trips to Western Europe, both sanctioned and unsanctioned, including to Italy and France. On one such trip to Paris in 1966, Mamardashvili met Louis Althusser.[20] The two philosophers maintained a warm epistolary friendship for many years after, up until Althusser's declining mental health and subsequent institutionalization for his wife's murder in 1980 made their continued correspondence impossible. Mamardashvili and Bellefroid made a pact that they would never publish in the journal that employed them, in that "bastion of insufferable propaganda" that had brought them both to Prague.[21]

When Mamardashvili returned to Moscow in 1966, the Soviet Union was in the twilight of its period of cultural freedom. Leonid Brezhnev had already been presiding over the Soviet Union for two years and the period of economic and cultural regression that would come to be known as Stagnation, including new waves of political and artistic repression, was already underway. Thus, when Mamardashvili's voice reappeared in Moscow, two years before the Prague Spring of 1968, it was already a voice from an inaccessible past. He brought with him to Moscow his fondness for Czech cinema, binders of notes on Proust, and a taste for European fashion and jazz. His lectures, in turn, preserved the freedom of thought and expression that had been available to him abroad, but that had already disappeared from Soviet civil discourse. Mamardashvili appeared in Moscow's institutions of higher education in the 1970s as a man out of time, as a cultural traveler from a more liberal past, adorned in both the fashion and ideas of an era that had already faded from the Soviet horizon of possibility.

It was Mamardashvili's voice, in particular, that became a defining symbol of the openness and intellectual pathos of the 1960s, as transposed into the 1970s. Volkova describes how he spoke in a "low, masculine voice with a slight Georgian accent, more like a Georgian intonation pattern, a complicated way of speaking, sometimes almost whispering to himself, but with each person in attendance believing that Mamardashvili was speaking for him and him alone."[22] The slow, deep, familiar tone of his manner of speech may have reflected the sincerity of artistic forms of expression during de-Stalinization; the boldness of his philosophical views may have recalled the short-lived artistic and intellectual freedoms of the 1960s. Grushin too describes Mamardashvili as a time traveler of sorts, though in the opposite direction. "Already by 1950," Grushin recalls, "[Mamardashvili] had achieved a vision of the world that we, through our collective efforts, reached only in 1990."[23] Just as Irina Shilova argues that the filmmakers of the 1970s sought to "destroy the fortress of isolation, to connect the past with the present, and to remind us of universal human problems," so did Mamardashvili's lectures seem to serve that same function for members of his audiences, bringing people together—students and filmmakers and hairdressers—in an auditorium for an hour or two, around ideas of duty, justice, and consciousness.[24] Upon reading recollections on Mamardashvili's lectures, one gets the clear sense that their philosophical content was secondary to the *experience*, to the feeling of having been part of a cultural event that defined an intellectual generation.

For Soviet philosophers, the 1970s was often a decade of ideological struggle and censorship, but also one in which scholars had access to "air vents," as Nina Iulina calls such ideological loopholes, through which they could carry out original scholarly work.[25] Indeed, Soviet philosophers were engaged in productive collaboration with the Tartu school of semioticians, as one such example, and in the optimistic account of Slobodanka Vladiv-Glover, Mamardashvili "single-handedly constructed a late East European (Georgian) version of poststructuralism."[26] Nevertheless, Mamardashvili was driven out of his academic posts with increasing frequency, too liberal for a university culture that was becoming increasingly circumspect. In 1974, on the orders of the Secretary of the Moscow Committee for Ideology, Mamardashvili was fired from *Problems of Philosophy*, where he had worked for over a decade.[27] It also became difficult for other scholars to cite Mamardashvili. In a letter from 1978, philosopher Nataliia Avtonomova wrote to thank Mamardashvili for his "utter and complete" influence on her work, but also to share with him the following regret: "all my citations of your work are systematically and outrageously cut out (the most recent, enraging incident occurred in my Introduction to Foucault's *The Order of Things*), but I hope that one day I might express the words of thanks I've written [to you] here in published form."[28]

In 1980, Mamardashvili gave his last lecture at VGIK. Volkova, who brought him to VGIK in the first place, recalls complaints from her Marxist colleagues over "that Georgian and his Kafka."[29] As she described it, "VGIK could not bear the power of his personality for long. The Department of Social Sciences rattled and moaned."[30] In Sokurov's words, "[Mamardashvili] shined so unbelievably brightly against the provincial background of VGIK that his expulsion was inevitable."[31] Around that time, Mamardashvili was called back to the KGB headquarters at Lubianka Square and informed that he was either to relocate to Tbilisi or leave the Soviet Union altogether. That same year he moved back to Georgia, although he returned to Moscow regularly for teaching jobs and conferences.

What is Consciousness?

Mamardashvili's philosophy was above all concerned with the problem of individual consciousness and its relationship to the world, to other minds, and to itself. Although most of his philosophical work was an attempt to describe and explain consciousness, he also believed that the study of consciousness can lead only to paradox and enigma. In 1989, for instance, he described how investigating the question of consciousness leads us into "a sphere of paradox to which it is impossible to grow accustomed."[32] In the same interview, when asked to define consciousness, he replied "I don't know" three times in a row before trailing off.[33] Philosopher Diana Gasparyan describes his view of consciousness as the "equivalent of a 'black box': we can see what is at its input and what is at its output; however, if we address what is inside it, we fall into insolvable contradictions."[34] Mamardashvili was not content, however, to say that we have no way of knowing the reality of our consciousness experience. While we may not have full access to the box, we can certainly glimpse inside, he argued. Philosophy is one way we can gain access to consciousness experience. Film, as we will see, is another.

The behaviorist metaphor of the black box serves as a reminder that Mamardashvili's work in this field was part of a long and contentious history in which there have been various paradigms of mind at play, ranging from spiritual and/or metaphysical interpretations to computational models that reduce the mind to the expression of brain function, or even neuroanatomy, alone. As early as the late nineteenth century and continuing through the mid-twentieth, the behaviorists sought to wipe out talk of consciousness altogether, arguing that only through the observation and testing of reactions to external stimuli can one construct an accurate picture of the mind. In this view, action and change come from the world and the mind is a result of, or even a misnomer for, responses and adjustments of the human organism to external stimuli. The phenomenologists of the twentieth century, by contrast, returned the investigation of experience to the first-person position, whereby it is consciousness alone that endows experience its intentionality and, by extension, its directedness onto things in the world. While Mamardashvili rejected the empirical and the phenomenological paradigms alike, he never proposed a comprehensive theory of mind or offered a summary of his own philosophical views. Perhaps his sudden death in Moscow's Vnukovo airport in 1990 preempted him from compiling and distilling his philosophical views; more likely, such a summary would have been wholly antithetical in the context of his philosophical style.

It is also important to keep in mind that Mamardashvili was working within the parameters of the philosophy of mind of his era, which placed the Soviet interpretation of Marxism as the official starting point for all analyses of conscious experience. According to the collectively authored *Philosophical Encyclopedia* (*Filosofskaia entsiklopediia*, 1962), which was published in Moscow during the period when Mamardashvili was living and working in Prague, "the question of the relationship of consciousness to matter comprises the main question of philosophy."[35] Here, consciousness is described as the means by which the real (objective) world from nature is reflected in the self. The idea of the objective world included not only the laws of physics, logic, and mathematics, but also the prevailing social structure and the influence it exerts on the human mind. A leading psychologist of the Stalin era, Sergei Rubenshtein, argued in his work from the 1930s and 1940s for the unity of consciousness and the external sphere, for a deterministic relationship between the external causes of the objective world and the internal make-up of human consciousness. If the consciousness of every individual is determined by "objective" external forces (e.g. social, economic, political), then human beings possess no genuine autonomy, in the Kantian sense. The Soviet picture of consciousness of the period, while much more complex than this summary allows, was often summarized by the Soviet (Marxist) proverb, "being determines consciousness," which would have appeared in some form in most introductory philosophy textbooks and courses of the era.

For Mamardashvili, consciousness was at its most basic level founded in a relationship between the thinking subject (the mind) and the external world. To have consciousness is to have awareness and experience of the external world. But this relationship is always reciprocal: the external world is necessarily filtered through the mind and, in turn, the mind is made possible only by virtue of the fact that there is an external world to know. Not only does the mind need a world to apprehend and the world must be apprehended by a mind, but both elements exist in relation to one another.

Indeed, Mamardashvili argued, mind and world are unified reciprocally such that consciousness is simultaneously a relationship of mind to itself. Gasparyan has formulated Mamardashvili's views in a similar vein as "a sameness of being and consciousness," in that one must be/exist to be conscious yet must be conscious in order to be/exist: in her words, "there will always be *consciousness* peeping out from behind *being*, and *being* peeping out from behind *consciousness*."[36] Mamardashvili himself attributed this idea to the Cartesian and Kantian traditions, where he reminded us that there was already an affinity between consciousness and being.[37] Where mind and world are concerned, Mamardashvili challenged the Soviet distinction inherited from Marx, which stipulated that it was "not the consciousness of men that determines their existence, but their social existence that determines their consciousness."[38] Only under favorable social conditions, as Lenin wrote, was it the case that "consciousness does not simply reflect the objective world, but also creates it."[39]

Because we need the tool of consciousness in order to think about the problem of consciousness at all, Mamardashvili continued by arguing that consciousness "refers to a kind of connection or relation of the individual to a reality that is above or beyond our everyday reality."[40] This further reality, he continued, is the apprehension of the self from outside the self—the task toward which a healthy consciousness must always be directed but can never fully achieve. Exploring consciousness is difficult and rarely yields clear answers, and thus Mamardashvili regularly called the meta-theory of consciousness "a struggle with consciousness."[41]

A guiding question of Mamardashvili's philosophy of consciousness is the extent to which we can access consciousness and, in a continuation of the Cartesian project, the type of knowledge we can gain from it. Just as Marx argued that social reality impedes human beings from having truthful access to their thoughts, so did Mamardashvili believe that "the things that happen inside us are the least accessible to us."[42] And although he believed that we cannot ever truly escape consciousness or, in turn, know consciousness, we certainly can *try*, reflecting on our phenomenological position through rigorous philosophical inquiry. This method involved "positioning ourselves at the edge of the world," becoming aware of what is external to us in order to become more aware of ourselves in turn.[43] The external world is necessary for consciousness, Mamardashvili explained, both because it provides context for conscious experience and because it offers the perspective that defamiliarizes us from our habits and ourselves, allowing each individual to "look at himself as if from a different world."[44] This is "consciousness as witness," as Mamardashvili called it.[45] It is the processing of seeing something wholly familiar in an unfamiliar light, including those dangerous existential habits that we find ourselves in when consciousness remains unreflected upon for too long.

Husserl too sought to examine the relationship between consciousness and the world, which in one instantiation can be formulated as a relationship between the natural attitude (or the way we take our subjective position in the world for granted) and things in the world (as they are known to, or constituted by, consciousness). Through Husserl's philosophical method of transcendental phenomenology, the phenomenologist leaves the "natural attitude" and examines the immanent experiences and data of consciousness from the first-person point of view. When paired with the phenomenological method, Husserl thought that such explorations could purify consciousness, and that this "pure consciousness" could go on to serve as a consistent and objective starting point for further research in a way that was analogous to the exactness of mathematical knowledge; moreover, that experience itself could be treated empirically. As Mark Rowlands puts it, "[Husserl] does believe that consciousness—experience in both empirical and transcendental roles—is *logically* prior to the physical world. Consequently, he also believes that an investigation of the structure of consciousness is *methodologically* prior to an investigation of the physical world."[46] For Mamardashvili, too, consciousness was methodologically prior to any other investigation, including, paradoxically, the investigation of consciousness itself.

Mamardashvili and Husserl were both, on a broader level, interested in clarifying the true aims of philosophy, and consciousness plays a decisive role in both their methods. However, unlike Gustav Shpet, who attended Husserl's lectures in 1912–13 and went on to become Russia's most prolific phenomenologist before he was arrested and shot during the height of the Stalinist purges, Mamardashvili's phenomenological language was not Husserlian. He did not use the term "natural attitude" when he spoke of the habituation of consciousness to its reality. He was also critical of Husserl's procedural requirement that phenomenological investigation be contained entirely within the first-person transcendental position—that "the level of the phenomenon itself serves as the final, end, and last reality and cannot be further developed through analysis."[47] Nor did Mamardashvili borrow his phenomenological vocabulary from Jean-Paul Sartre, of whom he was even more critical.

Mamardashvili was not a phenomenologist but, as Akhutin puts it, "he appropriate[d] its *orientation* in order to see, understand, and recreate it each time in its own way by some kind of exciting exertion."[48] Though he was well read in the phenomenological tradition and even contentiously referred to Marx as the first phenomenologist, Mamardashvili positioned himself outside the tradition of phenomenology. He articulated his approach as a broader plane of objective analysis, a new ontology that accounts for our constant confrontation with things that happen *by way of* (*posredstvom*) consciousness. *Being* itself, he said, "is an independent source of life, the mind, society, and history," and cannot be derived from a single point or as a continuous chain.[49]

To put forward another genealogy, we see how Mamardashvili's approach to what Husserl called the "natural attitude" was in fact closer to critical theorist and screenwriter Viktor Shklovsky's vocabulary of defamiliarization. In his landmark essay "Art as Device" ("Iskusstvo kak priem," 1917), Shklovsky described how poetic language shakes up our expectations and habits and thereby shakes off the automaticity of the everyday. In his words, "defamiliarization is to see the world through different eyes."[50] The potential of the poetic was critical for Mamardashvili, whose work rarely includes direct citations of philosophical texts but is ripe with references to poetry and literature. His favorite writers included Osip Mandelshtam, Andrei Platonov, and especially Marcel Proust, whom Mamardashvili saw as a great phenomenologist in his own right.

Film too served as an indispensable source of phenomenological and philosophical material for Mamardashvili. Film art could not only recreate "the time and space of consciousness," but when watching film he described how "perceptions and feelings are born in me that are not organic in their origins."[51] Shklovsky attributed to film art the power to produce perceptions and feelings that were somehow more external than perceptions and feelings from non-cinematic sources, perhaps much in the way that conscious experience arises from consciousness alone, and therefore seems to originate both from nowhere and from everywhere at once.

For Mamardashvili, consciousness came forth like a dressing-room mirror, in which we are constantly reflected back at ourselves from all angles, at all times. Indeed, the mirror was a favorite metaphor of Mamardashvili's, and he argued that although we come to know ourselves through consciousness' witnessing of itself, consciousness can never reflect directly on consciousness.[52] In other words, consciousness cannot become its own object; it cannot be *experienced* in the way we experience life, since consciousness is not the object of empirical knowledge.[53] The fact that in Russian the word *consciousness* (*soznanie*) is created by adding the prefix *so-* to the word *knowledge* (*znanie*) allows for a clever turn of phrase, as Mamardashvili said that "we can never turn the particle *so-* into the object of knowledge/consciousness."[54] Here we see how the concept of consciousness falls into paradox—this time in a linguistic turn—since grammatically it points at both knowledge and the awareness of that same knowledge. Semantically and phenomenologically, consciousness is a necessary part of consciousness. In their joint work *Symbol and Consciousness*, Mamardashvili and Piatigorsky argued that any study of consciousness must occur at the meta-philosophical level, since consciousness itself is not accessible to theory.[55]

For Mamardashvili, thus, consciousness appears to evade knowledge at every turn. The individual who goes out in search of his own consciousness will come up empty-handed, as will the individual looking for the glasses that he is already wearing, since the object of his search is in fact the mechanism of the searching. Although in his first book, *Forms and Content of Thought* (1968), Mamardashvili maintained that knowledge requires intersubjectivity, the impossibility of philosophical language to truly escape consciousness suggests a solipsistic structure in which both objects and reflective acts are the physical content of consciousness, a critique that also happened to be waged against Husserl's early work by German logician Gottlob Frege.[56] Moreover, the endless layers of consciousness, in which consciousness requires consciousness which requires consciousness ad infinitum, leads us into a logical conundrum that recalls Socrates' claims in *Parmenides* that even the Forms themselves participate in the qualities of which they are exemplars.[57] In this way, consciousness risks becoming a closed system that endlessly folds in on itself, as Mamardashvili reminds us that even the mind's retreat to "the edge of the world" always occurs within the confines of consciousness alone.[58]

One further difficulty for the practitioner of Mamardashvili's method is his view that an act of consciousness is available only in the moment of its actualization—that a fact of consciousness as the content of consciousness is available to the thinker only in the moment he is conscious of it, after which it is irretrievably gone. Mamardashvili regularly appealed to musical metaphors, whereby consciousness is fleeting, like a chord that is available only in the exact moment it is played. In *Symbol and Consciousness*, he described it in another metaphor: like a text that arises in the very act of its being read.[59] These metaphors are as useful for our understanding of Mamardashvili's philosophy as for our study of Mamardashvili as a cultural phenomenon. Although he gave several of his lectures in multiple places and those close to him report that he spent a significant amount of time preparing his presentations, those present among his audiences often describe the experience of seeing Mamardashvili speak as sharing the same ephemeral quality as a concert or theater performance: that they were witness to a unique and fleeting event, and that they were "included in the process of how thought is born."[60]

Is Consciousness a Place?

In a paper from 1987, Mamardashvili explained how he first took up questions of consciousness not for empirical reasons, but as an "attempt to reunite with what seemed to be a very dear and essential part of [himself], but that had somehow gone missing, forgotten."[61] Despite its many paradoxes and complications, and the claim that consciousness can never be its own object or an object at all, we have seen how Mamardashvili did attempt to describe consciousness ontologically—that is, what consciousness essentially *is*, and also where it is found.[62]

In his joint work with Piatigorsky, Mamardashvili described consciousness as the "only existing thing that is a non-thing," and describes its *thingness* in terms of its topology.[63] And although Descartes argued that the Ego was a thinking substance with no spatial extension, for Mamardashvili the human "I" has its own spatial configuration, akin to "a field."[64] In a 1988 presentation, Mamardashvili described consciousness as the *meeting place* for things we cannot connect in any empirical way. In a 1988 essay called "The Problem of Consciousness and Philosophical Purpose" ("Problema soznaniia i filosofskoe prizvanie"), he referred to consciousness as "a place (*mesto*), in the topological sense of the word."[65] Later on in the same work he said that "[consciousness] is a cosmological constant."[66] This final statement on consciousness seems to imply that if consciousness is some sort of space, then it is one with far-reaching and consistent properties and implications.

One way to answer the question of whether consciousness is a space would be to answer in the affirmative, and to say that its location, or space, is the brain. Indeed, the Soviet tradition of dialectical materialism understood consciousness to be "a property of highly organized matter, a function of that 'part of matter' that we call the human brain."[67] Again taking issue with Husserl's claim that pure consciousness, or transcendental subjectivity, could serve as an absolute and consistent basis for phenomenological research, Mamardashvili aligned himself closer to Freud on the role of the empirical in analyses of consciousness. He noted that Freud began psychoanalysis on the basis of empirical research in the study of the brain and neuroanatomy and, as Mamardashvili put it, "[Freud] does not describe the phenomenal world from within this world but tries to lay bare psychological mechanisms that are described in terms that cannot be found in the content of the phenomena themselves."[68]

In his lecture series on *The Aesthetics of Thinking* (*Estetika myshleniia*), Mamardashvili described the paradoxical condition of consciousness in terms of the Greek puzzle of aporia, which he described, etymologically, as an "impassable space."[69]

> It is interesting that it is [the concept of] "place" that figures in the word "aporia." Now recall the kind of place that I described to you as impassable. Here I am, standing and looking, and in its clarity my consciousness is witnessing, and to split it apart would be impossible, it is united, and I am unable to move neither right, nor left, nor straight ahead. As I said to you, it is in this situation that we first perceive ourselves as finite beings, without time. And when there is no time, only then do we perceive our own finitude.[70]

Though the empirical status of the topology of consciousness was up for debate, Mamardashvili was clear that the "space" of consciousness was, at the very least, both a phenomenological field for further theoretical work and a philosophical metaphor for the human condition.

Does Consciousness Have a Voice?

Mamardashvili not only assigned consciousness ontological status and topology but described it in terms of how it can be put into words: that is, how the space of consciousness can be recorded. Like Socrates, Mamardashvili was an avid proponent of the primacy of the methods of philosophy to examine the world and the mind. If consciousness is an awareness of the familiar as unfamiliar, then in order to examine the familiar as unfamiliar, the individual must use philosophical reasoning. In fact, for Mamardashvili, when consciousness is expressed as thought, it is done so through philosophical reasoning. When we think or talk about consciousness, we do so through philosophy. "Philosophy," he said, "is consciousness aloud."[71]

Philosophy, in other words, is a way to access consciousness, and to describe, analyze, interrogate, and seek to explain it. "Philosophy is a recording of consciousness," as Mamardashvili put it, and is therefore our best bet at accessing it.[72] Elsewhere, Mamardashvili argued that philosophy enables the individual "to report on himself to himself," and that it is the conceptual and semantic possibilities of philosophy that make this report both accurate and clear.[73] "Always and everywhere, philosophy is the language in which the witness of consciousness is deciphered," he said.[74]

If the practice of philosophy—or, the act of philosophizing—is a recording of consciousness, then what exactly is it recording? It is important here to keep in mind that for Mamardashvili, thought (*myshlenie*) is not reducible to consciousness; rather, thought is the voice of consciousness. Thought is "consciousness aloud."[75] Here again we see the influence of Descartes, for whom consciousness and self-awareness could be defined as thought (*pensée*), whereby thought is understood as "all those things which occur in us while we are conscious, insofar as the consciousness of them is in us."[76] In "Time and Space" ("Vremia i prostranstvo," 1990), Mamardashvili argued that consciousness expresses that which cannot be expressed or contained in other modes—for instance, through feeling.[77] It appears, thus, that thought is a product of consciousness, and philosophy is a recording of thought. Not all thoughts, of course, take the form of philosophy, and so Mamardashvili's description here does not seem to fully account for the range of thought that happens within us.

The paradoxes that Mamardashvili raised in his study of consciousness were intentional; they were not the products of faulty reasoning, but puzzles he presented intentionally to his readers as a way to think through the problem of consciousness metaphorically and poetically. He returned time and again to the idea that consciousness "refers to a kind of connection or relation of the individual to a reality that is above or beyond our everyday reality."[78] Specifically, he maintained that through consciousness, human beings are able to experience things that cannot be explained through an examination of physical processes alone.[79] Against the reductionist argument, he claimed that if an individual were to receive thoughts that were given to him through biological powers alone, then they wouldn't be *his* thoughts. They would be situations that occur in him, pure thoughts, pure love, pure etc., but they wouldn't be *his*.[80] Here the possessive *his* is constituted by something that points beyond the mechanistic or biological. Though Mamardashvili did not speak in spiritual terms, at the very least there is *something else* to human consciousness that transcends the empirical level. As Gasparyan puts it, "humans cannot 'derive themselves' from nature, and that between nature, as given to us, and humans, as given to themselves, there is an unbridgeable distance, a sort of a blank space or a gap."[81]

For Mamardashvili to claim that there was *something else* to consciousness was not only to go against the prevailing materialism of the day; it was also to go against the atheism of Soviet ideology. Mamardashvili stressed the possibility of transcendence and unknowability: the unknowability of consciousness, of the infinite, and of the potential for freedom and wonder within consciousness. He did not say that the *something else* was religious spirituality, but his framework at least allowed for that possibility. The extra, higher dimension of consciousness about which he spoke is what sets humans (at least, mentally) above all other living things; only human beings can have the *his* or *her* tacked on to their experience in the true, existential sense, he argued.[82] Consciousness was therefore something to be celebrated. It is joyful, it is spontaneous, and it is *the* great mystery of human life. Consciousness is not only what makes living (in the biological sense) possible, but it is also what makes living worthwhile.

Above all, Mamardashvili's work on consciousness was a celebration of the human mind and the power of thought. We see this both in his philosophical work and through the model of his own life, which was devoted to the public practice of "philosophy as consciousness aloud" at the front of the classroom, for all to see.[83] In his interpretation of the Socratic model, Mamardashvili lived the examined life by living the conscious life: to think consciously and act with conscience, and to use the language of consciousness as the tool we have been given against the world. Anything less and we are merely biological automata, sinking into the barbaric and nihilistic inclinations of society that he would discuss in detail in his interviews from the 1980s. Being a human being—not just a body with a mind, but an individual (*lichnost'*)—is something we must constantly work at, Mamardashvili argued. It is a battle that must be constantly fought and can never be won.[84]

The Lonely Voice of MM

When Mamardashvili arrived on the faculty at VGIK in the fall of 1976, a young Alexander Sokurov (b. 1951) was beginning his second year as a student in the Department of Directing. His diploma film was *The Lonely Voice of Man* (*Odinokii golos cheloveka*, 1978), a loose adaption of Andrei Platonov's short story "The River Potudan" (*Reka Potudan'*, 1936). The film combines fictional and documentary footage to detail the struggles of a young couple in their search for marital happiness in the traumatic aftermath of the Russian Civil War.

Oleg Kovalov points out that Sokurov's diaries from the time he was making *The Lonely Voice of Man* "seem to be filled with the atmosphere of midnight intrigue in the VGIK hostel," with references to Mamardashvili and others lecturing at VGIK in those years.[85] Like Mamardashvili, Sokurov was both celebrated and marginalized within the walls of the Institute. When the school administration discovered that he was adapting the work of one of the Soviet Union's most controversial writers, they ordered that the negatives to the film be destroyed. A single print was saved by the film's cameraman, Sergei Yurizditsky, who hid it in his dormitory and later arranged secret screenings for students and faculty. *The Lonely Voice of Man* was screened publicly only in 1987 at the Locarno Film Festival where it won the Grand Prix, the Bronze Leopard.

Following his graduation from VGIK, Sokurov began work at the Lenfilm studio in St Petersburg. In 1980 he directed *Demoted*, a short film of exactly thirty minutes. This time he based his screenplay on a 1976 short story of the same name by writer Grigorii Baklanov, best known for writing about the Soviet front. Sokurov's Lenfilm debut has by now all but disappeared into the celebrated expanse of his broader body of work; it is mentioned in few critical sources on Sokurov's work, and typically only in passing. Like *The Lonely Voice of Man*, *Demoted* too was banned shortly after completion and the negatives were ordered destroyed. Once again, the director's copy was smuggled out and saved from destruction; this illicit copy, now badly faded with age, is the only remaining celluloid original.[86]

Demoted takes place over twenty-four hours in the life of a former state traffic inspector who has recently been demoted to taxi driver. This "day in the life"-style portrait, in which we follow the driver on his daily routes, is arranged in disjointed fragments that muddle the time and space of the narrative, crafting St Petersburg as a space of chance encounters, impossible distances, enigmatic exchanges between strangers, and illuminated night-time spaces. On the particular day captured in the film, we watch the driver wake up, perform callisthenic rituals in a field on the way to the airport, and then shuttle two students back to their dormitory in the city. Although it is morning when he rises and overcast as he drives to the airport, the scenes in his cab take place at night. After delivering his passengers, the driver stops at a movie theatre to see a film; when he exits it is already morning. Dmitrii Savelev describes the wispy and disorienting arrangements of *Demoted* as Sokurov's "dream logic."[87] Indeed, we might view the temporal and spatial leaps as if we were peering into the driver's slumbering mind, traversing the city in his cab and meeting faces from his past and present as he sleeps.

For Aleksandra Tuchinskaia, the driver "experiences his loss of his power as a catastrophic injustice."[88] This power shift that drives the narrative of the film—the shift from high-ranking civil servant to service worker—employs the return trajectory of Lenin's mythical slogan of classless power reciprocity, according to which any cook could run the state. What this Soviet platitude left out, of course, is that by extension any head of state could as easily be demoted to the position of cook or, in the case of *Demoted*, taxi driver. Sokurov's driver is a stand-in for both these stories at once: he is a carnivalistic representation of this slogan, simultaneously personifying institutional power and the loss of that power. His personal setbacks are revealed over the course of Sokurov's thirty-minute portrait—the loss of his career, a troubled relationship with the daughter who is deceiving him, and broader existential disillusionment. These personal struggles are expressed through the trope of the road, by his erratic driving, and monologic outbursts.

Figure 1.1 The demoted taxi driver in the early morning light.

The driver's setbacks are, in turn, poeticized by the cinematic geography of St Petersburg, which is composed almost entirely of dark or partially illuminated spaces: the driver's bedchamber at night, the lamplit streets of the city, and a crowded movie theatre. While Baklanov's short story takes place in the middle of the day, where the sun is so bright that the taxi driver must put on his sunglasses, *Demoted* is dominated by the overwhelming darkness of the cinematography (see Figure 1.1). The night-time streets of the city, along which the driver travels, are lined by street lamps, oscillating traffic lights, and buildings lit by spotlights.

The murky light of Sokurov's St Petersburg prevents characters not only from seeing one another, but from engaging with each other in any authentic way. Characters speak to one another, but in such a way as if they are addressing only themselves. As the driver eats a sandwich at the airport café, a former colleague expresses the opinion that "people cease being people when they no longer feel pain—not just their pain, but the pain of others."[89] The sincerity of his humanism is cast into doubt by the fact that he expresses it in-between full-mouthed bites, with breadcrumbs spewing from his lips as he muffles the syllables of his inauthentic humanistic declaration. He receives no response from those listening. In this and other moments of the film, personal interactions in

Demoted oscillate between the existential noise of the film's soundtrack and the resulting silence of its inter-personal dialogue. The possibility for authentic human interaction is repeatedly thwarted by monologues and the rumble of passing trains, while conversation is reduced to silent expressions, unanswered questions, and mouths stuffed with food.

Personal relationships in the film are likewise fractured, frustrated, or absent. In the closing scene of *Demoted*, the driver leaves a movie theatre and comes upon his former subordinate running laps on a track. New snow has fallen that night and covers the empty stadium. The young runner is in excellent shape; he runs regularly to be physically prepared for whatever the future might hold. The day is coming and he will be ready. "But for what?," the driver provokes. The young man gives no answer. The film cuts to documentary footage of a ship on the river.

The most significant of the film's monologues occurs at the film's halfway-point, as the driver laments his family troubles on a late-night airport run. This segment makes up both the longest shot and sequence in the film. After a bout of reckless driving, the driver pulls his cab to a halt under a railroad bridge. Through the static on the dashboard transistor radio we hear a solitary male voice with a slight Georgian accent. For just over two minutes, the radio plays a fragment of a lecture by Merab Mamardashvili—the second-longest monologue of the film. This particular clip was taken from a conversation with Vladimir Tretiakov, a classmate of Sokurov's at VGIK who interviewed the philosopher for an unfinished film on the Decembrist movement. As the whistle from an approaching train sounds, the camera slowly zooms in to a close-up of the radio as we hear Mamardashvili's voice speaking of the nature of the rule of law and ethical questions surrounding the Decembrists.

Mamardashvili's voice would have been recognizable to the select viewers who found themselves in front of Sokurov's film in those years. They had most likely heard him lecture, and many would have known him personally, either through VGIK connections or elsewhere. For Savelev, the inclusion of this soundtrack is a comment on Mamardashvili's own troubled history at VGIK, as the "demoted philosopher" who was eventually driven out.[90] Although *Demoted* (and perhaps even Mamardashvili's own life) lends itself to an obvious populist reading, in which the career setbacks of the protagonist foretell the collapse of the Soviet system that has both given him and taken away his power, Nancy Condee correctly points out that *Demoted* is not a class-driven adaptation of Baklanov's story.[91] This despite the fact that the downcast and devalued driver is played by amateur actor Ilia Rivin, a Soviet everyman who would go on to appear in three other films by Sokurov in the 1980s.

We open up new possibilities for interpreting the film if we consider the inclusion of Mamardashvili's voice in Sokurov's film as more than just an aesthetic choice, but as a comment on the existential position of the driver. Instead of reading Sokurov's narrative tapestry as bound by the logic of the dream, as Savelev contends, I argue that *Demoted* encourages us to view it as guided by the logic of consciousness. That is, that the content of the consciousness of the driver—his stream of thoughts—is expressed through the images of the film. Upon moving from the dream model to a *model of consciousness*, the seemingly unconnected and impossible coincidences of the film (e.g. meeting former subordinates, the bizarre behavior of the people he encounters and their dream-like movements and expressions) go from being disconnected (dream-like) to representing the normal fluidity of human mental states, in this case the driver's. The prevailing darkness of the film's cinematography is not symbolic of sleep-time, in turn, but a representation of the driver's muddied mind as he fumbles his way through his new social and civil role. Like an individual unable to step outside of his own experience, the driver is unable to escape the stream of consciousness narrative that reminds him of his former life. We are trapped inside his mind, together with him. "Where do you think you're going?" he yells at another car. "You can't escape!"[92]

The cacophony of the audio space of the film further mirrors the driver's moment of existential crisis. We hear the roar of trains and car engines, the echoing female voice over the loudspeaker in the airport, and the sound of planes passing overhead. The noise of the driver's consciousness is loud like the rapid acceleration of a car engine or the deafening rumble of a passing train. In "The 'Third' Condition" ("'Tret'e' sostoianie," 1989), which he published in the film journal *Screenplays* (*Kinostsenarii*), Mamardashvili points to a moment in Andrei Platonov's *Foundation Pit* (*Kotlovan*, 1930) in which the consciousness of so-called "comrade cripple" Zhachev is broadcast for him while he struggles to answer back.[93] Platonov writes: "Sometimes Zhachev could not bear the melancholic despair in his soul and would yell over the noise of his consciousness that streamed through the loudspeaker: 'Stop that sound! Let me speak!'"[94] As Mamardashvili argued, each of us must find a way to confront the static inside our minds.[95]

Existential turmoil is represented by the noise of engines and static in *Demoted*, and it is telling that as soon as Mamardashvili's voice speaks the word consciousness on the radio a train rumbles by and drowns out the remainder of the sentence. In fact, "consciousness" is the last word we hear before the camera cuts to a take of the driver speaking with a traffic guard, a former subordinate, while the train passes by. The sound of the train fades away and we again see the pair speaking, but instead of hearing their conversation, the sound of Mamardashvili's voice returns. He speaks of justice and fairness. "But what is the difference between justice and law?" we hear before the voice fades away for good.[96] The distortion of the noise of consciousness' loudspeaker, or the loud diegetic sounds of the film, is counteracted by the film's musical score. The simple trombone score that plays in the background offers a single, comprehensible, and confident voice.

A further layer of textual commentary is delivered in the movie theatre scene. The film that the driver stops in to see is Sokurov's own banned diploma film, *The Lonely Voice of Man*. We see the driver, now sitting with his wife and daughter in the theatre, and the editing toggles between showing scenes from the film and close-ups of the faces in the audience. Two scenes from *The Lonely Voice of Man* appear in *Demoted*: the first when the young couple see each other for the first time again after Nikita's return from the front; the second when the newlyweds discuss the family that they will never have. The movie theatre scene is a clear moment of protest on Sokurov's part; it would have been impossible for anybody to step into a theatre in 1980 and watch clips from the director's shelved diploma film. As Savelev puts it, "by inviting *The Lonely Voice of Man* on the screen, Sokurov undertakes the act of recollection-resurrection of the demoted [protagonist] and as it were the film that was declared to not exist. He is preempting time, legalizing his *Lonely Voice*."[97] The power play in *Demoted* is extended to both a meta-reflexive and self-reflexive level as a victory over power and over censorship from above, in both the inclusion of the only extant sound bite from a film that was never authorized and the inclusion of nearly two minutes of a film that was supposed to have been eradicated.

That the driver's demotion becomes an opportunity for existential rebirth is signaled primarily through the use of documentary footage of water, including the opening and closing shots of a passenger ship cruising down a river, both of which are also featured in the beginning of *The Lonely Voice of Man*.[98] Water brings with it the archetypal weight of rebirth, resurrection, and redemption, and the watery scenes that open and close the film signal the unexpected optimism of this transitional moment. These shots are complemented with water imagery in the form of the remaining snow of spring in a field, and a water balloon that the driver holds in his hands while lying in the snowy grass (see Figure 1.2). He lies down in the snow while waiting to pick up a passenger at the airport, a roadside baptism at the start of a transfigured profession. In his notes on the first day of shooting, Rivin described his character in *Demoted*

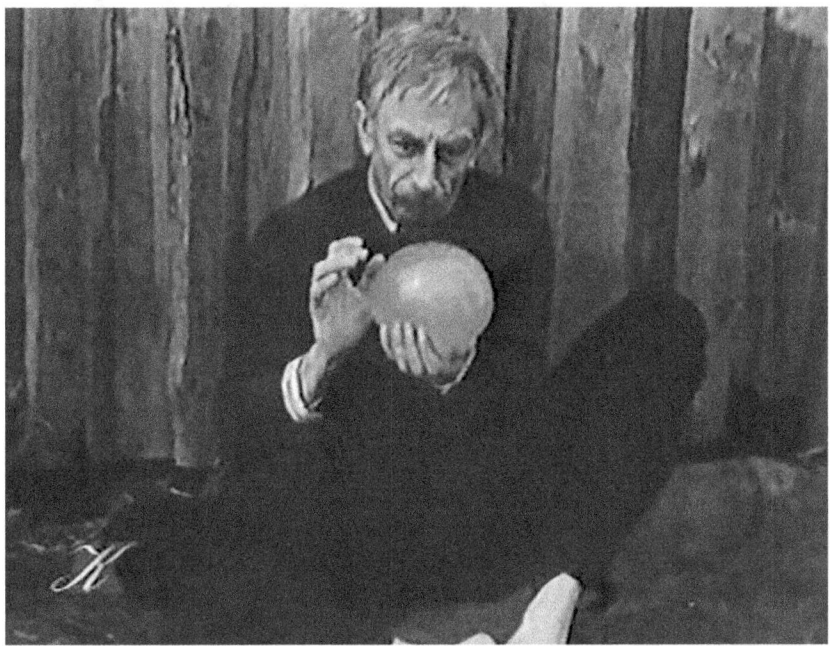

Figure 1.2 Water imagery in *Demoted*.

as guided by an unconscious inner sensation of rebirth after a period of psychological and familial dejection.[99] It is not in vain that the driver in *Demoted* keeps saying, "I just want to celebrate (*voskhishchat'sia*)," where the verb in Russian for "celebrate" emphasizes the act of being elevated and enraptured by something, and shares the same prefix as the word for "resurrection" (*voskresenie*). The protagonist does not make clear why or what he wants to celebrate but perhaps, like Mamardashvili, he will celebrate being itself.

At the end of his broadcasted monologue in *Demoted*, Mamardashvili says that "the spoken word has great significance. The word is a social fact."[100] Although the conversations in *Demoted* are rarely conversations at all, often beginning and ending as monologues and receiving only one-word responses or strange looks, the film posits a different model of recognitive transmission. It is not conversation that is privileged, but the transmission of the word itself—not just any word, but the authentic word, even if that word receives no response or is broadcast fleetingly over the radio of a cab. For Mamardashvili, only the authentic word was worth transmitting; "The communist word has no meaning," he used to say to Bellefroid.[101] The insertion of Mamardashvili's voice in *Demoted* signals toward a broader significance of the word, reaching beyond the genre of populist portrait to the status of consciousness itself. In the next chapter we will investigate the status of the literary word in Mamardashvili's work from the 1980s, the decade he taught at the Higher Courses and Tbilisi State University.

Notes

1. David J. Chalmers, "Facing Up to the Problem of Consciousness," *Journal of Consciousness Studies* 2, No. 3 (1995): p. 3.
2. Mamardashvili and Piatigorskii, p. 31.
3. The temporal exception here is Chapter Six, on Vadim Abdrashitov and Alexander Mindadze, who are part of an earlier generation but about whom Mamardashvili wrote.
4. Stanley Cavell, "'What Becomes of Thinking on Film?' (Stanley Cavell in Conversation with Andrew Klevan)," in *Film as Philosophy. Essays in Cinema after Wittgenstein and Cavell*, ed. Rupert Read and Jerry Goodenough (New York: Palgrave Macmillan, 2005), pp. 167–209.
5. See, for instance: Tirons; Sokurov, "Pamiati Meraba Mamardashvili;" and Volkova, "Paola Volkova o tom, chto bol'she ne povtoritsia," Arzamas Academy, Course No. 9, http://arzamas.academy/materials/217.
6. Viktor Vizgin, "My vse ego tak liubili: vspominaia Meraba Mamardashvili," Mamardashvili.com, 2009, http://mamardashvili.com/about/vizgin/2.html.
7. Balaian.
8. Volkova, "Paola Volkova o tom, chto bol'she ne povtoritsia."
9. Merab Mamardashvili Personnel File. 1976. Fond No. 1, Inventory No. 8-L, Storage No. 223. Archives of the Gerasimov Institute of Cinematography.
10. See, for example: Denis Dragunskii, "Filosofiia bez trepa," *Russkii zhurnal* (Oct. 6, 2010), http://www.russ.ru/layout/set/print/Mirovaya-povestka/Filosofiya-bez-trepa; Diana Gasparian, *Filosofiia soznaniia Meraba Mamardashvili* (Moscow: Kanon +, 2013), p. 35; Sedakova; Mariia Vagina, Mnenie.ru (Dec. 24, 2012), http://mnenia.ru/rubric/culture/shestidesyatnikam-zdes-ne-mesto/; V. P. Zinchenko, *Posokh Osipa Mandel'shtama i trubka Meraba Mamardashvili* (Moscow: Direkt media, 2013), p. 123.
11. Valerii Zalotukha, "My nazyvali kursy litseem," in *Professiia – kinematografist*, ed. P. D. Volkova, A. N. Gerasimov, and V. I. Sumenova (Ekaterinburg: U-Faktoriia, 2004), p. 178.
12. Sokurov, "Pamiati Meraba Mamardashvili."
13. Riazantseva.
14. Qtd Alena Mamardashvili, "'Eto v pervuiu ochered' reaktsiia udivlennogo cheloveka, kotoryi v izumenii podnial brovi ...,'" *Chastnyi korrespondent* (Sept. 17, 2010), http://www.chaskor.ru/article/alena_mamardashvili__

eto_v_pervuyu_ochered__reaktsiya_udivlennogo_cheloveka_kotoryj_v_ izumlenii_podnyal_brovi_20497.
15. Dularidze, "Stranstvuiushchii filosof."
16. Alexander Prokhorov, "The Unknown New Wave: Soviet Cinema of the Sixties," in *Springtime for Soviet Cinema. Re/Viewing the 1960s*, ed. Alexander Prokhorov (Pittsburgh: n.p., 2001), p. 8, http://www.rusfilm. pitt.edu/booklets/Thaw.pdf.
17. Aleksandr Volkov, "Redaktsiia zhurnala 'Problemy mira i sotsializma' 1958–1990. Vospominaniia sotrudnikov i sovremennikov. Chast' I," *Russkii zhurnal* (Oct. 9, 2013), http://russ.ru/pole/Redakciya-zhurnala-Problemy-mira-i-socializma-1958-1990.
18. Mamardashvili, "Moi opyt netipichen," p. 359.
19. Bellefroid.
20. There is a chance Mamardashvili and Althusser's first meeting occurred earlier, sometime between 1962 and 1966. See: Annie Epelboin, "Perepiska Meraba Mamardashvili s Lui Al'tiusserom," in *Vstrecha: Meraba Mamardashvili i Lui Al'tiusser* (Moscow: Fond Meraba Mamardashvili, 2016), p. 57.
21. Bellefroid. On Mamardashvili and Althusser's epistolary friendship, see: Miglena Nikolchina, "Inverted Forms and Heterotopian Homonymy: Althusser, Mamardashvili, and the Problem of 'Man,'" *boundary2* 41, No. 1 (2014): pp. 79–100.
22. Volkova, "Ob"iasnenie neob"iasnimogo," p. 209.
23. Qtd A. Mamardashvili, "'Eto v pervuiu ochered'.'"
24. Irina Shilova, . . . *I moe kino* (Moscow: NII Kinoiskusstva/Kinovedcheskie zapiski, 1993), p. 138.
25. Nina Iulina, "Taking in the Past at a Glance. An Interview with N.S. Iulina," *Russian Studies in Philosophy* 48, No. 1 (summer 2009): p. 57.
26. Slobodanka Vladiv-Glover, "Poststructuralism in Georgia. The Phenomenology of the 'Objects-Centaurs' of Merab Mamardashvili," *Angelaki: Journal of the Theoretical Humanities* 15, No. 3 (Dec. 2010): p. 28.
27. Riazantseva describes the Aesopian nature of that encounter as follows: "Merab explained that he had been 'removed' from the journal [*Problems of Philosophy*] with high esteem, with appreciation for his work, and had even been given a trip to an excellent sanatorium in Crimea as a parting gift." See: Riazantseva.
28. Nataliia Avtonomova, "Letter to M. Mamardashvili," Feb. 3, 1978.
29. Volkova, "Merab na vysshikh kursakh," in *Merab Mamardashvili: "Byt' filosofom – eto sud'ba . . . ,"* ed. N. V. Motroshilova, A. A. Paramonov, and E. V. Petrovskaia (Moscow: Progress-Traditsiia, 2013), p. 281.
30. Ibid.
31. Sokurov, "Pamiati Meraba Mamardashvili."
32. Merab Mamardashvili, "Soznanie – eto paradoksal'nost', k kotoroi nevozmozhno privyknut'," in *Kak ia ponimaiu filosofiiu*, ed. Iu. P. Senokosov, 2nd edn (Moscow: Progress – Kul'tura, 1992), p. 85.

33. Ibid.
34. Diana Gasparyan, *Merab Mamardashvili's Philosophy of Consciousness* (Takoma Park, MD: PhotoPressArt, 2012), p. 97.
35. F. B. Konstantinov (ed.), "Soznanie," in *Filosofskaia entsiklopediia*, Vol. 5 (Moscow: Iz-vo "Sovetskaia entsiklopediia," 1962), p. 44.
36. Gasparyan, p. 23.
37. Mamardashvili, "Problemy analiza soznaniia," Mamardashvili.com, Lecture No. 10, http://www.mamardashvili.com/archive/lectures/consciousness/10.html.
38. Karl Marx, "Preface," in *A Contribution to the Critique of Political Economy* (Moscow: Progress, 1977), https://www.marxists.org/archive/marx/works/1859/critique-pol-economy/preface.htm.
39. Qtd Konstantinov, p. 45.
40. Merab Mamardashvili, "Problema soznaniia i filosofskoe prizvanie," in *Kak ia ponimaiu filosofiiu*, ed. Iu. P. Senokosov, 2nd edn (Moscow: Progress – Kul'tura, 1992), p. 42.
41. See, for instance: Mamardashvili and Piatigorskii, pp. 29 and 37.
42. Mamardashvili, "Problema soznaniia i filosofskoe prizvanie," p. 52.
43. Mamardashvili, *Vvedenie v filosofiiu*, http://psylib.org.ua/books/mamar02/index.htm.
44. "Problemy analiza soznaniia."
45. Ibid.
46. Mark Rowlands, *Externalism* (Chesham: Acumen, 2003), pp. 60–1.
47. "Problemy analiza soznaniia." In a cycle of lectures called "Questions of the Analysis of Consciousness" delivered at Moscow State University between 1972 and 1974, Mamardashvili sought to demonstrate that there are conditions of consciousness that actuate themselves independently of the level of phenomenological analysis, and therefore cannot be described from within the boundaries of phenomena alone.
48. Akhutin, p. 26.
49. "Problemy analiza soznaniia."
50. Viktor Shklovskii, *O teorii prozy* (Moscow: Sovetskii pisatel', 1983), p. 271.
51. Merab Mamardashvili, "Vremia i prostranstvo," Mamardashvili.com, https://mamardashvili.com/archive/interviews/timespace.html.
52. See, for instance: "Problema soznaniia i filosofskoe prizvanie," pp. 42–3.
53. Mamardashvili and Piatigorskii, p. 31.
54. Merab Mamardashvili, "Besedy o myshlenii," Mamardashvili.com, Lecture No. 7, http://mamardashvili.com/archive/lectures/thinking/bm07.html. The English *conscious* also shares "knowledge" as its root, coming from the Latin *scio*, meaning "to know."
55. *Simvol i soznanie*, p. 31.
56. On Frege's reading of Husserl, see Rudolf Bernet, Iso Kern, and Eduard

Marbach, *An Introduction to Husserlian Phenomenology* (Evanston, IL: Northwestern University Press, 1993), pp. 22–4.
57. Gasparyan discusses the logical conundrum that occurs when consciousness is treated as an object of consciousness. Gasparyan, pp. 81–2.
58. *Vvedenie v filosofiiu.*
59. *Simvol i soznanie*, pp. 65–6.
60. Volkova, "Paola Volkova o tom, chto bol'she ne povtoritsia."
61. "Problema soznaniia i filosofskoe prizvanie," p. 41.
62. Ibid., p. 50.
63. *Simvol i soznanie*, p. 26.
64. Ibid., p. 26.
65. "Problema soznaniia i filosofskoe prizvanie," p. 48.
66. Ibid., pp. 154–6.
67. Konstantinov, p. 44.
68. "Problemy analiza soznaniia," p. 49.
69. Mamardashvili, *Estetika myshleniia*, ed. Iu. P. Senokosov (Moscow: Moskovskaia shkola politicheskikh issledovanii, 2000), p. 71, http://rumol.ru/files/library/books/mamardashvili/m.mamardashvili_estetika%20mishleniya.pdf.
70. Ibid.
71. "Filosofiia – eto soznanie vslukh," p. 57.
72. "Problema soznaniia i filosofskoe prizvanie," p. 53.
73. Mamardashvili, "D'iavol igraet nami, kogda my ne myslim tochno ...," in *Kak ia ponimaiu filosofiiu*, ed. Iu. P. Senokosov, 2nd edn (Moscow: Progress – Kul'tura, 1992), pp. 126–8.
74. "Filosofiia – eto soznanie vslukh," p. 57.
75. Ibid., p. 67.
76. René Descartes, *Principles of Philosophy*, trans. Valentine Roger Miller and Reese P. Miller (Dordrecht, Holland: D. Reidel Publishing Company, 1983), p. 5.
77. "Vremia i prostranstvo."
78. "Problema soznaniia i filosofskoe prizvanie," p. 42.
79. Ibid., p. 43.
80. Ibid.
81. Gasparyan, p. 21.
82. "Problema soznaniia i filosofskoe prizvanie," p. 43.
83. See, for instance: "Filosofiia – eto soznanie vslukh," p. 57.
84. Mamardashvili used the word *lichnost'* in his writing on consciousness as early as the 1970s, when the term was considered a contentious, and in some contexts forbidden, topic of bourgeois reflection. For one example, see his 1977 presentation "Philosophy and Personality" ("Filosofiia i lichnost'") at the Institute of Psychology (Russian Academy of Sciences, Moscow). The text of his talk was posthumously published as Mamardashvili, "Filosofiia i lichnost'," *Chelovek* 5 (1994): pp. 5–19.

85. Oleg Kovalov, "We in The Lonely Voice," in *The Cinema of Alexander Sokurov*, ed. Birgit Beumers and Nancy Condee (London: I. B. Tauris, 2011), p. 217.
86. On the film's extrication from destruction, see Dmitrii Savel'ev, "Krugi razzhalovannogo," in *Sokurov. Chasti rechi* (St Petersburg: Seans, 2011), p. 37.
87. Savel'ev, p. 42.
88. Aleksandra Tuchinskaia, "Annotatsiia," Ostrov Sokurova, http://sokurov.spb.ru/isle_ru/feature_films.html?num=4.
89. Sokurov, *Razzhalovannyi* (Mosfil'm, 1980).
90. Savel'ev, p. 40.
91. Nancy Condee, *The Imperial Trace: Recent Russian Cinema* (Oxford: Oxford University Press, 2009), p. 167.
92. Sokurov, *Razzhalovannyi*.
93. Andrei Platonov, *Kotlovan* (St Petersburg: Lenizdat, 2014), p. 180.
94. Ibid., p. 89.
95. Merab Mamardashvili, "'Tret'e' sostoianie," in *Kak ia ponimaiu filosofiiu*, ed. Iu. P. Senokosov, 2nd edn (Moscow: Progress – Kul'tura, 1992), p. 168.
96. Sokurov, *Razzhalovannyi*.
97. Savel'ev, p. 40.
98. Sokurov began his career in the mid- and late 1970s making TV documentaries for the Gorky television station and would explore the documentary mode throughout his career, for instance in *Russian Ark*. See: Jeremy Hicks, "Sokurov's Documentaries," in *The Cinema of Alexander Sokurov*, ed. Birgit Beumers and Nancy Condee (London: I. B. Tauris, 2011), pp. 13–27.
99. Il'ia Rivin, "Razzhalovannyi. Iz pis'ma ispolniteliu glavnoi roli I. Rivinu," in *Sokurov. Chasti Rechi* (St Petersburg: Seans, 2011), p. 475.
100. Sokurov, *Razzhalovannyi*.
101. Bellefroid.

CHAPTER 2

Ivan Dykhovichnyi's *The Black Monk* (1988): Madness, Chekhov, and the Chimera of Idleness

Mamardashvili was hired at the Higher Courses in the early 1980s, where he taught courses in Ancient Philosophy, European Thought, and Foundational Questions of World Philosophy.[1] The Higher Courses was founded in 1960 explicitly as a center for post-baccalaureate training and had the reputation for being the intellectual alternative to the professionalism of VGIK, with a curriculum that aimed to facilitate broad intellectual training for its students: "a one-of-a-kind lycée, bringing together the best intellectuals of the day," according to director Alexander Mitta.[2] In the 1980s, in particular, the tenures of some of the institution's most notable instructors overlapped, including established intellectuals from a range of fields: pioneer of Soviet cosmonautics Boris Raushenbakh, psychiatrist Arkadii Avrutskii, philosopher Lev Gumilev, and linguist and semiotician Viacheslav V. Ivanov.[3] Some of these scholars, for instance Gumilev and Mamardashvili, and also animator Yuri Norshtein, had come to the Higher Courses because they were (for political reasons) removed from positions elsewhere, meaning that, quite literally, students who attended lectures at the Higher Courses had the opportunity to hear speakers that they could not hear anywhere else.

Moreover, film students at the Higher Courses already had undergraduate degrees and were often in their thirties or older, thereby bringing to their work the experiences and wisdom of their lives and careers before their turn to cinema. Before enrolling in the Higher Courses, for instance, Aleksandr Askoldov completed a degree in literary studies, Alexei Balabanov worked as an Army interpreter in Africa and the Middle East, and Konstantin Lopushansky was a professor of theatre at the Leningrad Conservatory.[4] The result was a diverse space for intellectual debate, a formula that, in many cases, attracted intellectual misfits—both among the students and the faculty.

Dykhovichnyi passed through the Higher Courses in 1980–2, as Mamardashvili was beginning his lectureship there. Just before his death in 2009, he described his relationship to his former teacher with palpable nostalgia: "Just ask my wife or my children, and they will tell you that I talk about [Mamardashvili] more frequently than about people I see every day."[5] His debut feature was an adaptation of Anton Chekhov's *The Black Monk* (*Chernyi monakh*, 1988), a film that anticipated the associative markers of excess, fragmented narrative, and camera stylization that would in the 2000s earn Dykhovichnyi a name as a leader in Russian cinematic postmodernism.

For Mamardashvili, Chekhov served as a literary exemplar of the representation of consciousness in literature. He referenced Chekhov in several of his lecture series, in particular in his cycle of lectures on Marcel Proust, which he delivered during the 1984–5 academic year to students at Tbilisi State University. In this chapter, I will examine philosophical affinities between Dykhovichnyi's *The Black Monk* and a single movement in Mamardashvili's expansive Proust cycle: the twenty-seventh lecture, in which he weaved together his thoughts on mental illness and the significance of the concept of indivisibility for consciousness, using Chekhov's novella *The Black Monk* (1893) as a literary example of madness.

Two Monks

In the 1970s, Ivan Dykhovichnyi (1947–2009) was best known in the context of Moscow's illustrious and nonconformist Taganka Theatre, where he spent a decade in the actors' troupe. Though he had a degree from the Boris Shchukin Theatre Institute, in 1980 he left acting and enrolled in the postgraduate program at the Higher Courses. For two years he trained as a director under the tutelage of the father of modern Russian comedy, Eldar Riazanov—the man who singlehandedly transformed the New Year's holiday with the premiere of his 1976 film *The Irony of Fate* (*Ironiia sud'by*), a film that has been televised in Russia every holiday season except during Gorbachev's anti-alcohol campaign. Dykhovichnyi's first feature after graduation was *The Black Monk*, which won the award for Best Debut of the Year from the George Sadoul Culture Fund in 1989.

Chekhov's *The Black Monk* tells the story of Andrei Kovrin, a weary scholar of psychology who travels to the country to rest his nerves at the estate of his former guardian. The head of the estate in question is Yegor Pesotsky, a renowned horticulturist with splendid gardens, who is father to a restless and dispirited daughter, Tania. While walking in the garden one evening, Kovrin sees the apparition of a monk dressed all in black. They begin speaking regularly, although only Kovrin can see or hear him. The monk tells the scholar that he is a genius chosen by God to "serve eternal truth," and this gives Kovrin a renewed sense of purpose and energy.[6] After Kovrin and Tania marry, the young bride overhears her husband conversing with the monk and sends him for psychiatric treatment. Kovrin is cured of his hallucinations, but he also loses his creative power. Two years later, Kovrin is living with another woman when he receives word of Pesotsky's death. As he reflects on his former life, Kovrin sees the monk one last time and collapses dead.

In 1893, Chekhov described *The Black Monk* as "a medical story, an *historia morbi*" of a man afflicted with the disease of "megalomania."[7] Chekhov took up mental illness and personality disorders as the driver of plot in other works, including his celebrated short story "Ward No. 6" ("Palata No. 6," 1892), and "Ariadne" ("Ariadna," 1895), a tale of a calculating and manipulative young woman who lacks the capacity for love. Claire Whitehead details how critical receptions of Chekhov's *The Black Monk* have been anything but straightforward, ranging from debates over where the sympathies of the omniscient narrator lie (with Kovrin, Pesotsky, or Tania?) to dissatisfaction with the overall literary quality of the work. Where genre is concerned, Rosamund Bartlett and others have described the novella's mitigated relationship to realism, where Chekhov's narrator blends his introduction of precise temporal and spatial detail with the genre of the supernatural, thereby "persuading the reader to see a mimetic relationship between the real world and the story world."[8] Dykhovichnyi wrote the screenplay for *The Black Monk* together with director Sergei Solovyov, who had by that time completed his tenth film and accepted his seventh international prize. Dykhovichnyi and Solovyov's screenplay faithfully retains the plot line of Chekhov's novella, removing only a few narrative details for the sake of cinematic brevity.

By the early 1990s, both Dykhovichnyi and Solovyov had become leading names in Russia's cinematic wave of postmodernism. Dykhovichnyi's position in this regard was solidified in 1992, with the release of his Russian–French co-production *Moscow Parade*. In an era of political volatility and anemic film financing, *Moscow Parade* was a return to, and pastiche of, the grand myths and style of high Stalinism. The film stars German actress Ute Lemper, styled as a farcical inversion of Federico Fellini's Anita Ekberg, bathing not in a fountain but under a bottle of Soviet champagne. *Moscow Parade* is an extended play on the excesses of the Soviet myth, where citations from film, music, and daily life of the late 1930s—that moment of aesthetic and political suspension before Hitler invaded the Soviet Union—are layered and inverted so as to produce the logical opposite of excess: emptiness, as expressed in the direct meaning of the Russian title *Prorva*, or *void*. Dykhovichnyi's citational trajectory would peak in 2009 with *Europe-Asia*, based on a play by the Presnyakov Brothers. The film is a compilation of cinematic, cultural, and literary references, ranging from cameo appearances by media personality Ksenia Sobchak and St Petersburg rock icon Sergei Shnurov to a character's confession, in the spirit of Dostoevsky, that "I killed the old pawnbroker." Dykhovichnyi died from lymphoma three months after the premiere of *Europe-Asia*, having directed ten full-length films over his career.

In contrast to the expansive pastiche of *Moscow Parade* and *Europe-Asia*, *The Black Monk* is an introspective and psychological film. The perspective of the camera is disorienting and regularly shifts position and point of view, a tactic that matches the fragmented cinematography we find in Dykhovicnhyi's films from the 2000s, in particular *Inhale-Exhale* (*Vdokh-Vydokh*, 2006). However, *The Black Monk* lacks the centrifugal force of cultural citation that is typical of the postmodern, and which styled Dykhovichnyi's later work. Instead, the camera functions in a radically centripetal way, representing primarily the interpersonal relationships of the characters and their inner worlds, at times taking up the perspective of individual characters in the narrative.

In one early example of the camera's flexible interiority, the character of Tania, played by Tatiana Drubich (who had a year earlier appeared in Solovyov's *ASSA*), walks through the family orchard. She speaks directly to the camera, addressing it as if it were Kovrin (see Figure 2.1). The camera moves around the garden with her. Kovrin's coat is draped over

Figure 2.1 Tania seems to address Kovrin by addressing the camera.

her shoulders and we hear his voice, originating as if from directly behind the camera. We are led to believe that they are walking around the orchard together, moving between trees and under branches. The close proximity of the camera to Tania lends a sense of intimacy between interlocutors, and the viewer is drawn into that relationship. Their conversation lasts several minutes and just as the viewer has become comfortable with the established perspective, the camera pans right and we see Kovrin standing further down a garden path, smiling at Tania as she approaches him. With this move, it is revealed that the camera was not capturing a one-on-one conversation between Kovrin and Tania, in fact, but that the camera movement represented an externalized form of Tania's inner monologue or, in other words, a cinematic representation of her inner state.

The film is ripe with such games of perspective. At several points the camera tracks through the house, slowly and intentionally, as if it from the perspective of a house guest exploring the halls. The camera pauses on haphazard arrangements of furniture, interiors thick with fog, and billowing curtains, hinting both at the rainstorm in the distance and the supernatural legend of the black monk. The film's unattributed, first-person tracking shots are long and deliberate. The camera's constant searching from an unreliable and undefined perspective imparts the tension, boredom, and eventually madness that has descended on the estate. By way of contrast, Whitehead explains how the narrator in *The Black Monk* offers specific temporal and spatial references—how many steps from one place to another; how much time has elapsed—as a way to verify the realism of the narrative against the supernatural plot line of Kovrin and his apparitions.[9]

At the level of structure, we might see the flexible interiority of the camera in Dykhovichnyi's *The Black Monk* as a strategy for conveying the inner thoughts of the characters without relying on Chekhov's use of inner monologue and an omnipotent third-person narrator. In the novella, we see Kovrin's descent into madness unfold over nine parts. If in Part I of Chekhov's original we get the sense that Kovrin might find peace in the country and by Part VII Tania sends him for treatment, by Part IX he is living with another woman. In the final paragraph he dies, ostensibly of some kind of hemorrhage, "with a blissful smile frozen on his face."[10] Chekhov's narrative omnipotence allows us access to Kovrin's inner thoughts and his conversations with the monk, whose voice is only heard in Kovrin's own head. How can that kind of access be translated into the language of cinema without appearing forced or campy on the screen? The disorienting movement of the camera in Dykhovichnyi's *The Black Monk* is an elegant solution.

Yet Dykhovichnyi's *The Black Monk* does not simply translate Chekhov's style into cinematic realism. Even the structure of the film is disorienting and dream-like. There is little distinction between day and night, and characters move in and out of sleep, dozing off in chairs even during conversations, only to be awoken the next time the camera falls on them. The film's aesthetic motifs are often repeated and reflected back on themselves, in different contexts, as a means of amplifying the mood of the film. When Kovrin sees the black monk for the first time, for instance, we hear the sound of a heartbeat, but see nothing; the heartbeat, in turn, is a repetition of the sounds of pounding and pulsing that we hear throughout the film, whether from the sound of rain or footsteps. At the end of *The Black Monk*, Tania's suggestion to her ill husband, "I think you should drink some milk," is repeated several times, like a distorted record skipping in the background.

The centripetalism of the camera in Dykhovichnyi's *The Black Monk* is perhaps most striking in Kovrin's interactions with the monk. When Kovrin speaks to his apparition, he directly addresses either the camera or an inanimate object in the room with him, for instance a billowing curtain or his own shadow. When we hear the monk's voice, we recognize it as Kovrin's own voice, only softer and more confident; in speaking to the monk, Kovrin is speaking to himself. "Funny, you repeat the very things that I think in my own head," he tells the monk. "It's as if you were looking and listening into my innermost thoughts."[11] Kovrin is aware that the monk is a product of his consciousness, because the monk tells him so. "The legend, the mirage, and me—it's all a product of your overactive imagination. I am a phantom," the monk explains.[12] In both Chekhov's original and Dykhovichnyi's screenplay, Kovrin's so-called madness is accompanied by a significant level of reflection and self-consciousness. In the film version, the shared identity of Kovrin and the monk is visualized in the way the camera regularly refers back to Kovrin when representing the monk. The ambiguity built into Chekhov's novella led his contemporaries to question his intentions, asking whether the story was supposed to elicit empathy for Kovrin's struggle or impart the message that "we should not prevent people from going out of their minds."[13]

Both Chekhov's and Dykhovichnyi's narratives also pair the presence of Kovrin's hallucinations with agency. Kovrin not only recognizes his hallucinations as such, but he *chooses* them, primarily because he realizes that his sickness is tied to his creative abilities. After his treatment, Kovrin chides the Pesotskys for treating his visions as a parasite rather than a part of himself:

Now I've become just like everyone else. I have become mediocrity; I no longer take pleasure in living. Oh, how cruel you've been to me! Yes, I saw hallucinations, but what harm did they cause to anyone? Answer me: What harm did they cause to anyone?[14]

Kovrin simultaneously delights in the fantasies of his madness and rationalizes his mental state with soberness of mind. The ending of the story adds a further layer of ambiguity, as the blood that flows from his throat at the moment of death is consistent with literary representations of tuberculosis, suggesting that it was not a supernatural force that killed him but a physical ailment. For Mamardashvili, the ambiguity present in *The Black Monk* offered not only a sophisticated portrait of madness, but a starting point for philosophical reflection on questions of individuality, creativity, and, most importantly, the importance of the concept of indivisibility to the philosophical method.

Madness as a Philosophical Problem

Mamardashvili's series of lectures on Marcel Proust, which he delivered under the title *The Psychological Topology of the Way* (*Psikhologicheskaia topologiia puti*), was one of his most expansive lecture cycles.[15] It was also one of his last. During the 1984–5 academic year, he presented the Proust cycle over thirty-six lectures to students at Tbilisi State University. Proust's novel *In Search of Lost Time* had not yet been translated into Russian in its entirety, and thus Mamardashvili's materials for his lectures were taken from his own translation from the French, for an audience unlikely to have read the original. While his lectures in Moscow were known for drawing enthusiastic crowds, sometimes in the hundreds, according to one source there were at times no more than a dozen students in attendance at his lectures on Proust.[16] One report from these lectures indicates that audience members felt offended upon hearing Mamardashvili begin in Russian and not Georgian, a move the philosopher defended by arguing that Proust's prose could not be accurately articulated in the Georgian language.[17] In actuality, the mood of the Georgian intelligentsia did not begin to swing in that direction until closer to 1988, when Georgian audiences were likely to react negatively to hearing a prominent Georgian-born philosopher deliver a lecture in Russian.

We have seen how a common theme among Mamardashvili's lectures was the associative structure through which he connected ideas, whereby he moved through topics in circular patterns rather than through linear forms of argumentation. His lectures on Proust were no exception. In

The Psychological Topology of the Way, the reader is confronted with a thicket of questions and paradoxes posed by the philosopher, not for the purpose of obfuscation, but because paradox was integral to his philosophical method. Paradox, for Mamardashvili, provided both philosophical content and poetic form. Nowhere was the role of paradox more apparent than in Mamardashvili's work on consciousness. In a lecture from 1988, he defined consciousness as "that which makes more consciousness possible."[18]

For a thinker who took such great pains to unwrap and rewrap the nature of consciousness in a variety of contexts and mediums, it is no surprise that Mamardashvili would eventually take to analyzing the so-called "defects" of human conscious experience. He discussed the topic of mental illness at length at least twice in his work. The first mention appears in the eighteenth meeting of a cycle of lectures he delivered at VGIK between 1978 and 1980, called *A Sketch of Contemporary European Philosophy* (*Ocherk sovremennoi evropeiskoi filosofii*). The next occurs in the twenty-seventh lecture of the Proust cycle at Tbilisi State University. In both instances, Mamardashvili turned to the example of Andrei Kovrin, the protagonist of Chekhov's *The Black Monk*, as a literary example of the fragility of identity—of "a person who has died in terms of his individuality after being treated for his illness."[19]

Kant, whom Mamardashvili admitted to placing on a "godly pedestal," categorized mental illness within the domain of philosophy and even created a taxonomy of illnesses of the mind, distinguishing between categories like illness and weakness, or derangement and deficiency. Only in the most serious cases, in which self-treatment through force of the will was unsuccessful or could not be attempted, should one resort to psychiatric or medical treatment for mental illness, Kant argued. Although Mamardashvili never spoke about specific kinds of mental illness or suggested interventions (or non-interventions) in the way Kant did, Mamardashvili too seemed to view mental fortitude primarily as a philosophical problem, if only because he viewed consciousness as a philosophical problem. Not unexpectedly, madness was, like many of the other things he set himself toward defining, essentially indefinable. "If we were able to define madness, then it wouldn't be madness," Mamardashvili said in his "Kantian Variations" lecture cycle, which he delivered at the Institute of Psychology in Moscow in 1982.[20]

Mamardashvili also seemed to draw an analogy between the unity of conscious experience in Kant and the indivisibility of individuality, using a brief analysis of Kovrin as a literary example. In the tradition of Kant, Mamardashvili argued for the unity of consciousness, meaning that the "I think" must accompany all cognition in order for an individual to make any sense of the world.[21] Kant's articulation of the role of consciousness as the structuring agent of human experience and knowledge was the foundational point from which Mamardashvili built his own philosophy of consciousness. In order for consciousness to serve this unifying function, it must be present at all times: it must be indivisible.

Mamardashvili extended this view of indivisibility from consciousness to the notion of individuality, or *lichnost'* in Russian. He argued that "very often curing somebody of a mental illness is the same as killing him as a creative being."[22] In *Sketch of Contemporary European Philosophy*, he continued:

> While [Kovrin] was ill, his illness served as the condition for productive and original work by his consciousness and his psyche. However, something happened that affected his illness; it was not done innocently, it changed the very essence of the path his psyche was on. It changed it to such an extent that when he was restored to health, the individuality [*lichnost'*] in him died.[23]

The human creative ability, or what he called the "creative pathos," is also indivisible. Just as moral categories like goodness, beauty, truth, and justice cannot be divided, nor can the creative pathos be split or conceived of as existing in parts.[24] For Mamardashvili, in fact, goodness, justice, and the like were not concepts but metaphysical phenomena (*iavleniia*) with the "characteristics of being," and in *Psychological Topology of the Way* he summarized the indivisibility of these and other phenomena in a single line: "Everything exists *at once*, if all exists at all."[25]

Mamardashvili's view of indivisibility had important ethical implications as well. Indivisible values like goodness or truth can be achieved only by already participating in them, he argued. Having goodness as your goal and striving toward goodness "means that goodness already exists in the soul of the person who is striving toward it."[26] He explained that we tend to understand morality by separating "the goal" and "the means," without realizing that the highest moral concepts are their own means: "The goals of goodness are reached by goodness itself."[27] In short, there are no external ways to achieve goodness except by just *being good*. In this view we will recognize Plato's conception of the forms as always becoming, and our participation in them also as acts of becoming. Philosophical thinking requires the concept of indivisibility, where "the goal of a law is the law itself," Mamardashvili argued.[28]

Continuing with the ethical dimensions of the concept of indivisibility, Mamardashvili also discussed situations where the truth is manipulated under the false banner of goodness, truthfulness, or justice. One must not, he argued, lie in order to make people think one is *good*, because that lie will never translate into *goodness*. Nor must one calculate how to become *good* and then try to achieve that *goodness* in stages, he continued, since *goodness* and other such values are indivisible and absolute. Mamardashvili emphasized that goodness is not part of our faculty of calculation (*raschet*), which deals explicitly in increments and calculations. While the rational act of calculation presupposes that the object of calculation is divisible, virtues like goodness, truthfulness, and justice are indivisible and therefore can never be the object of calculation. Mamardashvili used the term *calculation* pejoratively to describe attempts to out-think or out-reason the intrinsic indivisibility of moral values. I can strive toward *good* only by being good, and the very act of my striving *by doing good* means that I am already participating in *goodness*.

The idea of indivisibility was thus important for Mamardashvili's concept of mental illness, as creativity is also an "all or nothing" endeavor. In cases where creative genius goes hand in hand with mental illness, curing the symptoms of the illness (e.g. hallucinations, depression) means undermining the genius as well. Mamardashvili's connection of madness and creativity here was not particularly novel, as the many platitudes on the "fine line between genius and madness" remind us.[29] Bolder, however, was his extension of the concept of indivisibility from the Good (an idea that takes us back to the Greeks) to human individuality, treating individuality holistically and in terms of the unity of apperception that is necessary to his Kantian (in this regard) vision of consciousness. After all, the possibility of removing a part of someone's consciousness and still retaining that consciousness sounds nonsensical, since we already tend to think about consciousness as a unified "function," and we cannot turn parts of consciousness on and off at will. The more difficult claim to accept is Mamardashvili's argument that effecting any change to somebody's individuality—the curing of hallucinations, in the case of Kovrin—is akin to destroying the identity of that individual and stripping them of individuality altogether, as Mamardashvili argued in *A Sketch of Contemporary European Philosophy*.[30]

For Mamardashvili, the main conflict in *The Black Monk* occurs between Kovrin's individual consciousness and his creativity (the scholarly work he was undertaking). When Kovrin realizes that the monk is a figment of his imagination, he responds with wonder that he "didn't know [his] imagination was able to create these kinds of amazing phenomena."[31] The monk represents both the source of his creativity and his own self-reflection on that creativity, and it is a reality of his mind that he readily accepts. His creativity is bound to, and indivisible from, the sickness that will eventually kill him. Mamardashvili pointed out that those who forced treatment on Kovrin failed him twice over, first by destroying his individuality and second by robbing him of the potential for any future creative work. He continues that when

> we meddled with his individuality through such experimental means . . . , means that are located in some sort of proportion to the object and in the power of their proportionality to the object they destroy its natural course and cause us to lose the very thing we should have discovered. After all, we never discovered what was trying to express itself through his illness; we failed to achieve this and at the same time killed his individuality.[32]

In other words, Mamardashvili argued that in Kovrin's case madness was not so much a deficiency as it was a state of consciousness.

Mamardashvili's commitment to indivisibility of both consciousness and individuality also appears to be at odds with the dualism he at times took up, in particular in an interview from 1990 during which he argued that "the spirit is one and the body is another."[33] Rather than commit Mamardashvili to a Cartesian-like dualism, however, we might productively read this statement in the context of a larger series of binaries, or paradoxes, traceable through his work. Together with "body and soul," for instance, he speaks of "thought and reality" and "individual and history."[34] Binaries exist even within terms, for instance the problem of language, which is necessary for human civilization, on the one hand, and yet unable to fully express the human experience, on the other. Mamardashvili describes these problems as "philosophical dilemmas," where each comprises "a fundamental unresolvable aporia."[35] He relied on dualistic pairs as a way to define the negative space of philosophical investigation—the epistemological blank spots formed by questions that are unanswerable, and which always lead us into "insolvable contradictions."[36]

The convoluted nature of Mamardashvili's views of indivisibility notwithstanding, he was clear that there are serious moral and existential consequences for those who calculate the truth through means other than truthfulness. "Everything that I do in relation to others according to rational calculation will inevitably come back to me and destroy me," he said in *The Psychological Topology of the Way*.[37] In this regard, his view was similar to the Hindu and Buddhist idea of karma, though Mamardashvili preferred the term "the sum of life" (*summa zhizni*). Like in the idea of karma, in "the sum of life" each individual and every action plays a small role in a broader picture of cause and effect, a picture that continues on even after individual lives end. Mamardashvili described the "sum of life" as indivisible and dynamic, but also as part of a broader, collective indivisibility. "As members of this indivisible movement, we exist outside the borders of our own individual lives," he explained.[38]

While you may not suffer for your wicked deeds directly, or even in your own lifetime, Mamardashvili added that your wickedness will come back to you at some point on the historical continuum, perhaps "to [your] children, who are a part of [your] history."[39] For Mamardashvili there were few things more terrible than a misdeed, whether legal or moral, that goes unpunished. This view was born not out of any particular jurisprudential stance on his part, but out of his concern for the integrity of the self—out of his belief that a transgression not met with acknowledgment and resolution results in the loss of the self itself. In *The Psychological Topology of the Way*, he described the horror of genocide not in terms of its victims, but in terms of the fractured selves of the perpetrators. "Just try and you will see how much of your own potential—how much of your freedom and curiosity—you will destroy," he warned those seeking to escape punishment for their crimes.[40] We cannot ignore the likeness of Mamardashvili's views here to Fedor Dostoevsky's characters and their appetites for punishment, as if only in risking the self—by dangling the self on the precipice of criminal anonymity—can one recapture the creative potential from the clutches of nihilism.

Just like consciousness and language, freedom counted among the characteristics that Mamardashvili assigned to human beings alone. "In our cosmos," he wrote in "The Problem of Man in Philosophy" ("Problema cheloveka v filosofii"), "the phenomenon of freedom exists only through the human form."[41] And again, like consciousness and language, freedom was defined by the paradox inherent to human life. "Freedom cannot be expressed verbally," he continued, as "it is something that is done by man. Freedom is that which is created by freedom."[42] Language is simultaneously necessary for human connection and civilization, as we will see in the chapters that follow, but also unable to express the human condition in any satisfactory way.

In the case of *The Black Monk*, Kovrin's self too is intimately tied up with his creative freedom. When Kovrin sees the monk, he feels powerful and productive; once he is treated for these visions, his mind becomes muted and his life mundane. Russian philosophers like Vladimir Solovyov, Petr Chaadaev, Pavel Florensky, Aleksei Khomiakov, and Nikolai Berdiaev took up the question of creativity and creative freedom as philosophical problems in the nineteenth century, as Yuri Lotman would later do in the twentieth. In his 1981 essay "Rhetoric" ("Ritorika"), for instance, Lotman described two forces at play in the construction of culture, "as if there were two consciousnesses in place of one."[43] While the first force operates as a discrete system, where texts "come together like linear chains of interconnected segments," in the second the text itself is primary, and like a ritual or a scene in a play the complexity of the picture comes together to form a living whole that carries the meaning of the piece.[44] For Mamardashvili, thus, *The Black Monk* was a striking example of the power of the human mind to create, in terms of consciousness, as well as the fragility of that very mind and the genius of which it is capable. The tension between the discrete and the whole, as Lotman described it, came forward more specifically as a struggle between the explainable and the unknowable, between constructing a philosophical theory of consciousness and that unknowable "something else" that makes human consciousness so extraordinary and so mystifying to philosophers and scientists alike.

Mamardashvili was essentially arguing for a non-physicalist reading of consciousness in a political and cultural context dictated by the reigning physicalism and materialism of the day. His subtle resistance here is twofold. First, the self indeed possesses autonomy outside of social forces; second, it is in that autonomy of thought that our basic humanity lies. To whom does he turn in this regard but again to the father of modern moral autonomy, Immanuel Kant. In *Kantian Variations*, Mamardashvili talked about how Kant used the turn of phrase "to be sensibly mad" (*s tolkom sumasshestvovat'*), which he understood as "to engage in a special form of the unthinkable."[45] In Mamardashvili's reading, Kant used the concept of madness as representative of the unavoidable antinomy of the human condition: that we are thinking, feeling, and rule-governed beings living in a world that we cannot fully comprehend, with noumenal selves that exist outside time and nature, and governed by rules that we do not fully grasp—a feeling that Kant expressed in the *Critique of Practical Reason* as a sense of wonder in the face of "the starry heavens above and the moral law within."[46] Madness can be a sensible reaction in the face of the unknowable, or simply a state of the human condition. For Mamardashvili, madness described the condition of the individual caught in the unavoidable paradox of human conscious experience.

Meteorological and Horticultural Expressions of Mind

The relationship between consciousness and text (literature, film, etc.) was one of mutual expression for Mamardashvili. Consciousness can be expressed in texts, for instance in the work of Proust, which he regularly cited as displaying the movements and cadences of consciousness. He thought that as readers, we are able to pick out patterns of consciousness in a text or the absence of consciousness from them.[47] Consciousness and text are mutually expressive, but we should stop short of drawing them into a one-to-one relationship; we can never say that a certain part of a text *is*, or *contains consciousness*, he said.[48] Even the deepest textual analysis can only give us a glance into consciousness, and not every text is "constructed with consciousness," as Mamardashvili put it.[49]

As we saw in Chapter One, Mamardashvili described consciousness as a space existing mostly outside the borders of language. It is a "certain special dimension in which the objects and events of the world are described."[50] The most vivid spatial configuration in Chekhov's *The Black Monk* is the Pesotsky estate, whereby the topology of the garden is an important vehicle for the representation of psychological states in the novella. The gardens on the estate are described as a series of sections radiating three-quarters of a mile from the house to the river. Near the house there is a courtyard and an orchard. Beyond the orchard is a vast formal English garden, and beyond that there are fields, "from which one could hear the cry of quails."[51] The property ends at the river with "a precipitous clay bank where pine trees grew with bare roots, like hair-covered paws. The water below gave off an unfriendly shine."[52]

The sections of Pesotsky's gardens, in turn, represent different states of well-being for Kovrin. The house does not calm Kovrin's nerves, as "[i]n the country he continued living the same nervous and unsettled life he had lived in the city."[53] The garden near the house was different, "pleasant and gay even in bad weather."[54] Pesotsky's formal gardens were stifling environments of oppression, and in moving through the changes in landscape, Kovrin moves through different emotional states, from happy to constrained, from freedom and creativity to societal restraint.

This was especially true of the decorative part of the garden, which even Pesotsky himself dismisses scornfully as containing "every caprice, exquisite monstrosity, and mockery of nature."[55] Trees are twisted and trimmed into monstrous shapes and planted in rigid patterns, "like soldiers," distorted from their natural forms to such an extent that one could identify their type only by examining them closely and intently.[56] Bartlett describes the tension between representations of nature in *The Black Monk*, where Pesotsky's gardens include both spaces of nature- and human-made monstrosities, or what Bartlett describes as "a highly ambiguous manifestation of human 'culture.'"[57] Donald Rayfield offers an imperial reading of Chekhov's use of horticulture, both in *The Black Monk* and in other works by the author, arguing that "the extraordinary size and wealth of the garden, with its merciless regimentation and its energetic, monomaniac owner . . . desperate about the succession to his estate, make it inevitable that one should see it as Russia under the rule of the Tsar."[58]

We also might read the imposed structure of the formal gardens as a stand-in for society's admonition of Kovrin's hallucinations. It is in the field, at the edge of the gardens, where Kovrin feels most at peace and where he first sees the black monk, "among the hollow murmur of the pines."[59] After his first vision, "he laughed loudly and danced the Mazurka. He felt happy. Tania and all the guests noticed that today there was something different in his face. He had a radiant and inspired look about him, and they found him very interesting."[60] We might read the various divisions of the garden in Chekhov's *The Black Monk* as each correlating to a different layer of self, or state of mind, from the natural freedom he experiences in the field to Tania's desire that he conform to societal expectations, as if he were an ornamental shrub she could prune and shape. In this reading, the topology of the novella's landscape might function as that very "sum of life" that Mamardashvili used to describe the totality of consciousness, individuality, and human life. All the parts of the garden are also parts of Kovrin's self, are manifestations of his emotional and social experiences. As Tania expresses her relationship to the garden: "Our entire life has gone into this garden. I don't dream of anything except apple trees and pears."[61]

In Dykhovichnyi's film version of the story, there is no such contrast between parts of the garden or the manner of its tending. The different spaces of the garden in Chekhov's original are intentionally blended into one another in the film, where the various settings of the film's action are constructed as gradations of one and the same space. For instance, the Pesotsky estate is staged as an extension of the garden: the curtains are floral and the smoke from the garden fires rolls into the house, as if the gardens extend into the house and vice versa. When Tania encounters Kovrin speaking with the monk, she is watching him through those floral curtains, as if she too is in the thicket of the garden.

In Dykhovichnyi's film, thus, topology is not emotionally coded, in that particular spaces are not connected to particular emotions. We are given no indication that Kovrin feels oppressed in the formal garden and the house, while happy in the smaller garden adjacent to the house, as he does in the novella. The garden of the film is not even divided into distinct sections but represented vertically: the estate is located at the top of a hill, and in one scene, balls roll down the hill down a path, emphasizing layering and height rather than horizontality or symbolism.

Mamardashvili believed that consciousness could be expressed in text, and in the *Aesthetics of Thinking* he included film in this broad category.

If we were to read Dykhovichnyi's *The Black Monk* side by side with Mamardashvili's writing about Chekhov's *The Black Monk*, we might start by remembering how Mamardashvili took to heart Kant's view that there are no layers to consciousness and, by extension, argued that there are no layers to self or to creativity either. The landscape of Dykhovichnyi's *The Black Monk* lends itself to this vision of indivisibility not just in the structure of the gardens, which are represented as an indivisible whole: Kovrin's madness is also captured in the cinematography of the film through the use of water imagery and weather states. Rain and wind, in particular, are essential to the mood of the film. The rainstorm in the opening scene of the film gives way to smoke from fires meant to warm the fruit trees from the impending frost. The sound of rain dominates the film's soundtrack. When a pair of rowdy partygoers knocks over a croquet set, the wooden balls go tripping down the cascading stone walkway of the steps that lead to the family estate. This scene both reinforces the importance of verticality in Dykhovichnyi's film, as well as mimicking the earlier sounds of rain on those very stones.

The cameraman for *The Black Monk* was Vadim Yusov, internationally known for his work as the cinematographer on several films by Andrei Tarkovsky. Yusov was behind the camera for Tarkovsky's *Andrei Rublev* (1966), which is often cited as a textbook example of the on-screen poetics of water and natural framing devices. Tarkovsky was among Dykhovichnyi's instructors at the Higher Courses for Scriptwriters and Directors, and we can see the influence of his teacher not only in his use of water, but in the way that Kovrin is framed in several scenes (see Figures 2.2 and 2.3). It does not rain at all in Chekhov's original, but the film is dominated by the sound, signs, and threat of rain. We might view the "indivisible movement" (*nedelimoe dvizhenie*) of consciousness, in other words, as mirrored by the incessant flow or presence of water in the film.[62]

Figures 2.2 and 2.3 Two monks: Dykhovichnyi's Andrei Kovrin (left) and Tarkovsky's Andrei Rublev (right).

Figures 2.4 and 2.5 Kovrin speaks to the camera when he speaks with the monk.

Yet another significant difference between Chekhov's and Dykhovichnyi's texts is the viewer/reader experience of the monk. While in Chekhov's novella we experience the monk through the description of the omniscient narrator, in Dykhovichnyi's film our perspective of the monk corresponds to Kovrin's own. When the monk appears in the film, the camera fixes on Kovrin, often as a close-up (see Figures 2.4 and 2.5). We hear only Kovrin's voice, speaking as the monk. In other words, the camera attempts to place the viewer within Kovrin's own mind, as the monk is a representation given to his consciousness alone.

Donald Rayfield argues for how gardens and orchards make up an important part of reality in Chekhov's work more broadly, functioning as a stage-setting, an emotional metaphor, as a microcosm of Russia, and as models for the narrative structure of his stories. In Rayfield's view, Chekhov assimilated the essence of garden design—"to disguise boundaries, to claim the whole horizon as part of the garden, to avoid straight lines and final points, to bring the perambulating visitor unsuspecting back to the point where he entered"—into his craft of writing, building his literary constructions as one builds a garden.[63]

When Mamardashvili used the image of the garden, he did so as a metaphor for the unknowable distance between mind and world, between consciousness and self-consciousness, and for other paradoxes of human consciousness. In an interview from 1990, when asked if there was any pure space of philosophical reflection, he deferred to the metaphor of the garden. The inner life of any individual, Mamardashvili argued,

> is not an inner organization of space but ... pathways in one's inner garden, and no matter where you turn, you are moving around with yourself, and it is nearly impossible to organize things externally in such a way that they correspond to that internal picture.[64]

Here the metaphor of the garden represents consciousness as a physical space, one to which we have exclusive access, but one in which we also have limited freedom of movement. There are pathways there and we move about them, but like in a large garden or park, there is always the chance that one might take the wrong path or find that no path exists where we might like one to be. The metaphor of the garden can illustrate our limited access to knowledge about our own inner lives.

There was also a public component to Mamardashvili's metaphor of the inner garden. We will remember that for Kant, mental illness was a social phenomenon: it was a product of the Enlightenment, the result of unfavorable social conditions, and the effect of societal stress on the human mind.[65] Character was something that we could will and cultivate through practice, restraint, and design; this is apparent in the third and final section of *Conflict of the Faculties* (1798), which he titled "On the power of the mind to master its morbid feelings by sheer resolution." In Patrick Frierson's summary of this work, "Kant allows that what we might call mental illnesses can be due to physically diagnosable causes, but he reserves the term 'mad' for those disorders that do not have a discernible physical cause."[66]

Mamardashvili focused on the Kantian concept of the "chimera of superfluity," which he summarized as "knowledge that is superfluous to morality about how the secret and higher world is structured."[67] Upon reading further, we see that Mamardashvili seems to have had in mind individuals who mix the truths of philosophical inquiry with personal gain. Those suffering from the "chimera of superfluity" are engrossed in their own aspirations and advantage, and act according to the misconception that higher powers—the structure and truths of the world—exist for them alone. He attributes this not to illness or madness, but to a kind of trickery, or fanaticism, which makes use of a cunning and devilish form of "judgment" (he uses both *rassuditel'nost'* and *raschet*) that "always lands on its feet."[68] Mamardashvili's definition grafts nicely onto the character of Kovrin, who too is convinced that the monk has sought him out so that he might "serve eternal truth."[69] Mamardashvili's discussion here of the "chimera of idleness" also serves to highlight his broader view on the human existential position in the world, and the separation of philosophical and/or scientific truths from the meaning of any individual life. "The world has nothing to do with us," he said in 1990, "and thank God."[70]

In his discussion of the chimera of idleness, Mamardashvili also drew a comparison with the lived experience of his Soviet reality. He compared the unscrupulous reasoning of "artful judgment" to the anonymous denunciation letters he used to receive, presumably during his editorial days at *Problems of Philosophy*. These kinds of denunciations, he recalled, are "familiar to any person who has done editorial work in journals or publishing houses, which are always surrounded by psychopaths."[71] The imagery of pathways in one's inner garden takes on a political dimension, serving as a metaphor for cultivating inner freedom against the restrictions of the outside world—more specifically, of Mamardashvili's Soviet reality. In the last decade of Mamardashvili's life, the concept of indivisibility, and the problem of consciousness in general, took on a profoundly political dimension. In Chapter Three, we will look at the more explicitly political works Mamardashvili wrote at the end of his life and his time at Tbilisi State University in the late 1980s.

Notes

1. Volkova met Mamardashvili in the 1970s and took up the role of his Moscow patron of sorts, helping him find teaching positions first at VGIK, and later at the Higher Courses.

    An earlier version of parts of this chapter appeared as: Alyssa DeBlasio, "'Nothing in Life But Death': Aleksandr Zel'dovich's *Target* in Conversation with Tolstoy's Philosophy on the Value of Death," *The Russian Review* 73, No. 3 (2014): pp. 2–21.
2. Aleksandr Mitta, "'Gamburgskaia shkola rodilas' u menia na kukhne.' Interview with Vlad Vasiukhin," *Kinoshkola Aleksandra Mitty*, 1999, http://mitta.ru/otzyvy/statji-i-publikacii/36-a-mitta-gamburgskaya-shkola-rodilas-u-menya-na-kukhne.

    Like many Russian institutions of higher education in the immediate post-Soviet period, the reputation of the Higher Courses was compromised in the late 1990s when government funding dried up and the institution became tuition-dependent, and therefore could no longer afford to offer spots to only the most talented candidates but to those who could afford to pay.
3. Mamardashvili reportedly got along particularly well with legendary Soviet *auteur* Andrei Tarkovsky, who ran masterclasses in directing at the Higher Courses in that decade. On the relationship between Mamardashvili and Tarkovsky, see: Volkova, "Ob"iasnenie neob"iasnimogo," pp. 224–5.
4. Between 1985 and 1996, the average directorial debut age jumped from 26 to 37 years old, about which Nancy Condee writes in *The Imperial Trace*, pp. 72–3.
5. Ivan Dykhovichnyi, "Ty beresh' tam sily," in *Professiia – kinematografist*, ed. P. D. Volkova, A. N. Gerasimov, and V. I. Sumenova (Ekaterinburg: U-Faktoriia, 2004), pp. 418–19.
6. Anton Chekhov, "Chernyi monakh," in Lib.ru, ed. Aleksei Komarov, n.d., http://www.ilibrary.ru/text/985/index.html.
7. Anton Chekhov, *Polnoe sobranie sochinenii i pisem v tridtsati tomakh*, Moscow, 1974–83, *Sochineniia*, Vol. 8, pp. 488–9.

8. Claire Whitehead, "Anton Chekhov's 'The Black Monk': An Example of the Fantastic?," *The Slavonic and East European Review* 85.4 (Oct. 2007): p. 604. See also: Rosamund Bartlett, "Sonata Form in Chekhov's 'The Black Monk,'" *Intersections and Transpositions: Russian Music, Literature and Society*, ed. Andrew Wachtel (Evanston: Northwestern University Press, 1998), pp. 58–72.
9. Whitehead, pp. 605–6.
10. Chekhov, "Chernyi monakh."
11. Ibid.
12. Ibid.
13. Chekhov, *Polnoe sobranie sochinenii*, Vol. 8, p. 494.
14. Chekhov, "Chernyi monakh."
15. Merab Mamardashvili, *Psikhologicheskaia topologiia puti*, ed. Elena Mamardashvili (Moscow: Fond Meraba Mamardashvili, 2014).
16. Akhutin, p. 22.
17. Dmitry Leontiev, "Life as Heroic Effort: Merab Mamardashvili's Psychological Topology of the Way," *Transcultural Studies* 5 (2009): n. 3. Mamardashvili's daughter, Alena Mamardashvili, refutes this claim, explaining that his apology for speaking in Russian at the beginning of this lecture was at this time an indication of his "good Georgian (and one might even say aristocratic) upbringing and his unprecedented politeness." Alena Mamardashvili, "A. Mamardashvili to DeBlasio," September 27, 2018.
18. Mamardashvili, "Problema cheloveka v filosofii," *Silentium* 1 (1991): p. 239.
19. *Psikhologicheskaia topologiia puti*, p. 661.
20. Mamardashvili, *Kantianskie variatsii*, p. 65.
21. *Kantianskie variatsii*, pp. 38, 245, and 142.
22. *Psikhologicheskaia topologiia puti*, p. 661.
23. *Ocherk sovremennoi evropeiskoi filosofii*, pp. 343–4.
24. *Psikhologicheskaia topologiia puti*, p. 660.
25. Ibid., p. 657.
26. Ibid., p. 658.
27. Ibid., p. 657.
28. "Problema cheloveka v filosofii," p. 235.
29. *Kantianskie variatsii*, p. 36.
30. *Ocherk sovremennoi evropeiskoi filosofii*, p. 354.
31. Chekhov, "Chernyi monakh."
32. *Ocherk sovremennoi evropeiskoi filosofii*, p. 344.
33. Merab Mamardashvili, "Drugoe nebo," in *Kak ia ponimaiu filosofiiu*, ed. Iu. P. Senokosov, 2nd edn (Moscow: Progress – Kul'tura, 1992), p. 327.
34. Ibid., pp. 327–8.
35. Ibid., p. 327.
36. Gasparyan, p. 97.
37. *Psikhologicheskaia topologiia puti*, p. 662.
38. Ibid.

39. Ibid.
40. Ibid.
41. "Problema cheloveka v filosofii," p. 239.
42. Ibid.
43. Iurii Lotman, "Ritorika," in *Ob iskusstve*, ed. Grigor'ev (St Petersburg: Iskusstvo, 1998), p. 406.
44. Ibid.
45. *Kantianskie variatsii*, p. 163.
46. Immanuel Kant, *Gesammelte Schriften*, ed. DeGruyter (Berlin: Reimer, 1910), 161, NaN-6.
47. Merab Mamardashvili, "Evropeiskaia otvetstvennost'," in *Soznanie i tsivilizatsiia* (St Petersburg: Lenizdat, 2013), p. 40.
48. Mamardashvili and Piatigorskii, p. 40.
49. Ibid.
50. Ibid., p. 42.
51. Chekhov, "Chernyi monakh."
52. Ibid.
53. Ibid.
54. Ibid.
55. Ibid.
56. Ibid.
57. Bartlett, p. 65.
58. Donald Rayfield, "Orchards and Gardens in Chekhov," *The Slavonic and East European Review* 67.4 (Oct. 1989), p. 537.
59. Chekhov, "Chernyi monakh."
60. Ibid.
61. Ibid.
62. *Psikhologicheskaia topologiia puti*, p. 662.
63. Rayfield, pp. 544–5.
64. "Odinochestvo – moia professiia."
65. On Kant and psychology, see: T. E. Weckowicz and H. P. Liebel-Weckowicz, *A History of Great Ideas in Abnormal Psychology*, Vol. 66 (Amsterdam: Elsevier, 1990), pp. 81–9.
66. Frierson, p. 16. Patrick Frierson points out that Kant's views on mental illness are difficult to lay out for a modern audience, both because he changed his position over the course of his life and because the terms and categories he used either no longer exist or exist in significantly altered forms in present-day psychology and psychiatry. Frierson, "Kant on Mental Disorder," *History of Psychiatry* 20, No. 3 (2009): pp. 1–23.
67. *Kantianskie variatsii*, p. 30.
68. Ibid.
69. Chekhov, "Chernyi monakh."
70. "Odinochestvo – moia professiia," p. 560.
71. Ibid.

CHAPTER 3

Dmitry Mamuliya's *Another Sky* (2010): The Language of Consciousness

In the years leading up to his death, Mamardashvili's work took a turn toward geopolitical and social philosophy. He spoke openly about Bolshevism, Soviet demagoguery, the need for civil society in Soviet space, and the anti-historicism of the prevailing ideology, which he viewed as "a form of thought that postulates ideals in such a way that they can never effectively interact with the real."[1] In 1987 he was allowed outside the Soviet Union for the first time in two decades and began giving lectures abroad, including two visits to the United States. The new freedoms of the perestroika and glasnost reforms of the late 1980s are apparent in the political turn of Mamardashvili's work from this decade; the return of the "living legend," as one philosopher called him, to Georgia in 1980 may have also played a role in this trajectory, allowing him the geographical and political distance necessary to speak in ways he could not have while living in Moscow, under the scrutiny of his colleagues and the authorities.[2]

In Georgia in the 1980s, questions of identity and independence garnered significant public interest, as Georgians took to the streets to protest against Soviet rule and prepared for the contentious parliamentary elections of 1990. The nationalist rhetoric of a "Georgia for Georgians" among the supporters of prevailing candidate Zviad Gamsakhurdia anticipated the successful 1991 referendum to restore Georgia's pre-Soviet independence, just months before Gamsakhurdia became the first democratically elected president of the country of just under five million citizens. The trajectory of late-Soviet politics and culture "stung and worried" Mamardashvili, and the situation in Georgia and the Soviet Union more broadly aroused in him "a sense of horror and the desire to ... think, understand, and see some kind of broader principle behind it all," as he expressed it.[3] He spoke out against nationalism and ill-directed patriotism in interviews and at political conventions, and Gamsakhurdia is reported to have called Mamardashvili "the main enemy of the Georgian people" after censoring an interview with the philosopher that was set to appear on national television in 1990.[4]

A student who attended Mamardashvili's lectures in Tbilisi during this decade was Dmitry Mamuliya (b.1969), a philosophy major at Tbilisi State University writing a thesis on the concept of proportion in Kant. More than a decade later, Mamuliya enrolled in the Higher Courses for Scriptwriters and Directors, where he completed the workshop of Irakly Kvirikadze and Andrei Dobrovolskii. Mamuliya remembers in Mamardashvili's image and presence "a feeling of ease in the face of uneasy questions," a feeling that found expression not in the language of philosophy but in prose or musical composition.[5] In this chapter, I will look at Mamuliya's 2010 feature debut, *Another Sky* (*Drugoe nebo*), as a portrait of the "sickness of consciousness" about which Mamardashvili spoke when he discussed Soviet society and politics in the 1980s. *Another Sky* is a cinematic simulation of a world in which language has failed, and where an impassable rift has developed between mind and world—between the inner world of the individual and the social consciousness that Mamardashvili thought was critical to a healthy society.

The New Quiet One

The protagonist of Mamuliya's *Another Sky* is Ali, a Tajik shepherd living on the Uzbek steppe. When his herd begins dying off he sets out in search of the wife who left him and their infant son nine years earlier. With nothing but several old photographs, her former address, and a memory of generic physical details ("black hair, black eyes"), father and son arrive in Moscow and take up work as migrant laborers: Ali in a cement plant; the boy in a sawmill. Death follows them to the capital and soon after their arrival the boy is killed in a logging accident. Ali eventually locates his wife and the estranged couple drive off together in silence.

The slow, deliberate pacing of *Another Sky* earned Mamuliya a spot among a group of younger Russia-based directors that gained notoriety between roughly 2007 and 2010 for their boldly understated debut features. This cohort came to be known as the "new quiet ones" (*novye tikhie*) and includes Alexei German Jr, Boris Khlebnikov, Kirill Serebrennikov, Alexei Popogrebsky, and Ivan Vyrypaev.[6] The title, "new quiet ones," refers to the tendency of these directors to feature understated psychological drama, moody minimalism, a slow and deliberate narrative pace, and an emphasis on social themes. This cinematic trend was mostly over by the end of the decade, and especially by the start of the 2011–12 protests for free elections in Russia, after which the quiet aesthetics of the noughties (*nulevye*) generation were no longer seen as an adequate response to Vladimir Putin's contentious third term as President of Russia.

Another Sky is the quietest film of the "new quiet ones." The film is, quite literally, about the absence of voice, which takes cinematic form as the absence of on-screen dialogue. The dialogue in the film amounts to just under ten minutes in total; twenty minutes elapse before a single word is spoken. The film includes less than ten minutes of non-diegetic soundtrack, made up of one musical theme repeated four times. Interpersonal interactions, even between family members, are truncated into short sentences with unfulfilling, matter-of-fact answers. "How will we find her in such a big city?," the boy asks his father. "We'll find her," is his only response. When answers are given, they only confirm or deny, thereby pre-empting the possibility for interpersonal connection altogether. "Is my mother beautiful?" – "Yes." "What is your wife's address?" – "I don't know."

While *Another Sky* was too austere to have been screened in Russian cineplexes, it played to positive reviews among its intended audience of critics and festivalgoers. The film won several important prizes in 2010, including the Grand Prix at the International Festival of Auteur Cinema in Batumi (Georgia), the award for Best Musical Score at Kinotavr (Russia), three prizes (including the FIPRESCI) at the Cottbus Film Festival (Germany), and Special Jury Mention at Karlovy Vary (Czech Republic). The film was released at the end of a decade that featured several important films about migrant labor in Russia, and it premiered at the Kinotavr Film Festival in 2010 together with Yusup Razykov's *Gastarbeiter* (2009).[7]

On the one hand, Mamuliya's filmmaking shares some of the *auteur* conventions of the Kazakh New Wave of the late 1980s and early 1990s, which Elena Stishova has argued was more innovative and influential on Russian-trained filmmakers in the post-Soviet period than films produced in Russia.[8] Films of the Kazakh New Wave, including the work of Amir Karakulov, Rashid Nugmanov, Darezhan Omirbaev, and Ermek Shinarbaev, tend to privilege mood over dialogue; experimentation over mainstream cinematic devices and genres; non-professional actors and natural sets; and dialogue in national languages instead of Russian. *Another Sky* contains all these elements, but what sets Mamuliya apart from other directors, both of the Kazakh New Wave and the Russian "new quiet ones," is the philosophical weight he places on silence and expression. Silence is not only an aesthetic tool in *Another Sky*, but an acute symptom of existential and social crisis. Moreover, the crisis present in Mamuliya's films does not manifest itself in the reshaping of post-Soviet space and history, as in the Kazakh New Wave, but is an abstracted crisis of the contemporary moment—one that is as dematerialized as the presentation of Moscow in Mamuliya's film. Silence is a marker for collapse in the interpersonal and social realms, an empty space that signifies the absence of authentic connection in a globalizing world.

When Ali eventually finds his wife at the end of *Another Sky*, there is no emotional reunion or long-awaited reconciliation. The film concludes with an extended sequence of silent profiles, the camera alternating between Ali and his wife as they sit silently in the car or examine their own faces in the mirror. She steps out to wipe her make-up off in a public bathroom, only to reapply it defiantly, bearing an accidental but unmistakable likeness to Anna Akhmatova—the poetess of the Soviet metropole. Mamuliya has described how the poetic device of the gesture and the mirror were more powerful than words.[9] In an alternate ending to the film, which the director shot but chose not to include, Ali drives his wife to a remote location and shoots her dead.[10] The present ending to the film is no less a death; the film closes with five minutes of silence as Ali rides alongside the wife he has not seen for nine years.

The style of Mamuliya's filmmaking blends his interests in philosophy and prose. In the 1990s and 2000s he authored an award-winning screenplay and several collections of poetry and prose, some published under the pseudonym Leo Luriia, and for four years he was editor-in-chief of the literary almanac *Logos* (published in Russia and Japan). In 2005 he enrolled in Kvirikadze and Dobrovolskii's workshop at the Higher Courses, and in 2012 he co-founded the Moscow School of New Cinema, a cinematic laboratory merging philosophy, visual studies, and filmmaking.[11] The Moscow School of New Cinema takes up an overtly philosophical objective: to "give students back 'their eyes'" and teach them to view film from a philosophical perspective.[12] It "will not only teach students to do, but to *see*," Mamuliya explained. "A director should feel reality with the tips of his fingers, then he can sculpt his cinema from reality. Our school will teach *cinematic tactility*."[13]

The Moscow School of New Cinema has positioned itself as a formal alternative to the traditional film-school experience, in the way that the Higher Courses for Scriptwriters and Directors had done in the 1960s, accepting older students who were often coming to film after establishing careers in other fields. When asked about his students, Mamuliya replied that

> intellect is of no consequence here. They should be people with life experience ... For instance, a dentist who dropped everything to take up filmmaking—this is the ideal student for our school ... If we give him the feeling that he can lay his troubles out on film, then we have done our jobs.[14]

Just as Mamardashvili argued that the ideal philosopher is not a philosopher by training, for Mamuliya the ideal director comes to the art of filmmaking as a way to organize and interpret an earlier catalog of life experience.

Mamuliya has expressed a similar approach in the way he blends the cinematic and philosophical modes in his work. "It's not like I took leave of philosophy to begin filmmaking," he said in 2015. "Philosophy is not a profession."[15] For Mamardashvili, philosophy was, at its best, a practice found in the habits of everyday life, and especially among those with no formal philosophical training.[16] "I have been convinced time and time again that philosophy is best understood by those who know nothing about it and are encountering it for the first time," he wrote.[17] Both Mamardashvili's and Mamuliya's views in this regard are an echo of Plato's seventh letter, in which Plato describes how philosophical knowledge cannot be transmitted or even taught, but "occurs like a flare-up in consciousness that cannot be repeated."[18] In Mamuliya's case, as we will see for Zeldovich and other directors, Mamardashvili's philosophical method offered a way of understanding the relationship between philosophy and film such that it was not his philosophy that was impactful so much as it was the way he engaged in the practice of philosophy.

In his defense of philosophy as a way of life, Mamardashvili attacked the dogmatic discourse of academic philosophers, in particular what he saw as the linguistic and poetic paucity of official Soviet philosophy of the day. He viewed this as the artificial language of philosophy *as a profession*, which was external to philosophy proper. Philosophy proper, he continued, had more in common with the language of human thought and consciousness: "Always and everywhere, philosophy is the language in which the witness of consciousness is transcribed."[19] Mamardashvili used the term *philosophy* here in its Socratic meaning: a love of wisdom and inquiry into the fundamental questions of human existence, employing not the terminology that one gains in philosophical education but the faculties given to us by virtue of our being born human. This tension between a shared, universal language of thought and an externally imposed language, one with political or ideological motivations, is at the heart of the existential collapse in *Another Sky* as well.

The Language of Consciousness

One of Mamardashvili's explicitly political works is his lecture "Consciousness and Civilization" ("Soznanie i tsivilizatsiia"), which he delivered in 1984 in the Georgian port city of Batumi. In it, he warned of an impending "anthropological catastrophe" with the power to irreparably change, and even destroy, civilization as we know it.[20] He was not referring to a natural or industrial disaster, although the Soviet Union had a history of both such kinds of catastrophe. Mamardashvili instead seemed to have in mind a moral apocalypse at the level of consciousness, in which "something vitally important [to human civilization] could be irreparably broken."[21] In a later work from 1989, he referred to the same condition as "sick consciousness," which he identified as a leading malady of Soviet life at that time.[22] For Mamardashvili, sick consciousness was a way of relating to the external world that is insular, selfish, and disconnected from concepts like civic duty and the greater good. "The people themselves are sick, and this is apparent in the way they react to what is happening around them, to themselves, to those in power, and to the surrounding world."[23] He likened this kind of consciousness to being trapped in a room covered in mirrors, where instead of seeing the way out you see only the multiplied reflection of your own image.[24] Mamardashvili went on to argue that while sick consciousness was a problem of Soviet mentality, it above all affected people living on Russian territory.

In the 1970s and 1980s, Georgia was known for having an unusually vibrant civil society, much more so than the imperial center.[25] Georgian civil discourse, in turn, often pivoted on conversations surrounding Georgian nationalism and support for the Georgian language. Ronald Grigor Suny describes how in 1978, for instance, when the draft of the Georgian constitution was set to include an amendment that would make the Russian language equal to Georgian, demonstrators disputed the clause so passionately that Eduard Shevarnadze, First Secretary of the Georgian Communist Party, agreed to their demands and had the clause removed.[26] Activist and author Irakli Zurab Kakabadze has written about the unparalleled vibrancy of Georgian intellectuals of the post-Stalin period, including film director Otar Iosseliani, writers Guram Rcheulishvili, Erlom Akhvlediani, Jemal Karchkhadze, and philosopher Zurab Kakabadze, all of whom "started to articulate the vision for the new Georgian 'Alter-Modern'" in the period between the Stalinist Thaw and the Velvet Revolution.[27]

Mamardashvili had been living in Moscow since before his eighteenth birthday, and his professional training, as well as most of his professional career, had taken place in the context of Moscow academia. He was eloquent when speaking and writing in Russian yet nonetheless described Russian as a foreign language for him, comparing it to his proficiency in Spanish and French.[28] Historian Filipp Makharadze has written about how in the mid-nineteenth century, the Georgian language "gradually lost significance in the eyes of Georgians themselves, since knowing only their own language Georgians could not enter state or public service."[29] In an interview from the 1990s, Mamardashvili attributed the relative poverty of the Georgian language not only to the small size of the Georgian nation, but to a historical lack of energy and importance devoted to the national language.[30] Up to the 1860s, fewer than 180 books had been printed in the Georgian language; there was no permanent Georgian theatre, not a single Georgian scientific or cultural institution, and there were only three printing presses in the country, only two of which even had the technology for Georgian typeface.[31] The centralization of the Soviet system changed this and, at certain historical moments, brought prestige and resources to printing texts in national languages. Still, writing in Georgian would have significantly limited Mamardashvili's audience, and some of the texts that were important to his work, for instance the novels of Proust, had not even been translated into Georgian. Mamardashvili gave his first lecture series in the Georgian language during the 1989–90 academic year in Tbilisi, but died before he could complete the course.

In interviews, Mamardashvili was clear about the important role of his Georgian identity to his work and career. He survived the Soviet system the way he did precisely because of his Georgian nationality, he argued.[32] Working between two languages and countries offered, if not freedom, then at least flexibility that Georgian philosophers used to their advantage. Some of the more controversial works of Hegel scholar Konstantin Bakradze, for instance, appeared in the Georgian language decades before they appeared in Russian translation. Most of Mamardashvili's political publications from his later period were presented first as lectures in Georgia, and only later published in Russian periodicals. Though not delivered in Georgian, his 1984–5 lecture series on Proust at Tbilisi State University was rich with biblical metaphors, references to the concept of "individuality" (*lichnost'*), and other nods to bourgeois literature and culture, from Proust to the Bible. Despite avoiding politics for much of his career in Moscow, Mamardashvili was expatriated because he had become too political. But once he arrived in Tbilisi, he became more political than ever.

The political trajectory of Mamardashvili's career deserves special mention, in particular the way it has been oversimplified as a move from Marxism in his earlier writing to humanism in his later work. Miglena Nikolchina argues that when Mamardashvili first met Louis Althusser in the 1960s, both philosophers were undertaking "rigorously antihumanist Marxian analyses," but that in the decades that followed, his thought appears to move in the opposite direction.[33] Viktoriia Faibyshenko's framework is helpful in this regard, as she interprets the avoidance of

Figure 3.1 Mamardashvili in the film *Should the Sighted Lead the Blind?* (Vladimir Bondarev, 1989). © Merab Mamardashvili Foundation.

humanism in Mamardashvili's early Marxist period as a strategic choice: as "the only real political action" he could take, as Mamardashvili himself put it.[34] In a letter from 1968 to Althusser, he wrote:

> In a situation like ours, it is best not to have any political title. For us, good politics is to depoliticize philosophy, insofar as we aren't able (censorship, ideological pressure, totalitarianism, etc.) to create, develop, and publish serious work on politics, or to act politically in any real sense, and so we refrain from politics as such and, in general, in every sense.[35]

We might contrast this position with that of Walter Benjamin, with whom Mamardashvili shares a number of similarities, but who wrote in 1913 that "in the deepest sense, politics was choosing the lesser evil."[36]

In light of Mamardashvili's above letter to Althusser, we can view the various "negative" moves of his career—his refusal to participate in the Soviet project, the bold and unprecedented manner of his lectures, and his rejection of the language of dialectical materialism and of the Georgian and Russian languages in general—as similar political moves, which violated the norms of Soviet scholarship not through antagonism, but in calculated refusal. His own apophatic descriptions of himself as an "antihumanist," as "atypical" within the Soviet context, and as someone who "watched politics from a distance," even as late as 1988, also play into this trope.[37] The irony of this stance, however, was that at the same time Mamardashvili insisted that a civil sphere was impossible within the conditions of Soviet reality, he was seen as a beacon for the very possibility of such a sphere.

Mamardashvili believed that *Homo soveticus* "knew no national borders" and that "truth is higher than Nation," but his correspondence with Althusser makes it clear that he saw himself not among the narrow category of Soviet philosophers but as part of a broader philosophical dialogue.[38] At the same time, in later interviews he regularly expressed sentimentality for his Georgian origins, not only in his fierce criticism of Russian political practices of the day, but in the weight he attributed to the early, formative experiences of his youth in Georgia.[39] He referred to this as his "impossible love for Georgia," a love he had only felt one other time—for France.[40]

Mamardashvili's nostalgia for Georgia did not prevent him from being critical of the Georgian intelligentsia, and he argued that the secular, civil society that existed in the post-Stalin period had already evaporated in Tbilisi by the end of the 1960s. In an interview from 1990, while talking about street culture and the norms of public etiquette in Georgia, he declared that in the Soviet period every Georgian "saved himself, and for this reason we [Georgians], on the whole, made it through as individuals, but our public sphere was destroyed."[41] In the same interview, he wrote about the neglected state of Tbilisi's public spaces as a metaphor for the Georgian public's abandonment of civil society: "An entry hall [*pod"ezd*] that nobody gives a damn about is the external expression of a structure of understanding oneself and the kind of external environment you are willing to accept and tolerate."[42]

The answer to the public dilemma Georgia faced was to be found at the local level. In a 1990 interview for the newspaper *Georgian Youth* (*Molodezh' Gruzii*), Mamardashvili said that Georgians must "create local precedents for a different way of life and action," and that "the struggle must happen not for nationalistic attributes, but for the freedom of the people."[43] Although he appeared to agree with Benjamin's conclusion from 1940 that the "'state of emergency' in which we live in is not the exception but the rule," for Mamardashvili the solution was not a revolutionary response "to bring about a real state of emergency," but social engagement at the interpersonal level—at the level of the *pod"ezd* and of *lichnost'*.[44]

In the context of his philosophy, which was strongly influenced by Kantian cosmopolitanism, Mamardashvili privileged the universal process of becoming cultured over the culture of any particular nation. "The human is a being that is constantly in the process of becoming," he argued, "and the whole of history can be described as the history of efforts to become a person."[45] He described, as Plato did, how "the human being is a continuous effort."[46] Moving toward culture (toward civility, and understanding, and toward cosmopolitanism) and away from national and personal interests was a way for civilization to fight against the "barbarism of the present day."[47]

In Alexander Arkhangelsky's documentary miniseries *The Department* (*Otdel*, 2011), which traces the renaissance of Soviet philosophy in the 1960s and 1970s, Elena Nemirovskaia describes a conversation she had with Mamardashvili after his return to Tbilisi in the 1980s. "You love Georgia, but Georgia doesn't want you," she told him. "Birthplace is an accident," he replied. "But the soul is immortal."[48] Mamardashvili often referred to himself not as a Georgian or Soviet philosopher, but "a citizen of an unknown country."[49] Just as he distanced himself from both the Georgian and Russian languages, he preferred to see himself as a human being first and foremost, although there is no doubt that national and local concerns played a defining role in his politically charged work from the 1980s. National concerns also appear to have played a role in the changing relationship of the Russian media to Mamardashvili in the 2000s. Erik Solovyov observes that starting around 2007, surrounding the lead-up to the Russo-Georgian War of 2008 over the administration of South Ossetia and Abkhazia, documentaries about Mamardashvili began to appear less frequently on Russian television.[50]

Language served an important function not only in Mamardashvili's intellectual biography, but in his investigation of consciousness. This was especially the case in his joint work with Alexander Piatigorsky, *Symbol and Consciousness* (*Simvol i soznanie*, 1973–4/1982), in which the authors discussed how working with problems of consciousness was, in many ways, like working with problems of language. True, they argued that consciousness had an important pragmatic aspect and therefore required its own method, while other fields like linguistics, psychology, and epistemology were primarily theoretical.[51] Nonetheless, they agreed that, like the study of consciousness, the study of language always happens in relation to itself:

[A]ny attempt to describe it already contains those very conditions, means, and the genesis point that we are trying to explain in the first place, and for this reason we feel that the science of linguistics must take the fact of language as an integral and indivisible unit, from the point of view of its origins.[52]

While we use our faculty of consciousness to investigate consciousness and our faculty of language to discuss the roots of language, Mamardashvili and Piatigorsky went on to argue that we do not truly understand the nature of either, and therefore cannot speak about either with any certainty. They demanded that any investigation into consciousness first bracket questions of the nature of language in order to avoid the confusion that the problem of language necessarily brings to the table.

What exactly was the relationship between consciousness and language for Mamardashvili? In Chapter One, we saw how he assigned consciousness a peculiar kind of ontological status: he saw it as a meeting place, a spatial configuration akin to "a field."[53] He also described it in terms of its potential to be articulated: how it can be put into words, or how the space of consciousness could be recorded. Like Socrates, Mamardashvili was an avid proponent of the primacy of the methods of philosophy to examine the world and the mind. To examine consciousness—to examine the familiar as unfamiliar, the inaccessible as accessible—one must rely on philosophical reasoning. Philosophy, he argued, is a way to access consciousness (insofar as it is accessible), to describe, analyze it, interrogate it, and seek to explain it. Philosophy is a "grammar" of the mind that allows for the transmission of some ideas while prohibiting the full definition of others, since consciousness can never be fully expressed in natural language.[54] Elsewhere he described the language of philosophy as "a recording of consciousness"—as the best attempt we have at giving voice to human thought.[55] The language and approach of philosophy enables the individual "to report on himself to himself," and the conceptual and semantic possibilities of philosophy are what make this report both accurate and clear.[56] "Always and everywhere," Mamardashvili argued, "philosophy is the language in which the witness of consciousness is deciphered."[57]

If philosophy is the language of consciousness, then it is reasonable to assume that philosophy can tolerate a certain amount of paradox and opacity, as consciousness is never given to us clearly. This view of philosophy might explain why Mamardashvili's work appears at times to intentionally disorient its audience through language play, both in the fragmentary nature of its structure and in the performative style of his delivery. When his friend and colleague Paola Volkova asked him, "Why is your speech so complicated, Merab?," he answered that "it is very important to strive to overcome language," in the sense that the language of the everyday can never be the same language through which consciousness is expressed.[58] In this way, Mamardashvili's philosophical style sought to mimic the structure he attributed to the process of consciousness itself. "There is nothing wrong when a thought without an answer turns in your head," he said. "Let it turn there. And in this turning of the thought is the very work of life."[59] Language signals both the potential for expression while also setting limits for thought, and language games are one way to experiment with those limits. Although he thought that we cannot gain direct access to consciousness, Mamardashvili did identify certain linguistic constructions that indicate and overlap with conscious acts. Phrases that contain their own referent, for instance *I think that . . .* or *I suppose that . . .*, have the ability to "tell us something *about* a conscious state but not tell us what consciousness *is*."[60]

Mamardashvili argued that language, together with consciousness, is a faculty given only to human beings; the robust potential of language is a defining feature of human existence.[61] Language "mediates the practically powerless efforts of the individual," Mamardashvili explained, and "allows him to formulate his own thoughts, that is, allows him to think that which he thinks."[62] Although Mamardashvili discussed philosophy as the language of consciousness, he also seemed to argue that there is no natural or necessary overlap between the linguistic form of consciousness (i.e. the language of consciousness) and natural language (i.e. the language we speak). If this is true, then we are unable to treat language as an extension of conscious processes and are, in turn, unable to use natural language as an indication of what consciousness experience looks like, or how it might sound.[63] Mamardashvili never claimed to be building a philosophy of language, and so it was not up to him to answer these questions; language is just one problem he raises along his path to his primary interest in human conscious experience. However, given what we know about Mamardashvili's attraction to the trope of the unknowable and of the absurd, which we will look at more closely in Chapter Four, we have reason to assume that his statements here on language were made in the same spirit.

It is also important to note that Mamardashvili's own language changed significantly depending on his audience—his writing was complex and technical in his academic publications, conversational and repetitive in his lectures, and provocative and personal in his interviews. He seemed acutely attuned to problems of audience, genre, and voice, and language was one of the primary tools with which he navigated this difference. While he did not venture an answer that sought to explain the intricacies of language and language acquisition, he thought that language, like consciousness, was part of what makes human life distinctively human. And like consciousness, any investigation of language would undeniably lead to unresolvable paradox and endless questioning.

Russia is not Europe

In his writing on sick consciousness from the 1980s, and especially in "The 'Third' Condition," Mamardashvili emphasized the role of language in the anthropological catastrophe of Soviet society of his day. "Sick consciousness is also a problem of language," he wrote, since it impedes communication between individuals and within communities.[64] This was a condition that affected Russia most severely, he argued. As a Georgian living in Russia and identifying in large part with Europe, it makes sense that by "Russia," Mamardashvili had in mind not an ethnic or nationalist definition, but a Soviet or imperial one, whereby "Russia" referred to "a social-economic phenomenon, called by the name 'Russia,' which includes Uzbeks, Georgians, etc."[65]

Mamardashvili did not give concrete examples of the kind of breaks in communication he had in mind. He instead described its corrosive effects on consciousness, on the possibility for interpersonal communication and, by extension, on self-knowledge—the result being a kind of epistemological and moral impasse that philosopher Alasdair MacIntyre described in his work on American moral philosophy at the same historical moment, *After Virtue* (1981).[66] It is no surprise that for Mamardashvili, the problems in Soviet society could be traced back to deficiencies in the processes of thought and language: "Even when we want to think, when there is the desire and impetus for thought, nothing comes of it. Something has already broken in the foundation of language itself."[67] We will remember from Chapter One how, for Mamardashvili, the only way to gain access to consciousness is through the mind of others, through "enriching yourself with the unfamiliar, the external 'other,' that the things we think are confirmed and exist."[68] When we lose our connection to others, we lose access to ourselves.

Another Sky depicts one such impasse, a world in which individuals are inaccessible to one another. The absence of language is the symptom of their sickness, represented on screen by the dramatic paring down of the audio dimension of the film. Mamardashvili wrote that "consciousness is thought aloud," and in *Another Sky*, consciousness is without language; we hear nothing but those sounds that compete with consciousness and, ultimately, drown it out. In this way, *Another Sky* shares Mamardashvili's concern that Russian society is moving toward a sickness of consciousness that will be difficult to cure and that risks stifling the social and cognitive fabric of society.

The longest verbal transmission of *Another Sky* measures approximately forty-five seconds long when, about halfway through the film, a television broadcast relays breaking news on the spread of the H1N1 virus, a reference to the global Swine Flu pandemic of the spring and summer of 2009. The overt analogy at play with the reference to H1N1 is, of course, that Ali's presence in Moscow is like that of an unwanted virus. He is regularly rounded up by the authorities, stripped naked, and hosed down with chemicals in a decontamination chamber reserved for migrants, vagrants, and nomads. The authorities are looking not only to rid him of contaminable diseases but to rid Moscow of him altogether. The film narrative takes place in the city's invisible spaces—its loading stations, brothels, back roads, work sites, and barracks. The rusted doors of a shipping container reveal a makeshift dormitory lined with bunk beds, where a dozen guest workers rest between shifts. The bodies who populate the film's public scenes do not tell a story of Moscow as a business or cultural center, but as a crossroads of invisible labor and its victims: we see silent networks of workers toiling on construction sites and in forests, riding busses to work in the pre-dawn hours, moving the cement that builds the city, and seeking bureaucratic support in damp and dimly lit basement offices.

The use of the television transmission serves as a point of connection between the events on screen and Ali's inner world, while also reinforcing the lack of communication in the film's narrative. The H1N1 broadcast scene is followed by a scene with a logging machine ripping through the forest, the same machine that takes the life of Ali's son. When Ali learns that his son has been killed, the television is on, but this time the sound is muted. Neither does Ali speak to anyone about his son's death, both because he chooses not to and because the language barrier between him and most of Moscow prohibits it. The film cuts from one silent scene to another, where expressions and snippets of television broadcasts serve in place of dialogue and, ultimately, in place of Ali's mourning. Critics have referred to the "rhythmic influence" of filmmaker Alexander Rekhviashvili and his *Georgian Chronicles of the XIX Century* (1979) on *Another Sky*, though the first five minutes of Rekhviashvili's film contains more conversation than the entirety of *Another Sky*.[69]

If the film is verbally silent, it is loud with the sounds of Moscow. We hear the endless buzz of transit: loudspeakers, car engines, rolling luggage, and feet shuffling over hard floors. The sounds of labor and mobility drown out everything else, leaving no room for thought or reflection. There is work, there is movement, and there is more work. There are no hints of the monuments, towers, and spires that so often serve as literary, cultural, and visual metonymies for the city and the entire country—a gesture toward the landscape of Venedikt Erofeev's *Moscow to the End of the Line* (*Moskva-Petushki*, 1973), in which the inebriated narrator has walked the city but not once seen the Kremlin. The only recognizable locale in the film is the Kazan station—the hub of long-distance travel to and from the metropole.

When language does penetrate the sounds of the city in *Another Sky*, the language of meaning is always Tajik. Even with the assistance of an interpreter, Ali is able to communicate only the most basic details about his wife in Russian to the police. When he visits the morgue archives in search of information, records on the deceased are bundled arbitrarily and piled on the floor of a basement room, with no apparent logic to their storage or reverence for the lives they represent. Information about his wife comes only by word of mouth through countrymen, always in Tajik. Moscow, as a city and as a symbolic system, is inaccessible to Ali. If language makes thought possible, as Mamardashvili argued, then the absence of language indicates a lapse in consciousness.[70] In Alexander Sokurov's *Demoted*, consciousness breaks through every crevice it is afforded—through the blare of traffic, over the radio, at the movie theatre, and in the reflection of a human face in a balloon. In *Another Sky*, conversely, filmmaker Dmitry Mamuliya has created a world in which the metaphorical absence of consciousness—the absence of human connection, the way that the sounds of the city drown everything else out—is represented through the absence of language.

At the same time, there is no romanticizing of Ali and his family. Although it has been a convention of new wave cinema to privilege national language, settings, and actors over exported (i.e. Russian or European) themes, the film's early shots on Ali's family farm do not paint the steppe in a nostalgic light. *Another Sky* opens as Ali and his son load sick and dead goats into a truck as a plane passes overhead; as they drive, cars and motorcycles pass them noisily on the road. Perhaps Ali's family life has been poisoned by his wife's disappearance; perhaps it is that human relationships anywhere, be it Moscow or the steppe, are fragile and fractured. The vices of contemporaneity have permeated the Uzbek countryside as a stack of hundred dollar bills that Ali has saved for their journey, an amount nearly equal to the price placed on his deceased son in the Moscow sawmill. On the steppe, as in Moscow, there are no glimpses of goodness between human beings, no tender moments even among family relations. In the way that Sokurov's *Demoted* resists a populist reading of the protagonist's reverse trajectory through the Soviet ranks, so does *Another Sky* privilege existential and conceptual problems (e.g. silence, lack of communication, language) over social commentary.[71]

The trope of liminality in *Another Sky* is equally present in the film's cast. The actors mirror the hybrid identities and professions of the characters they represent. After searching in vain for actors among migrant workers in Moscow for the role of Ali (they were all too expressive, Mamuliya lamented), the director settled on Habib Boufares—a Tunisian construction worker-turned-actor living and working in France.[72] The role of Ali's son is played by Amirza Mukhamadi, an Afghan refugee attending school in Moscow. For the role of Ali's wife, Mamuliya cast Mitra Zakhedi, an Iranian living in Berlin for over two decades. Mamuliya chose her on her "look" alone after an extensive search for actresses.[73]

In 2018 Mamuliya described his first encounter with Mamardashvili. It took place in the hallway of the Institute of Philosophy in Tbilisi, which at the time was called the Institute of Marxism-Leninism:

> A handsome man in a light, stylish dress shirt walked toward me. He was smoking a pipe. He didn't look like a philosopher. I knew exactly what a philosopher should look like [the soles of his shoes] worn through. Down the hallway walked Merab—a dandy, a fop. There weren't any holes in his soles. He didn't look like the other philosophers. On that fall day he simply walked right past me, leaving the strong smell of tobacco smoke in his wake. In that smell and in his aura, something slowly began to crystalize, which I was subsequently able to identify as my own 'I.' It was connected with a kind of mood that began to accompany me from that day on.[74]

Mamardashvili was not teaching regularly in those years, and Mamuliya described how the philosopher spent most of his time "somewhere in his own back wings [of the Institute]."[75] Nonetheless, Mamuliya wrote about how he "fell under [Mamardashvili's] influence, then out from under it, and then back under it."[76]

Mamuliya describes the city of Moscow with the same metaphor of the theater, as having both a public façade and a back wing, hidden from view. In Moscow, one can avoid the extravagance and "positivism" of the city's façade by wandering around its unconscious, "as if in a labyrinth."[77] *Another Sky* takes place in these underground and liminal spaces, which have been intentionally sublimated by the city's public face. "We live in a fictitious world," Mamuliya writes, "and if we don't see that it's fictitious, well then we don't exist either."[78] By stripping Moscow of the signs that make it in any way distinctly Moscow or even Russia, the setting of the film can better serve as a stand-in for the broader crisis nodes of globalization. By filming in Moscow without showing Moscow, in other words, Mamuliya extends the reach of his parable to other places and times.

When Mamuliya writes of anthropological catastrophe, he describes it as "the most terrifying kind of corruption," a "voluntary, spiritual corruption, where everything has been sold off in advance, and at the level of the mind."[79] Within these conditions of consciousness, "the person who has been sold off at the level of the mind and who has lost his image [*obraz*]" is forced into a context in which "his utterance is turned into a weapon, strengthening that very thing against which you might stand."[80] While Mamuliya does not explicitly use the word consciousness, for both him and Mamardashvili the concepts of mind, thought, and language figure fundamentally in their respective visions of the main maladies of the contemporary era.

In *Another Sky*, the absence of language translates into an absence of communication altogether: not just verbal communication, but the complete lack of connection between human beings. We also see how, in a very Mamardashvilian sense, the lack of language translates into an absence of self-knowledge. The cold logic of Moscow's anti-humanism permeates the film, and the human being is emptied of consciousness—of knowledge of both himself and others—in the nowhere setting of Mamuliya's anti-Moscow. "A barbarian is a man without language," Mamardashvili writes, and Mamuliya has created a portrait of this contemporary barbarism: displayed not through physical violence or unrestrained fanaticism, but by the absence of language, personal connection, self-knowledge, and, by extension, the absence of consciousness as Mamardashvili understood the term.[81]

Both Mamuliya and Mamardashvili seem concerned about a perceived loss of civilization, understood as a kind of quality of communication and interaction. For both, language—communication, openness, understanding—is a fundamental component of civilization. And like the symbolic abstraction of Moscow in *Another Sky*, Mamardashvili's work expanded the experience of his reader outside the Soviet context, into the inaccessible (at the time of his lectures) category of European-ness. As Miglena Nikolchina distils it, in Mamardashvili's work the concept of "Europe is shorthand for human being."[82] In Mamardashvili's own words, the adjective "European" refers not to territorial affiliation, "but is a different slice of human existence, in the sense that Europe is not a geographic notion. European can be present in Tokyo but absent in Moscow; Europe can be present in Hong Kong but absent in Moscow."[83] In a lecture he delivered in Paris in 1988 under the title "European Responsibility" ("Evropeiskaia otvetstvennost'"), he defined "Europe" as those civilizations that are governed by the rule-of-law state and the inner voice first recorded in the Bible.[84] Within this definition, Soviet Russia was European neither in the first category, nor in the second: "[T]he Enlightenment bypassed Russia," he explained.[85] For Mamardashvili, Europe was an aspirational concept. His idea of the human being, however, came from Plato, as that which "always is and never becomes and what becomes and never is."[86]

Within the "extended effort" of being human, the spoken word took up an important function.[87] Mamardashvili viewed the spoken word as a social fact. Not just any word, but the authentic word: "the communist word has no meaning," he used to say to Pierre Bellefroid.[88] Language is how we translate the paradox and profundity of consciousness into the world, and only the authentic word was worth transmitting. While we can easily take issue with Mamardashvili's definition here of authenticity in language use, it is important that we recognize his emphasis on language as the vehicle of the transcendent, since metaphysics is expressed "in the genius of [natural] language."[89]

Mamuliya's most direct homage to his teacher appears in the title of the film itself. *Another Sky* shares a name with an interview that Mamardashvili gave to the journal *Latin America* (*Latinskaia Amerika*) in the year of his death, the year he died of heart failure in the customs terminal of Moscow's Vnukovo airport on his way home to Tbilisi from Europe. The tropes of exile and transit in *Another Sky* were also part of Mamardashvili's life and work. Especially in the last decade of his life, he was candid about the cost of positioning himself as neither ideologue nor dissident, neither Russian citizen nor émigré. "I am not afraid of a civil death [*grazhdanskaia smert'*]," he wrote in 1990, reflecting on troubles he had faced during his career. "My oppressors back then were themselves Georgians—the lies, aggressive ignorance, and the vigilante justice of the ruling contingent of my own people. It was precisely because of them that I and others like me went into internal emigration."[90] Mamardashvili employed the concept of "civil death" to describe his position in the Soviet system, and he articulated the practice of philosophy as his own preparation for death.[91]

While the idea of "civil death" hinges on the absence of public/social structures in Russian and Soviet space, it does not address what comes after that death—the possibility of the transcendent within Mamardashvili's thought. Though Mamardashvili rarely spoke in spiritual terms, the transcendent played an important role in his understanding of consciousness. In Chapter Four we will look at the search for the transcendent and its path through the absurd, in both Mamardashvili's work and the final film by director Alexei Balabanov, *Me Too*.

Notes

1. "The Civil Society," p. 5.
2. Qtd Iu. P. Senokosov, "Merab Mamardashvili: Vekhi tvorchestva," *Po kom zvonit kolokol*, July 6, 2009, https://www.mgarsky-monastery.org/kolokol.php?id=1104.
3. "Soznanie i tsivilizatsiia," p. 7.
4. Dularidze, "Merab Mamardashvili segodnia."
5. Dmitrii Mamuliia, "Mamuliia to DeBlasio," June 9, 2018.
6. Khlebnikov first used the term *"novye tikhie"* to describe the filmmaking of his contemporaries at the 2011 annual Kinotavr Film Festival in Sochi, Russia. On the "new quiet ones," sometimes also called the Russian "New Wave," see: Justin Wilmes, "From *Tikhie* to *Gromkie*: The Discursive Strategies of the Putin-Era Auteurs," *Russian Literature* 96–8 (2018): pp. 297–327.
7. On films about migrant workers in the first decade of the 2000s, see: Alena Solntseva, "Ten' gastarbaitera," *Seans* 43/44 (2010), http://seance.ru/n/43-44/novyiy-geroy-gastarbayter/ten-gastarbaytera/.
8. Elena Stishova, "Ekh, dorogi ... ," *Iskusstvo kino* 10 (October 10, 2001), http://old.kinoart.ru/archive/2001/10/n10-article19.
9. Dmitrii Mamuliia, "Dmitrii Mamuliia: 'Neponimanie – samyi vazhnyi organ,'" *Seans* (June 11, 2010), http://seance.ru/blog/dmitriy-mamuliya-neponimanie-samyiy-vazhnyiy-organ/.
10. "Mamuliia to DeBlasio."
11. Incidentally, Kvirikadze studied at VGIK when Mamardashvili was teaching there, and Dobrovolskii and Mamardashvili were colleagues at the Higher Courses in the 1980s.
12. Sergei Bondarev and Dar'ia Goriacheva, "Kinobizon pogovoril s Dmitriem Mamuliei i Gennadiem Kostrovym o shkole i industrii," *Moskovskaia shkola novogo kino*, http://www.newcinemaschool.com/kinobizon-pogovoril-o-shkole-s-dmitriem-mamuliev-i-gennadiev-kostrovyim/.
13. Ibid.
14. Ibid.
15. Dmitrii Mamuliia, "Dmitrii Mamuliia: Nikto ne ponimaet, gde nakhoditsia i zachem. Interview with Larisa Maliukova," *Novaia gazeta*, July 7, 2015, http://www.novayagazeta.ru/arts/2805.html.
16. Mamuliia addresses the issue of poetry and philosophy being above, or outside of training, in: Dmitrii Mamuliia, "Shpion, osedlavshii tigra. Dmitrii Mamuliia i ego fil'm 'Drugoe nebo' Interview with Dmitrii Volchek," Svoboda.org (July 15, 2016), http://www.svoboda.org/content/transcript/2100742.html.
17. "Esli osmelit'sia byt'," p. 198.
18. Mamardashvili, "Kak ia ponimaiu filosofiiu," in *Kak ia ponimaiu filosofiiu*, ed. Iu. P. Senokosov, 2nd edn (Moscow: Progress – Kul'tura, 1992), p. 19. For Plato's reference to the love of knowledge as a spark, see: Plato, "Letter 7,"

Plato, *Letters*, 341d, http://www.perseus.tufts.edu/hopper/text?doc=Perseus%3atext%3a1999.01.0164.
19. "Filosofiia – eto soznanie vslukh," p. 57.
20. "Soznanie i tsivilizatsiia," p. 8.
21. Ibid.
22. "'Tret'e' sostoianie," pp. 163–5.
23. Ibid., p. 163.
24. Ibid., p. 167.
25. Suny, p. 309.
26. Ibid.
27. Kakabadze.
28. "Evropeiskaia otvetstvennost'," p. 36.
29. Suny, p. 128.
30. "Odinochestvo – moia professiia," p. 555.
31. Suny, p. 128.
32. "Odinochestvo – moia professiia," p. 557.
33. Nikolchina, p. 82.
34. E. Mamardashvili, p. 83; Faibyshenko.
35. E. Mamardashvili, p. 20.
36. Qtd Buck-Morss, *The Dialectics of Seeing*, p. 12.
37. See, for instance: Mamardashvili, "Moi opyt netipichen," pp. 356–7.
38. "Odinochestvo – moia professiia," p. 549; Timur Selivanov, "Svobodnaia mysl' Meraba Mamardashvili: Interv'iu s issledovatelem filosofa," *Svobodnaia Gruziia*, http://svobodnaya.info/ru/society/1620-svobodnaya-mysl-meraba-mamardashvili-intervyu-s-issledovatelem-filosofa.
39. See, for instance, the following works by Mamardashvili: "Odinochestvo – moia professiia" and "The Civil Society," p. 4.
40. Paramonov.
41. "Odinochestvo – moia professiia," p. 551.
42. Ibid.
43. Mamardashvili, "Veriu v zdravyi smysl," Mamardashvili.com, https://www.mamardashvili.com/archive/interviews/common_sense.html.
44. Walter Benjamin, "Theses on the Philosophy of History," in *Illuminations. Essays and Reflections*, trans. Harry Zohn (New York: Schoken Books, 1968), thesis VIII.
45. "Evropeiskaia otvetstvennost'," pp. 40–1.
46. Ibid., p. 42.
47. Ibid., p. 41.
48. Aleksandr Arkhangel'skii, *Otdel* (2010), 8 series, Russia K, Episode 8, 20:20.
49. Paramonov.
50. Ol'ga Rolengof and Nabi Balaev, *Besedy o gruzinskom Kante*, video material, 2007.
51. Mamardashvili and Piatigorskii, p. 27.
52. Ibid., pp. 32–3.

53. Ibid., p. 26.
54. "Problema cheloveka v filosofii," p. 239.
55. "Problema soznaniia i filosofskoe prizvanie," p. 53.
56. "D'iavol igraet nami, kogda my ne myslim tochno ...," p. 126.
57. "Filosofiia – eto soznanie vslukh," p. 57.
58. Volkova, "Paola Volkova o tom, chto bol'she ne povtoritsia."
59. Fokina, 00:30.
60. "Evropeiskaia otvetstvennost'," pp. 38–9.
61. Ibid., p. 41.
62. Ibid.
63. Ibid. pp. 37–8.
64. "'Tret'e' sostoianie," p. 165.
65. "Problema cheloveka v filosofii," p. 232.
66. Alasdair MacIntyre, *After Virtue. A Study in Moral Theory*, 3rd edn (South Bend, IN: University of Notre Dame Press, 2007).
67. "'Tret'e' sostoianie," p. 165.
68. "Soznanie i tsivilizatsiia," p. 11.
69. Mamuliya studied for a year under Rekhviashvili. For a mention of the rhythmic influence of *Georgian Chronicles* on *Another Sky*, see: Mamuliia, "Shpion, osedlavshii tigra."
70. "Evropeiskaia otvetstvennost'," p. 41.
71. In an interview following the release of *Another Sky*, Mamuliia rejected a social reading of the film as commenting on the plight of migrant workers in Moscow. See: Mamuliia, "Situatsiia Ivana Il'icha," *Seans* (Sept. 22, 2010), http://seance.ru/blog/ivan-ilyich-situation/.
72. "Shpion, osedlavshii tigra."
73. Ibid.
74. "Mamuliia to DeBlasio."
75. Ibid.
76. Ibid.
77. Dmitrii Mamuliia, "'My zhivem v strashnoe vremia.' Interview with Maria Baker," Kinote.info (Dec. 7, 2010), http://kinote.info/articles/4063-dmitriy-mamuliya-my-zhivem-v-strashnoe-vremya.
78. "Shpion, osedlavshii tigra."
79. Ibid.
80. Ibid.
81. "Evropeiskaia otvetstvennost'," p. 41.
82. Nikolchina, p. 86.
83. "Problema cheloveka v filosofii," p. 240.
84. "Evropeiskaia otvetstvennost'," pp. 38–9.
85. "The Civil Society," p. 5.
86. Plato, *Timaeus and Critias*, trans. Robin Waterfield (New York: Oxford University Press, 2008), 27d5–28a1.
87. "Evropeiskaia otvetstvennost'," p. 42.

88. Bellefroid.
89. *Ocherk sovremennoi evropeiskoi filosofi*, p. 260.
90. "Veriu v zdravyi smysl."
91. Dularidze, "Stranstvuiushchii filosof."

CHAPTER 4

Alexei Balabanov's *The Castle* (1994) and *Me Too* (2012): Kafka, the Absurd, and the Death of Form

> Merab Mamardashvili taught the courses in philosophy at our institute. He didn't like speculating about mystical things, but at literally every one of his lectures he told us that there is an irrational side to humans . . . that we will never be able to analyze, because we don't have the necessary tools to do so.
>
> Yuri Arabov, screenwriter[1]

Mamardashvili's death in the late fall of 1990 went hand in hand with the end of the Soviet empire. Earlier that year, the Central Committee of the Communist Party had reluctantly given up its monopoly on political power, and elections had concluded or were underway in six of the Soviet republics. Just two weeks before Mamardashvili's death, the Georgian parliamentary elections established Zviad Gamsakhurdia as the first President of Georgia, a candidate against whom Mamardashvili had come out strongly and publicly in the debates leading up to the election.[2] In the years following glasnost, Mamardashvili's philosophical contributions primarily took the form of interviews, short essays, and public lectures, and were notable for their openness, pithiness, and engagement with the tectonic shifts in late-Soviet politics and culture. While the structure of human conscious experience remained a priority for him, his political work from the 1980s bears little stylistic or methodological resemblance to the closed, technical style of his earlier writing.

Among the final group of filmmakers to study with Mamardashvili at the Higher Courses for Scriptwriters and Directors was Alexei Balabanov (1959-2013). If Mamardashvili was part of the last generation of Soviet philosophers, Balabanov belongs to the last generation of Soviet-trained directors: he came of age in the Soviet system, served in the Soviet Army, and was at work on his first feature film as the Soviet system unraveled. His cinema has been said to take place in the "post-ideological" space of the 1990s, yet the "post" in his work often bears relation to the Soviet past: the narratives of his films are set against the historical backdrop of political and cultural collapse (e.g. imperial Russia on the eve of revolution or the

Soviet–Afghan War and its legacy), where new Russian values are forged from the rubble of Soviet consciousness.³

What is more, Balabanov's cinematic style and approach to directorial authorship foreground the tension of the modern subject in the absurd mode—the antinomy between the human desire to seek out meaning in the world, on the one hand, and the impossibility of its discovery, on the other. Like Samuel Beckett, from whose play he drew inspiration for his 1991 debut, *Happy Days* (*Schastlivye dni*, 1991), Balabanov has more than once been called "the last modernist."⁴ This title comes not only from his admiration for Beckett, Franz Kafka, the American modernists, and the literature of the absurd, but, according to Liubov Arkus, his modernism is revealed in his Cartesian desire to achieve "a complete expression of the self" through his film, a task that the director extended to his own life.⁵

In this chapter, I look at the role of the absurd in Mamardashvili's philosophy and in two of Balabanov's films, *The Castle* (*Zamok*, 1994) and *Me Too* (*Ia tozhe khochu*, 2012). A guiding theme of this book has been the question of how philosophical influence takes shape in cinematic form. We have looked equally at directors who cite Mamardashvili explicitly in their films and those on whom the philosopher's influence has been less direct. This chapter is an exercise in a different kind of influence. The sections that follow (on Balabanov and Mamardashvili, respectively) can be read together or separately, in or out of order, depending on the kind of dialogue the reader seeks. For a reading that emphasizes direct connections between the two, a side-by-side reading of the sections below can reveal conceptual and philosophical affinities between two thinkers who bookended what is arguably the defining crisis of Russian contemporaneity. In this approach, we are encouraged not only by the fact that Balabanov and Mamardashvili shared several months in the classroom, but that both found deep inspiration in the work of Kafka. At the same time, we have no reason to believe that Balabanov gave much thought to Mamardashvili after leaving the Higher Courses; as his first wife recalls, he "did not find the lectures of legendary philosopher Merab Mamardashvili particularly interesting."⁶ Reading the sections of this chapter separately, thus, offers a study of the guiding role of the absurd in the work of each, whereby the absurd was a narrative and aesthetic mode for Balabanov and a description of the fundamental condition of human life for Mamardashvili.

Road to Nowhere: Balabanov and Genre

Balabanov's popularity with audiences and critics has earned him "a special place in the history of Russian cinema," as Vlad Strukov puts it.⁷

He established himself in the 1990s both as an early box-office success story and a Russian-made *auteur*, as a filmmaker with a localized focus in post-Soviet space. Balabanov was educated as an interpreter and worked for several years in Asia and the Russian Far East before enrolling in Lev Nikolaev and Boris Galanter's Auteur Cinema experimental workshop for documentary screenwriting at the Higher Courses.[8] While his early films were mostly experimental literary adaptations and period-pieces, his 1997 blockbuster *Brother* (*Brat*) was a rare marriage of commercial and critical success, selling more than 400,000 legal copies in the first five months of its release and remaining to this day a cultural touchstone of the late 1990s among audiences and scholars of Russian film and culture.[9] Many of his films, including *Brother* and *Morphia* (*Morfii*, 2008), pay homage to his more experimental work and to the history of film itself through the use of cinematic devices like intertitles (*Morphia*) and black screens (*Trofim* [1995], *Brother*, and *Brother 2* [2000]); the insertion of documentary footage (*War* [*Voina*, 2002] and *Morphia*); the inclusion of film posters (*Dead Man's Bluff* [*Zhmurki*, 2005]); and the use of film equipment or the film process as a component of narrative (*Trofim*, *Brother*, *Of Freaks and Men* [*Pro urodov i liudei*, 1998], *Brother 2*, and *War*).[10]

In interviews, Balabanov regularly rejects many of the tools, or approaches, a critic might employ in order to understand his filmmaking. He speaks disparagingly about scripts based on values and ideas, about cinema for the purposes of open-ended philosophical meditation, and about films that "force [the director's] opinion on others."[11] In the case of *Me Too*, he also rejects the idea that he developed characters for the film at all, claiming instead that "those folks really acted that way; everything [in the film] is realistic."[12] Balabanov's elusive and provocative relationship to the Russian and international press, and in particular his antagonistic comments about genre conventions, has led some critics to argue that he never settled on a single genre over his career, and others to say that genre experimentation was at the foreground of his cinematic grammar.[13] In reality, beginning with *Brother*, Balabanov's trademark style is a mixture of both genre cinema and his own *auteur* style, which borrows strongly from his early study in modernism and, in particular, from the literature of the absurd.

Important to Balabanov's trademark style is the fact that each of his films can be characterized as a road movie of some kind. In *Happy Days*, a nameless hero wanders the streets of St Petersburg looking for a room to rent; in *Trofim*, which Balabanov shot to celebrate the centenary of the moving image for the *Arrival of a Train* (*Pribytie poezda*, 1995) compilation, the hero's journey occurs without the framework of the filmmaking process itself, from filming through post-production. *Brother* follows Danila's journey, in the genre of the *Bildungsroman*, from younger brother to street anti-hero, ending on a snowy forest road "to Moscow," as the film's final spoken line reveals. In *Brother 2* (*Brat 2*, 2000), that same road continues from Moscow to Chicago, where Danila battles the vices of American capitalism in the name of Russian exceptionalism.

Very often, however, the journeys that Balabanov's characters undertake feature an inverted or frustrated directionality, whereby the journey is guided by the mode of the absurd. One such example is his 1994 adaptation of Kafka's *The Castle*, a story of the modern subject at sea in a world without interiority. The genre of the absurd is, by definition, a frustrated road movie: characters set out in search of transformation, but their journey is incompatible with the nature of the world, which lacks any reliable mechanism for knowledge, progress, or resolution. Land Surveyor K in *The Castle* tries and fails to reach the always elusive castle, thereby failing to take up his duty as surveyor; in Kafka's earlier novel, *The Trial* (1914-15; 1925), a protagonist by the same name, Josef K, is shuffled through the absurdities of the legal system on charges he must accept but that are never revealed to him. The philosophical cornerstone of the absurd, Albert Camus' *Myth of Sisyphus* (1942), is founded on the story of how Sisyphus was sentenced to push a boulder up a hill for eternity, a man doomed to unending movement (the boulder rolls down each time he reaches the top) without the hope of meaning or progress.

Many of Balabanov's films feature movement without progress as a main element of narrative non-development. In *Brother*, *Dead Man's Bluff*, *Cargo 200* (*Gruz 200*, 2007), *Morphia*, and *The Stoker* (*Kochegar*, 2010), the director's trademark bandits and anti-heroes travel back and forth between key locations, often in snow and always to music.[14] In *The Stoker*, for instance, over 30 minutes is dedicated to the act of travel, in particular by foot; in *Me Too*, Balabanov dedicates the first 50 minutes of the 83-minute film to scenes in transit, and over 35 minutes of that time is spent in a car. Extra-long takes of walking and driving are the cinematic glue of Balabanov's trademark style, setting his work apart from Hollywood editing practices; they function as what his long-time editor Tatiana Kuzmicheva calls "the air within the film."[15] With the exception of *Me Too*, the repetitive travel sequences in these films shuffle characters back and forth, aestheticizing and ritualizing movement without progress as a hypnotic placeholder for character development. Bodies are used to draw and redraw meaningless maps, and the very act of repetitive movement takes on a Hesychast tinge in the otherwise spiritual vacuum of the worlds of Balabanov's films.

Balabanov's fourteenth and final feature film, *Me Too*, is less a film narrative than it is the plot of a game. A motley crew of sinners and saints sets out in search of a church bell tower reported to offer eternal happiness to those it accepts inside. The bell tower of happiness is located in a remote zone that some supernatural force has plunged into eternal winter, and armed guards at the perimeter are instructed to admit pilgrims "on the orders of the Archbishop." The characters travel in a single car, and later by foot to the tower, where each attempts to enter. Winners are accepted inside, their bodies transformed into a stream of smoke that escapes from the open roof of the bell tower; losers are struck down dead, admitted no further than the snowy field already strewn with bodies.

On the one hand, the travel narrative of *Me Too* inverts the standard Soviet cinematic trajectory, where progress involved an edifying journey from the periphery to the imperial and cultural center. On the other hand, in reversing this formula, Balabanov taps into an equally engrained set of clichés about the spiritual potency of the Russian provinces and the meditative potential of escaping the metropole, a narrative inherited from the Slavophiles and Leo Tolstoy alike. The winter landscapes present in *Brother*, *Morphia*, *Stoker*, and *Me Too* echo the nineteenth-century tradition of snowy settings in Russian prose, while also serving as narrative stand-ins for the apocalyptic and for nuclear winter.[16] In *The Stoker*, much of the film is spent following a fashionable young fur-saleswoman walk through the snowy streets in extravagant pelts, where her glamour and youth are juxtaposed against the crackling inferno of the film's fires and boiler rooms, where living spaces are warmed by "hellish stoves, fed with corpses."[17] In *Me Too*, Balabanov decouples the snowy landscape from any embedded positivist or metaphysical expectations, recasting the territory surrounding the bell tower as a ruin site that carries with it the potential for both destruction and salvation.

In Balabanov's narrative landscapes, spaces of spiritual refuge are often juxtaposed against the moral vacuum of the present, where religious symbols are repurposed as vessels for the morally ambiguous messages of Balabanov's films (see Figures 4.1 and 4.2). One of the more commented-on elements of *Me Too* is the spiritual symbolism of the protagonists' journey from St Petersburg to the Bezhetsky district outside the city of Tver, with critics referring to the film as a "Russian Orthodox road movie" or a "Russian Orthodox [version of Andrei Tarkovsky's] *Stalker*."[18] We would be remiss, however, if we failed to recognize the ambiguous nature of Balabanov's "zone"—not only has the cupola of the teetering structure been torn off, but the evidence presented in defense of the bell tower's power is the same evidence that might lead us to believe it is a hoax. Here

Figures 4.1 and 4.2 Remote winter landscapes and religious symbolism in Balabanov's *Me Too* and *The Castle*.

we are reminded of Camus' assessment that Kafka's work moves toward a "deification of the absurd," leading to a condition in which the source of hope becomes the very thing that precludes it.[19]

In the opening line of Kafka's *The Metamorphosis* (1915), an early foundational text in the literature of the absurd, Gregor Samsa awakes to find himself helplessly transformed into a hard-bodied insect. Mamardashvili argued that we feel no pity for Samsa upon reading of his transformation, not because Samsa does not deserve it, but because the genre of the absurd does not allow for pity. Kafka's writing represented the "impossibility of tragedy"—a world in which freedom was not restricted or refused, but conceptually impossible within the terms of the system.[20] His narratives lack both tragic pity and fear, the foundational emotions for achieving Aristotelian catharsis. They also lack heroes altogether. Gregor Samsa and Land Surveyor K are not "characters of a higher type" committing "action[s] . . . of a certain magnitude," as Aristotle described in the *Poetics*; they are unremarkable and anonymous men, without power or influence, and whose names refer us only back to the author himself, whether through partial anagrams or other alphabetical arrangements of the letters in the name Franz Kafka.[21]

Balabanov's anti-heroes share some obvious similarities with Kafka's protagonists, primarily in the competing tendencies of both toward ritualistic movement, on the one hand, and existential and spatial stasis, on the other. Like the nameless characters of Kafka's novels, Balabanov's anti-heroes are always on the move, but rarely in a way that yields progress. The dramatic irony of *The Metamorphosis*, likewise, is that there is little action in the story in-between Samsa's initial transformation in the opening line and his death at the end. In *The Castle*, irony is sustained by Land Surveyor K's perpetual search for the castle, and the fact that his chance of access is further diminished with every step he takes in its direction. Balabanov's anonymous anti-heroes are equally averse to introspection and their characters rarely undergo development. The fascination of the absurdists with the grotesque (insects, death, disease) as metaphors for the human condition also pairs well with Balabanov's own reliance on outcasts, hitmen, and bandits—a cohort of cinematic misfits that Nina Tsyrkun argues "turns the screen into a cultural dumping ground for the refuse of symbolism," and whose speaking names signal their brutish qualities (e.g. Bison in *The Stoker*).[22] In the literary mode of the absurd, human beings are outcasts by their very nature, endowed with a mind, a body, and a head, "hence, also a forehead, to beat one's hand on it," as Kafka wrote.[23]

Balabanov describes his own filmmaking as taking place within a genre he created, called "fantastical realism." He describes it as follows: "There is not a single set, absolutely everything is real. There is not a single actor, everybody plays themselves. I wrote the screenplay from their words and their stories."[24] The term "fantastical realism" was in fact coined by Dostoevsky, and Balabanov's method shares with Dostoevsky's work the narrative fusion of the sublime and the perverse, as well as the typological impulses that privilege historical/cultural archetypes over individual characters.²⁵ Moreover, just as Dostoevsky's essays and notebooks serve as a liminal space between his life and work, so does Balabanov repeatedly emphasize the non-fiction foundation of his filmmaking, saying about *Cargo 200*, *Me Too*, and other films that the screenplays were built on impressions, stories, and personal experiences—that "everything in the film is exactly as you would find it in real life."²⁶ This statement is best interpreted in the context of the absurd, both to the extent that Balabanov insists upon its truth and the extent to which it cannot be true.

Where the mode of the absurd is concerned, it is important to distinguish between a world without higher meaning (nihilism) and a world in which meaning is inaccessible (the absurd). In the latter, the transcendent is always present, but only in the sense that it is always out of reach, absent from all the places in which we go looking for it or present only in the imagination of those who seek it out. We find this visualized most acutely in the many ruin sites of worship and safety in Balabanov's films, ranging from repurposed churches and graveyards to private spaces where atrocious acts are committed, and where rituals of domesticity and prayer are layered against displays of extreme violence. We can also turn to the mode of the absurd to contextualize many of the similarities among Balabanov's films: protagonists who lack the capacity for development and introspection; movement without action; morally neutral zones and religious symbolism stripped of ritual; a clash between a lack of absolute meaning or justice, on the one hand, with a world that presupposes the search for that meaning, on the other. "There is plenty of hope for God—no end of hope," Kafka reportedly said in a conversation with Max Brod, "—only not for us."²⁷

At the same time, critics have described how *Me Too* does not fit neatly within the rest of Balabanov's work because it contains many of the narrative and aesthetic tropes we recognize from his earlier films while also including spiritual allegory and religious symbolism.²⁸ This line of criticism risks forgetting, however, that the hollowed-out edifices of the transcendent have always been present in Balabanov's filmmaking, be it the cemetery-turned-squatters' camp in *Happy Days*, the empty church in *Morphia* where Poliakov injects morphine to feed his addiction, or the prominent tattoo of a Russian Orthodox cross that adorns the arm of the mob boss in *Dead Man's Bluff*.

One way to reframe the relationship between *Me Too* and the rest of Balabanov's *oeuvre* is to consider the film in the context of *The Castle*. In the final section of this chapter we will look at how the stories of both films are essentially the same, each with a different ending. While the success of K's journey in *The Castle* is precluded at the start by the guiding mode of the absurd, in *Me Too* the transcendent is offered up to the viewer to interpret, and is visualized in the streams of smoke the tower emanates (and the accompanying sound effects) when a soul has been accepted. The question remaining at the end of *Me Too*, however, is the very puzzle that closes Balabanov's adaptation of *The Castle*: the question of "truth" and its role in cinematic discourse, whether at the level of narrative or in Balabanov's comments about his films and his own spirituality. In *The Castle* and *Me Too*—and, as we will see, for both Kafka and Mamardashvili as well—the ceaseless yet futile search for meaning that sustains the absurd does not only reflect the human condition, but goes so far as to break down expectations of form and genre themselves.

Mamardashvili and the Absurd

For Mamardashvili, the human condition was fundamentally absurd. This truth was evident particularly in the practice of philosophy, where every mental exercise into the nature of consciousness simultaneously holds the promise of knowledge *and* of lapsing into the unknown. Mamardashvili turned to Kafka's fiction as an example of this fundamental paradox—that sphere of incompatibility and contradiction that trails every investigation into human consciousness, insofar as human investigation into the structure of the world (and any meaning contained within it) is inherently incompatible with the very idea of being human. Mamardashvili's best-known work on the absurd is "The 'Third' Condition," in which he employed Kafka's position in the Western literary canon as an exemplar of the absurdity of human life and the contemporary historical moment.

Especially in his later work, Mamardashvili looked at human life in terms of its potential. He considered both the anthropological potential to achieve cultural forms of advanced civilization, on the one hand, and the philosophical potential to undertake phenomenological investigations of consciousness, on the other. On the other side of that vast space of potential, however, was a lack—a lack of civilization, of cultural awareness, of self-consciousness, and even of thought itself.

For Mamardashvili, the human experience was split between two worlds. There is the describable side, the world as we know it through everyday experience and that we describe in everyday language. There is also the "other side," which he referred to also as the "indescribable" and the "third side," and which represented the darker and unknown side of our familiar world: the "degenerative, or regressive" mirror image of the first, which negates the truths and expectations of the describable, and in which language is "dead."[29] Here Mamardashvili employed an epistemic or counterfactual lens, meaning that we should not take him to have believed that there is some other world out there in which all things are reversed, but rather, that the "other side" refers to a realm of logical possibility within a single, maximally inclusive human experience. In other words, the indescribable world is a logical reversal of the first—a conceptual space of possibility in which Mamardashvili played with how things *might turn out*, all within the philosophical landscape of human conscious experience as we understand it. If human life has the potential to advance, think, and reflect, it also has the potential to lapse into darkness and barbarism, and into the absence of thought and thinking about thought.

The "other side" was represented most acutely in Kafka's prose. Mamardashvili also called this the "third K," whereby the first K represented Descartes (from the Russian word for Cartesian), the second—Kant, and the third—Kafka. In the literary figure of Kafka, he found a representation of the maladies of the contemporary age: of an insular existence disconnected from community or any sense of greater good, a regressive condition that he called "sick consciousness" and that he identified as particularly prevalent within Soviet mentality.[30]

The literary function of the absurd in Kafka's work, to Mamardashvili's view, comprises "a comedy on the impossibility of tragedy, the grimace of some kind of otherworldly 'higher suffering.' It is impossible to take a situation seriously when a person is searching for truth the way he might search for the lavatory."[31] Mamardashvili also used the image of the "third" to describe unknowable, forgotten, and irretrievable meaning in speech acts. When we fail as subjects or the world fails us, we fall into the "third K," or the condition of the absurd. It was fitting that literature most aptly represented this space of negation, which Mamardashvili described in the *Aesthetics of Thinking* as "that which cannot be, which doesn't exist, which is nothing, and which cannot exist according to our understanding."[32]

Mamardashvili used the image of the zombie to describe the philosophical problem of the absurd. The zombie (*zombi*, in the original Russian) was a fitting metaphor for this realm of incompatibility, since the zombie simultaneously signifies both human life and its absence: it "looks like human life but can only imitate death."[33] The zombie metaphor aptly represents that logical other-world because it is both human-like but non-human; we can understand the idea of the zombie within the conceptual category of human life and at the same time understand it as a "degenerative, or regressive" version of the everyday, describable world.[34] It is striking that Mamardashvili's use of the zombie metaphor came over a decade before the image of the zombie would become important in debates on consciousness in contemporary analytic philosophy of mind, specifically in the work of David Chalmers, Daniel Dennett, and others.[35]

The greatest unknown, for Mamardashvili, was the question of consciousness itself. Consciousness is necessary for any robust definition of human life and accompanies all our thoughts and representations, yet could only be described in metaphors and contradictions, or through poetics and pauses. This was, for Mamardashvili, the paradox of the transcendental. The idea of the "other side" was also at the heart of how Mamardashvili grafted together Descartes' and Kant's positions. The transcendental, we will remember, always leads to paradox: to that unbridgeable gap between the internal condition of the soul (thought and desire) and the external condition of the material of our body, where human life is a philosophical mystery that sends us again and again into the sphere of paradox.

In Mamardashvili's summary of Kant's transcendental, he described "the world in relation to first principles of knowledge about that world, or a world that was formed by, and presupposed, inner sources of knowledge about itself."[36] Yet, while in the *Critique of Pure Reason* Kant argued that there are certain a priori concepts that are universal and necessary to make sense of human experience, for Mamardashvili the transcendental question highlighted above all the paradox of human experience. In other words, the transcendental did not lead to epistemological confidence about the nature of human experience, but to that unbridgeable, unknowable Cartesian gap between the soul and the body, and, by extension, between mind and world.[37] Here it is worth remembering Mamardashvili's memorable description of human life as the paradigm of this transcendental mystery, where "the walking example of the thing in itself is the human being."[38] We cannot fail to note that Mamardashvili's emphasis on Kant's transcendental, as in Descartes' *cogito*, is missing an important component: the absolute that sustains the system, or God.[39]

What views did Mamardashvili hold on the relationship of faith to the absurd? Mamardashvili was a Soviet philosopher and would not have been permitted to discuss the possibility of transcendent truths in any explicit way in his work, even if he had wanted to. However, he regularly appealed to religious language and demonstrated a deep knowledge of Christian stories, symbols, and philosophy. In his historical work on Kant and Descartes, he openly addressed their positions on God and the soul, at times using the words religion (*religiia*), God (*bog*), or soul (*dukh*) in nearly every sentence. The same held true for his lectures on the history of philosophy and culture, for which he wrote about the history of Christianity, the role of symbol in Christian imagery (e.g. the crucified Christ), and the role of faith as a philosophical problem. In his lecture series on Kant and

Descartes, religion was of predominantly historical and anthropological interest. He could not rely on faith as a way out of the absurdist paradox like Søren Kierkegaard, whereby the absurd was simultaneously the very condition of faith (the absurdity of the existence of the Godman), and also negated by leaps of that same faith. Mamardashvili was instead drawn to the anthropological focus of Kafka's absurd, whereby there is no possible "leap" outside the boundaries of one's own humanity.

Religious language played both an important historical and structural role in Mamardashvili's work. He used religious language to describe existential problems that he presented as non-religious in nature. On the one hand, he appealed to the symbolic resonance of religious vocabulary, which he argued had taken the place of ethical language in European culture and was necessary "to distinguish the psychological quality of good . . . from the good itself."[40] On the other hand, if we trace religious metaphors through his work, we see not only how Mamardashvili related to the religious paradigm, but we gain insight into his view on the anthropological and philosophical role of God, the soul, and faith in a higher being.

The language of religious metaphysics and the experiential mood of religious awe were, in fact, a part of the transcendental, and they contributed to the formation of moral conscience. Mamardashvili's approach in this regard blended Kant, Husserl, and the phenomenologists, but also took from the concepts of Buddhism, Daoism, and other Eastern religions and spiritual practices, in which he was likely influenced by his friendship and collaboration with Alexander Piatigorsky. Mamardashvili talked about an immortal soul and a universal soul, and also about eternal truths.[41] In a Platonic register, he described how human life is defined in great part by our striving toward these truths, and our negotiation of the relationship between our everyday being (*bytie*) and the metaphysical world of striving—striving to be absolutely good, absolutely just, absolutely this or absolutely that. We are split between these two worlds, as humans; that is our existential condition. Man is finite, but the effort of striving to become a human being is infinite. Because we can never reconcile this condition, even our goodness is essentially absurd. It is tempting to read religion into Mamardashvili, and in at least one textbook on the history of philosophy in Russia the authors interpret his vision of the endless striving of the human condition in explicitly religious terms: "To strive for what cannot be found in life—that is the human predestination. We can call this striving 'the eternal soul.'"[42]

The soul was real for Mamardashvili, though it was not a God-given spirit but the place where progress and striving found their source. The concept of the soul was inseparable from the concept of culture, he argued; the soul was a concept "from which I cannot escape."[43] Like the "third" side or "indescribable world," we are incapable of fully describing or controlling the ways in which the soul serves as the source of culture and inner life. He used the term "spiritual" (*dukhovnyi*) to describe the world that "surrounds human beings and their thought process. This is a world in which there are no hands of time, where it's impossible to pick out any single unit of meaning, as we might pick out a single letter in a word."[44]

Mamardashvili went as far as arguing that the act or thought, or the "I think" (*Ia mysliu*), was a spiritual act, and that all human cognition takes place within the bounds of the spiritual. In the 1989–90 political season in Georgia, during which he was active in debates over Georgian independence, Mamardashvili took this argument a step further. In response to Christian nationalism and the popularity of the "Georgia for Georgians" movement, Mamardashvili reportedly claimed in a public speech at the second meeting of the Georgian People's Front that "even a sacred concept like Homeland (*Rodina*) cannot be for us Christians higher than the Truth (*Istina*), which itself is God."[45] It is not hard to see how readers of Mamardashvili in the Aesopian climate of the 1970s misinterpreted him as a covert theologian, given his use of religious language to describe fundamental human processes like thought, cognition, and consciousness.[46]

The difference between philosophy and religion, for Mamardashvili, was that "philosophy, in contrast to religion, is unable to stop itself at the conditions of reverence, obedience, and respect. Philosophy (and thought in general) cannot and should not stand down for any reason."[47] He also took care to separate the concept of God in culture from the theological God. In culture, he argued, "God is a symbol of a certain power that acts in spite of our stupidity, ignorance, incapability, or refusal to understand conditions we are unable to reach through our own abilities, but which nonetheless exist as facts."[48] The miracle of life is located not in the moment of creation or in the promise of life after death, but in the existence of thought: "the very fact that one can have a thought is a miracle."[49] The main difference, of course, was that there is no absolute being holding everything together. Instead of divine order, Mamardashvili described the indescribable structure of the world as a kind of chaos "that is not behind us but surrounds every point of the cultural existence inside culture itself."[50]

For Mamardashvili, the absurd also had a strong political dimension. In his work from the late 1980s, he brought Kafka to his defense, arguing that "it was Kafka who described the state as enveloping us but [that] we can find it nowhere."[51] Kafka summed up the political and social climate of the twentieth century, Mamardashvili argued, where classical discourse on freedom no longer applied. The absurd could be found precisely in the fact that human beings were not tasked with choosing between freedom or determinism, but that determinism masked itself as freedom, such that any choice was already an illusion.

For instance, in *The Castle*, K is constantly asked to make such false choices, whereby the idea of some external law or truth—the very idea of the castle—always evades him. The world in which he does make choices, in turn, is constantly mocking him, placing him in positions that demean him in the name of necessity, such as the requirement that he take up lodgings in the schoolhouse, or the devoted tyranny of his assistants. K's world embodies the anti-tragic because there is no space for agency. As Roman Karst put it, "Kafka . . . dominates the imagination of his readers by simplifying and reducing the conditions of reality—we feel constricted and restive in the world created by him, and we yearn for the space and air of real life."[52]

Kafka did not appear in Russia until the mid-1960s, and was assailed by Soviet critics through the 1970s for ignoring the dangers of modern capitalism and for setting his novels in the metaphysical realm "in order to exclude from the outset the possibility of any [class] struggle."[53] The concern over the dangers of Kafka's absurdism extended into the 1980s, as Paola Volkova recalls how one of the complaints filed against Mamardashvili at VGIK described his negative influence on the students as follows: "Either they have read too much Kafka, or they have listened to that Georgian too much."[54]

We see how Kafka's literary environments provide a fitting structure for Mamardashvili's philosophy of the absurd. It is also easy to insert into the abstracted settings and characters of Kafka's stories the specific details of Soviet reality. For Kafka, as for Mamardashvili, it is impossible to fight for freedom, since the fight for freedom already presupposes the existence of some freedom, no matter how small. This is where Surveyor K makes his fatal error: he assumes there is a castle to begin with. In Balabanov's adaptation, he makes yet another error: he assumes not only that there is a castle and that he is in control of his search for it, but that he is the Surveyor to begin with.

Balabanov's Kafka

The mode of the absurd—for Kafka, Mamardashvili, and also for Balabanov—is a fundamentally human problem. When Gregor Samsa realizes that he has transformed into an insect in *The Metamorphosis*, the absurdity of his condition is sustained by the human realities that frame the narration: though he has lost the ability to speak, he relies on his inner faculties of language and reasoning to reflect on his condition; though his parents no longer see him as their son, he continues to experience human pains (the itch he cannot scratch), worries (concern over missing work), and pleasures (he is still moved by music). Samsa's new life as an insect in his old room, among his human furniture and personal effects, captures the guiding idea of the absurdist mode: that the absurd is only effective if it occurs within the logical and conceptual possibilities of human life. The same was true for Mamardashvili, and this was what made the images of the "zombie" and the "third side" such compelling metaphors for the existence of human consciousness and also for its absence.

The absurd helps to contextualize the role of movement and repetition in Balabanov's films, as well as his approach to the broader question of humanity, but it does not necessarily account for the way his films are coded with the concrete details of Soviet existence. If Kafka's narrative settings are emptied of localized meaning and his characters are broad signifiers of universal expressions of human futility, Balabanov's protagonists are vessels for a Russia-focused vision of Soviet and post-Soviet geopolitical, historical, and cultural trauma. He repeatedly asserts that time and place are essential for his art; that he makes films only from "what he knows," and that "all his films are about Russians," as he puts it.[55] To complicate matters, Balabanov repeatedly offers up his own experience as the organizing code of his art, populating his films with self-referential artifacts and plot twists: Soviet-era icons (songs, clothes, habits), his friends in cameo roles, and locations he frequented.[56] Although his filmmaking is self-referential and many of his films are indeed "films about films," his work rejects the postmodern, in that he seems to be interested first and foremost in the very thing that postmodernism most vehemently rejects: a grand narrative, a unifying gesture, and a strong statement about the artist as subjective ruler of their artistic domain.[57]

An example of one such unifying gesture in Balabanov's work is his repetition of character types, plot motifs, filming locations, and even cast members, all of which impart a sense of kinship among his catalog of films. In the case of his casting choices, we see actor Viktor Sukhorukov in six of Balabanov's early films; Aleksandr Mosin appears in five; Svetlana Pismichenko stars in *The Castle*, *Brother*, and *Morphia*; and Renata Litvinova appears in *Dead Man's Bluff* and plays the leading role in *It Doesn't Hurt* (*Mne ne bol'no*, 2006). Balabanov also worked on multiple projects with actors Sergei Bodrov Jr, Ingeborga Dapkunaite, Dmitrii Diuzhev, and Nikita Mikhalkov. His choice to cast popular icons, including rock musicians in *Brother* and *Me Too*, adds cultural weight to his repeated claims that his films are somehow an extension of reality. We might find another unifying gesture in the way he regularly engages literary adaptation in his work, ranging from his well-documented appreciation for John Steinbeck's *Of Mice and Men* (1937) to those scripts of his which find their inspiration in literature (i.e. *The Castle, Happy Days, The River* [*Reka*, 2002], *Cargo 200*, and *Morphia*).[58]

What is more, Balabanov's own comments about his method weave a meta-narrative across individual films. Joachim Neugroschel argues that the shock effect of Kafka's modernism presents itself through his use of *style indirect libre*, a form of third-person speech that collapses the perspectives of narrator and character, the codes of narrating and narrated.[59] This device is present in Kafka's language, but it is also useful for making sense of the relationship between Balabanov's films and Balabanov's rhetoric *about* his films, where he is suspiciously eager to encourage us to use his own biography as a key for understanding his art. For some critics, Balabanov's tendency to assert himself into his own work is an indication of his postmodernism, while for others it is his continuation of the Cartesian project, whereby all knowledge begins with a return to the self.[60] In fact, it is common misreading of Descartes to conflate his methodological skepticism with the conclusions at which he arrives; in other words, Descartes turns to the self (the mind) as the source of reliable knowledge only in order to demonstrate that there are in fact all kinds of other things that we have good reason to believe, among them the existence of God. Balabanov's rhetoric about his own filmmaking falls into that false Cartesian trap, and in interviews we see how he regularly and forcefully asserts his own subjective position as the genesis moment for interpreting the events on-screen, stripping away conclusions not generated from his authorial self and inserting his own name and image into his films.

An important component of Balabanov's method involves the connection he sees between the authenticity of on-screen emotions and the audience reception of his films as "real." Viktor Sukhorukov describes how, on the set of *Happy Days*, Balabanov ignored Sukhorukov's frozen legs so that his eyes would "translate that suffering."[61] In his final film, actress Alisa Shitikova ran through the snow naked on the set of *Me Too* for two days until her legs were bruised from exposure; though Balabanov used mannequins to represent the corpses scattered in the snow near the bell tower, the prostitute's suffering had to be real. Aleksei Medvedev describes how Balabanov's cinematic task was to blur the boundaries between genre and life, something that he accomplished through the use of pain.[62] The prostitute's brutal pilgrimage strips her of her vulgar femininity, such that once she arrives at the men's camp with frostbitten legs she is clothed in men's outerwear and welcomed around the campfire as a comrade among men. Not only is her long run one of the more startling scenes of the film, but at the end of *Me Too* we are led to believe that her penance was successful, since the bell tower accepts her in a puff of smoke.

Indeed, there are moments when Balabanov concedes that his repeated claims to the "truth" of his films are, in fact, part of his broader aesthetic approach to filmmaking. In one interview he explains that his goal is to make his audience engage with film at the level of emotion, and the role that literature plays in that process:

> I liked Kafka and Beckett because they didn't have any relationship whatsoever to the real world. My favorite thing is to create absolutely artificial worlds with absolutely realistic structures. A realistic structure creates a sense of authenticity, whereupon a fictitious character can make the viewers feel real emotions.[63]

There appear to be two different things happening in this statement. First, Balabanov highlights the tendency in Kafka and Beckett toward abstraction: how, as Roman Karst argues, Kafka embellished his characters with details from his private life and his home city of Prague, but then "habitually and systematically blurred his own tracks in the novels and tales, a practice already manifest in the universalism of his parables, in which the attributes of time, place, and human individuality are dissolved."[64] Second, in this statement Balabanov describes how he blends notions of the artificial and the real, the abstract and the precise, in order to achieve the balance of a world that is for its viewers both culturally relatable and subjectively acute. In her recollections of her work with him, Kuzmicheva suggests that Balabanov's search for a formula to produce on-screen "authenticity" ended up dictating the technical structure of his films. She describes how the tight shots and close-ups that critics have come to associate with his filmmaking style were in fact the technical by-product of his vision to film in those spaces (cars, apartments, around the kitchen table) that were part of daily Russian/Soviet experience, but in which the messiest and most "authentic" details of life often occur.[65]

At the close of *Me Too*, a character known only as "a member of the European Film Academy," played by Balabanov, collapses dead in the snow outside the bell tower. Earlier in the film, Balabanov's youngest son performs the brief role a boy who predicts whom the tower will and will not admit; in the end, the bell tower accepts neither the bandit, nor the filmmaker. *Me Too* concludes with a series of three deaths, all of which originate from Balabanov's image: the death of the character of the European filmmaker, the on-screen death of Balabanov in the role of the filmmaker, and Balabanov's performance of his own death, as he had already been diagnosed with an illness and would die not long after completing the promotion for *Me Too*.[66] The ending of *Me Too* is not only self-referential, but in the tradition of *style indirect libre* Balabanov collapses multiple levels of discourse—the character, the implied director/author, the process of making the film, and the history of cinema more broadly—into the perspective of filmmaker as storyteller, autobiographer, documentarist, and historian all at once.

Why, then, at the end of *Me Too* does the filmmaker die? Though Balabanov repeatedly rejects philosophical interpretations of his filmmaking, in a 2012 interview he described how the characters of *Me Too* "are tired, and sick of living here, and they must either commit suicide or fly off to happiness."[67] On the one hand, his comments recast Camus' famous declaration of his existentialist method, by which he extricated himself from the trap of the absurd by stating that "there is but one truly serious philosophical problem, and that is suicide."[68] On the other hand, here Balabanov once again describes his character's fate in terms of his own autobiographical self, claiming his on-screen death in *Me Too* as a form of punishment for his prior creative work. In multiple interviews, and especially toward the end of his life, he spoke about his own faith in relation to the narrative of *Me Too*.[69] "I've killed too many people in my films," he said in an interview from 2012, and "[it] hasn't really helped me achieve happiness."[70] These and other comments on Balabanov's part offer the viewer an enticingly simplistic invitation to interpret *Me Too* as part of his personal spiritual journey, an act of atonement for his cinematic soul in which he wrote his own demise and salvation into the narrative.[71]

Balabanov also spoke about the death of the cinematic form in relation to *Me Too*. On the occasion of the one-year anniversary of the film, he talked about the fleeting nature inherent to cinema, appearing to imply that films fall out of fashion more quickly (or have a more difficult time entering the cultural canon) than literary works.[72] *Me Too* was also the director's first and only film shot with digital technology. The high-definition RED camera that Aleksandr Simonov used for Balabanov's final film captured the unflattering and even grotesque physicality of his films in even greater dimension.[73] At the same time, this shift in cinematography was in itself another death of sorts, in that the director's passing in 2013 coincided with what at the time looked like the wholesale transition from film stock to digital technology in leading commercial film markets.[74]

Balabanov also inserted himself into his first film. Kafka died in 1925 before completing *The Castle*, meaning Balabanov had to decide how to end the story. At the close of the film, Balabanov's Surveyor is taken to a castle that turns out to be the hunting lodge of a character absent from Kafka's original, Mr Balabane. At the lodge of Balabane, whose name bears an unmistakable likeness to the director's own, the Surveyor is stripped of his identity and forced to switch places with another civil servant of the castle, Mr Brunswick. The Surveyor pleads with those around him, yet they no longer see him as his former self, recognizing him only as Brunswick. At the close of the film, our Surveyor—now Brunswick—is back at the tavern where the story began, and where it has just been announced that the castle has unexpectedly bestowed new privileges upon the Surveyor, an identity he no longer occupies.

Just as Mr Brunswick takes up the role as the "imposter Surveyor," so is Mr Balabane's lodge the "imposter castle" of the film. Upon entering Balabane's castle, we see that his family crest bears a two-sided silhouette, which is not unlike the well-known 1892 rabbit-duck illusion, except that the optical illusion associated with Balabane features the silhouette of a rabbit, on the one side, and a profile of Stalin, on the other. This same ambiguous symbol appears earlier in the film, hanging on the wall of the Surveyor's rented room, and serves as another indication in the story that the Surveyor's journey has been guided all along by forces outside his control. What is more, when we see the real castle on-screen, it appears comical, surrounded by artificial crags and a frothy, soapy lake, reinforcing not only the absurdity inherent to the film's plot, but the absurdity of visualizing the castle in the first place. Balabanov has referred to *The Castle* as his least successful film and expressed dissatisfaction with his version of the ending, but nonetheless describes the final third of the film—his completion of Kafka's unfinished novel—as its "only interesting achievement."[75]

In 2013 Balabanov was buried in St Petersburg's Smolensky cemetery, where he had filmed *Happy Days* and *Brother* in the 1990s. A little over a month after his death, the bell tower in Sheksna, where *Me Too* was filmed, collapsed. This perfectly absurd event—the collapse of the source of human happiness—has added yet another interpretive layer to the myths surrounding Balabanov and his filmmaking. In this regard, *Me Too* is a film best viewed not on its own, but in the context of Balabanov's broader body of work. Not only does it bring us full circle to his first feature, but the director's appearance at the end of *Me Too* lays bare his own *style indirect libre* one last time. In the case of *The Castle* and *Me Too*, both feature existential journeys whose interpretive validity hinges on the narrative insertion of the director: Mr Balabane as hidden hand in *The Castle*, and Alexei Balabanov in a minimum of two roles in *Me Too*, as both on-screen and off-screen filmmaker. At the same time, in the endings of both films Balabanov took his *style indirect libre* to its aesthetic extreme, whereby the competing layers of "truth" supply the film's epistemological framework and also make it difficult to settle on any definitive reading that does not risk taking too seriously the director's own stories about his method. The choice to interpret the Sheksna tower collapse as a sign from above, a mere poetic coincidence, or even the finale to one last comedy of the absurd—all are all perfectly reasonable within the intentionally ambiguous message of Balabanov's final film.[76]

Notes

1. Alisa Orlova, "'Faust' Aleksandra Sokurova: Kreditnaia istoriia d'iavola," *Tat'ianin den'* (Jan. 30, 2012), http://www.taday.ru/text/1445414.html.
2. On Gamsakhurdia, see: Mamardashvili, "Veriu v zdravyi smysl."
3. Andrei Plakhov has described Balabanov's work as "best characterized by the prefix 'post.'" Andrei Plakhov, "Balabanov kak prokliatyi poet," in *Balabanov. Perekrestki*, ed. A. Artamonov and V. Stepanov (St Petersburg: *Seans*, 2017), p. 11. Nancy Condee has also shown how Balabanov's early films were cultural signposts of the new post-Soviet era, as they sought to capture and describe the newly negotiated relationships between individuals and the state for the first post-Soviet generation (*The Imperial Trace*, p. 218).
4. On Balabanov as the "last modernist" in the Russian-language press, see Liubov' Arkus, "Balabanov kak poslednii modernist," Balabanovskie chteniia (St Petersburg and Moscow: *Seans*, 2015), http://seance.ru/balabanov/2015/conference/abstracts/arkus/; Mariia Kuvshinkova, "Piat' let bez Balabanova," *Takie dela*, May 18, 2018, https://takiedela.ru/2018/05/pyat-let-bez-balabanova/; Valeriia Ermakova, "Balabanov, Poslednii modernist," *Medium*, April 6, 2015, https://medium.com/@epinevalery/последний-модернист-2b5872f91383.

    Condee has also written about Balabanov's "iron modernism," visualized in his "fascination for the city, for machinery, industry, transport, metal landscapes, as well as his concerns with power, mastery, hierarchy, and (particularly in *Cargo 200*) paranoia" (Condee, *The Imperial Trace*, pp. 242–3).
5. Arkus.
6. Balabanova. It may be coincidence that at the first "Balabanov Readings" (*Balabanovskie chteniia*) in St Petersburg in 2017, Aleksei Medvedev cited Mamardashvili's definition of metaphor to set up a discussion of Balabanov's disputed relationship to the problem of genre. Aleksei Medvedev, "Zhanr kak metafora," in *Balabanov. Perekrestki*, ed. A. Artamonov and V. Stepanov (St Petersburg: *Seans*, 2017), pp. 79–90.
7. Strukov, p. 77.
8. Nikolaev was known for his work in the field of popular documentaries, and Balabanov expresses the early influence of this genre on his own education. In

particular, Balabanov referenced a documentary project by classmate Viktor Kossakovsky on philosopher Aleksei Losev, which Kossakovsky completed in 1989. See: Mariia Kuvshinova, "Aleksei Balabanov: Tak okazalos', chto ia zdes' zhivu," *Seans* (Feb. 25, 2014), http://seance.ru/blog/chtenie/balabanov_book_intrvw/.

9. The actual sales figures for *Brother* were much higher, since pirated VHS recordings of the film and its soundtrack (on CD and audio cassette) were disseminated by street venders "in huge quantities" upon its release. Dennis Danilov, "'V chem sila, brat?'. Piat' luchshikh fil'mov rezhissera Alekseia Balabanova," *Argumenty i fakty* (Feb. 25, 2016), http://www.spb.aif.ru/culture/person/v_chem_sila_brat_pyat_luchshih_filmov_rezhissera_alekseya_balabanova.

10. The program notes to Balabanov's *Morphia* from the 2009 Annual Russian Film Symposium briefly discuss the relationship of Balabanov's filmmaking to the history of cinema. See: "*Morphia* [*Morfii*]." Program Notes. University of Pittsburgh Russian Film Symposium, 2011, http://www.rusfilm.pitt.edu/2009/morphia.php. Condee also talks about Balabanov's filmmaking about the process of filmmaking in her review of *The Stoker*: "Aleksei Balabanov: *Stoker* (*Kochegar*, 2010)," *KinoKultura* 32 (2011), http://www.kinokultura.com/2011/32r-kochegar.shtml.

11. Evgenii Gusiatinskii, "Aleksei Balabanov: 'Vsegda zhivem v Rossii,'" *Iskusstvo kino* 7 (July 2007), http://kinoart.ru/archive/2007/07/n7-article2.

12. Alena Solntseva, "Govoriat, chto schast'e gde-to est'," *Stengazeta.net*, Oct. 3, 2012, https://stengazeta.net/?p=10008810.

13. On Balabanov and genre, see: Medvedev. On Balabanov's relationship to the press, see: Aleksei Balabanov, "Balabanov o Balabanove," *Seans*, No. 17/18, http://seance.ru/n/17-18/portret-4/balabanov-o-balabanove/; Gusiatinskii, "Aleksei Balabanov: 'Vsegda zhivem v Rossii.'"

14. On the combination of contemplation, travel, and music as Balabanov's "prominent cinematic signature," see: Condee, *The Imperial* Trace, p. 225. Andrew Chapman discusses the effect of music in Chapman, "*The Stoker*," University of Pittsburgh Russian Film Symposium, 2011, http://www.rusfilm.pitt.edu/2011/thestoker.html.

15. Tatiana Kuzmicheva, "Interview with the Film Editor Tat'iana Kuz'micheva by Anna Nieman," *KinoKultura* 59 (2018), http://www.kinokultura.com/2018/59i-kuzmicheva_nieman.shtml.

16. The theme of apocalypse puts Balabanov in line with other Russian *auteurs* of the twenty-first century, for instance Andrey Zvyagintsev, for whom the theme of apocalypse is a guiding aesthetic force.

17. Anna Nieman, "A Picnic on the Road to the Temple," *KinoKultura* 40 (2013), http://www.kinokultura.com/2013/40-nieman.shtml.

18. Aglaia Chechot, "Pozovi menia, nebo," *Seans* (March 15, 2012), http://seance.ru/blog/call-me-sky/; Nieman.

19. Qtd Neil Cornwell, *The Absurd in Literature* (Manchester: Manchester University Press, 2006), p. 186.
20. Merab Mamardashvili, *Neobkhodimost' sebia* (Moscow: Labarint, 1996), p. 186.
21. Aristotle, *Poetics*, trans. S. H. Butcher, 3rd edn (London: Macmillan & Co., 1902), pp. 21 and 23. Roman Karst writes of Kafka's biographical connection to his protagonists in: Karst, "Kafka and the Russians," *Perspectives and Personalities. Studies in Modern German Literature Honoring Claude Hill*, ed. Ralph Ley, Maria Wagner, Joanna M. Ratych, and Kenneth Hughes (Heidelberg: Carl Winter Universitatsverlag, 1978), p. 190.
22. Nina Tsyrkun, "Seansu otvechaiut: pro urodov i liudei," *Seans*, No. 17/18 (May 1999), http://seance.ru/n/17-18/rezhisser-film-kritik-2/pro-uro dov-i-lyudey/pro-urodov-i-lyudey-2/.
23. Franz Kafka, "The Bachelor's Unhappiness," in *The Metamorphosis, In the Penal Colony, and Other Stories*, trans. Joachim Neugroschel (New York: Simon & Schuster, 1995), p. 33.
24. Aleksei Balabanov, "Moe kino – eto novyi zhanr, fantasticheskii realizm. Vse igraiut sami sebia," Tass.ru (Sept. 10, 2012), http://tass.ru/opinions/inter views/1599012.
25. On the relationship between Balabanov's and Dostoevsky's employments of the term "fantastical realism," see: Dar'ia Ezerova, "'Ia tozhe khochu': mezhdu fantasticheskim i magicheskim realizmom," in *Balabanov. Perekrestki*, ed. A. Artamonov and V. Stepanov (St Petersburg: Seans, 2017), pp. 53–62.
26. Aleksei Balabanov, "Aleksei Balabanov: Ia ubil slishkom mnogo liudei v kino," RIA Novosti (Sept. 8, 2012), https://ria.ru/interview/20120908/745890762. html. Balabanov was also known for using unknown or non-professional actors in his films, sometimes finding them on location (Kuzmicheva).
27. Qtd Cornwell, pp. 193–4. On sourcing for this quote, see: Cornwell, p. 194.
28. Anisimova, "Aleksei Balabanov: Me Too (Ia tozhe khochu, 2012)," *KinoKultura* 30 (2013), http://www.kinokultura.com/2013/40r-ya-tozhe-khochu.shtml.
29. "Soznanie i tsivilizatsiia," pp. 12–13.
30. "'Tret'e' sostoianie," pp. 163–5.
31. "Soznanie i tsivilizatsiia," p. 16.
32. *Estetika myshleniia*, p. 162.
33. "Soznanie i tsivilizatsiia," p. 17.
34. Ibid., pp. 12–13.
35. For just one example of this vast literature, see: Daniel Dennett, "The Unimagined Preposterousness of Zombies," *Journal of Consciousness Studies* 2.4 (1995): pp. 322–6.
36. *Kantianskie variatsii*, pp. 133 and 145.
37. Ibid., p. 133.
38. Motroshilova, *Merab Mamardashvili*, p. 98.

39. On a discussion of the role and lack of the absolute in Mamardashvili's critic of Kantian transcendentalism, see: S. A. Nizhnikov, "M. K. Mamardashvili Ob osobennostiakh funktsionirovaniia religioznogo soznaniia," *Ezhegodnaia bogoslovskaia konferentsiia pravoslavnogo Sviato-tikhonovskogo gumanitarnogo universiteta* 25 (n.d.): pp. 172–5.
40. "Besedy o myshlenii."
41. Aleksandr Dobrokhotov writes about Mamardashvili and the universal soul in "Traditsiia bessmertiia: Mamardashvili kak filosof kul'tury," in *Izbrannoe* (Moscow: Territoriia budushchego, 2008), p. 365.
42. V. D. Gubin, T. Iu. Sidorina, and V. P. Filatov (eds), *Uchebnik filosofiia*, 2nd edn (Moscow: TON-Ostozh'e, 2001), p. 411.
43. "Problema soznaniia i filosofskoe prizvanie," p. 56.
44. Mamardashvili, "Byt' filosofom – eto sud'ba," p. 32.
45. Dularidze, "Merab Mamardashvili segodnia."
46. Among contemporary scholars, Igor' Evlampiev seeks to demonstrate how Mamardashvili was unconsciously influenced by the tradition and "spiritual atmosphere" of Russian religious philosophy. *Russkaia filosofiia v evropeiskom kontekste*, p. 418.
47. Mamardashvili, "Byt' filosofom – eto sud'ba," p. 32. See Sedakova for a discussion of Mamardashvili's use of thought as a form of resistance.
48. "Byt' filosofom – eto sud'ba," p. 38.
49. *Vil'niusskie lektsii*, p. 84.
50. "Mysl' v kul'ture," p. 145.
51. "The Civil Society," p. 5.
52. Karst, p. 189.
53. Qtd ibid., p. 188.
54. Volkova, "Paola Volkova o Merabe Mamardashvili."
55. Solntseva, "Govoriat, chto schast'e gde-to est'."
56. For example, the bathhouse sequence in *Me Too* was filmed in the *banya* that Balabanov visited every Wednesday, while several of his films feature scenes shot in his own Vasilevsky Island neighborhood of St Petersburg.
57. On Balabanov and the postmodern, see Plakhov, p. 11; Anisimova; Frederick H. White, "Aleksei Balabanov's 'Cinema About Cinema,'" *Essays in Honor of Alexander Zholkovsky*, ed. Dennis Ioffe, Marcus Levitt, Joe Peschio, and Igor Pilshchikov (Boston: Academic Studies Press, 2018), pp. 621–41.
58. On Balabanov and literary adaptation, see: White, p. 625.
59. Joachim Neugroschel, "Introduction," in *The Metamorphosis, In the Penal Colony, and Other Stories*, trans. Joachim Neugroschel (New York: Simon & Schuster, 1995), p. xiii.
60. On Balabanov and Descartes, see: Arkus; Ermakova.
61. Viktor Sukhorukov, "Portret. Aleksei Balabanov," *Seans* 17/18, http://seance.ru/n/17-18/portret-4/2505/.
62. Medvedev, p. 88.
63. Balabanov, "Balabanov o Balabanove."

64. Karst, p. 190.
65. Kuzmicheva.
66. "Aleksei Balabanov byl tiazhelo bolen i zhdal smerti," NTV (May 18, 2013), http://www.ntv.ru/novosti/596097/.
67. Solntseva, "Govoriat, chto schast'e gde-to est'."
68. Albert Camus, *The Myth of Sisyphus* (New York City: Alfred A. Knopf, 1983), p. 3.
69. See, for instance: Anzhelika Zaozerskaia, "Aleksei Balabanov: Ia khochu v rai, chtoby vstretit'sia so svoim papoi," (May 18, 2013), http://vm.ru/news/2013/05/18/aleksej-bababanov-ya-hochu-v-raj-chtobi-vstretitsya-so-svoim-papoj-196790.html.
70. Balabanov, "Aleksei Balabanov: Ia ubil slishkom mnogo liudei v kino."
71. On Balabanov's comments in this vein, see: Zaozerskaia.
72. Ibid.
73. Some accounts report that Balabanov had to be convinced to film in digital, and others suggest that he initiated the idea. On this question, see: Sergei Sychev, "Balabanov snimaet fil'm 'Ia tozhe khochu' v ekstremal'nykh usloviiakh," Filmpro.ru, March 22, 2012, https://www.filmpro.ru/materials/16286; Mariia Kuvshinova, *Balabanov* (St Petersburg: *Seans*, 2015), p. 174.
74. The Kodak company filed for bankruptcy in 2012 and Paramount eliminated new production on film stock in 2013. A few years later, however, this trend appeared to be correcting itself already; in 2017, cameraman Linus Sandgren won the Academy Award for Best Cinematography for *La La Land* (Damien Chazelle, 2016), the first award in five years for a cinematographer shooting in 35 mm.
75. Kuvshinova, "Aleksei Balabanov."
76. For a metaphysical reading of *Me Too*, see: Kuvshinova, p. 182. For an interpretation of the film through the lens of the director's psyche, see Gusiatinskii, "Bol'no, bystro," *Seans* (May 22, 2007), https://seance.ru/blog/reviews/ya-hochu-balabanov/.

CHAPTER 5

Alexander Zeldovich's *Target* (2011): Tolstoy and Mamardashvili on the Infinite and the Earthly

One of Mamardashvili's students at the Higher Courses in the 1980s was Alexander Zeldovich, a psychologist who had practiced for several years in Moscow before entering film school. Together with postmodernist novelist and dramatist Vladimir Sorokin, Zeldovich wrote the screenplay for *Target* (*Mishen'*, 2011) as a loose adaptation of Tolstoy's *Anna Karenina*. Set in an ambiguous, not-so-distant future, the film tells the story of a group of Moscow elites who visit a fountain of youth in the Altai region of southern Siberia. Philosophically, the film's focus on the moral dangers of eternity lends itself more closely to dialogue with Tolstoy's philosophy of death than with his novel; Tolstoy wrote over several decades about the spiritual and moral dangers of conflating the categories of the infinite and the eternal, and we can read *Target* as a philosophical case study of some of Tolstoy's most important ideas in this vein. Mamardashvili too spoke about the categories of the infinite and the eternal, arguing in particular that a proper understanding of the infinite was necessary for self-consciousness, for social relations, and, by extension, for any philosophical thinking to occur.

In this chapter, I offer a dual-voiced reading of Zeldovich's *Target*. First, I analyze the film in the context of Tolstoy's writing on the philosophy of death, where the categories of infinity and the eternal are critical for understanding the ethical and spiritual dimensions of his work. Second, I look at the film in the context of Mamardashvili's own views on infinity, which was among the more repeated terms in his lectures and which he viewed, in the tradition of Hegel, as the bridge between self-consciousness and being. By engaging film, philosophy, and literature across genres and historical periods, I hope not only to open up new ways of reading Zeldovich's film, but to argue for a robust understanding of the philosophical potential of the film image as a dynamic space of philosophical encounters.

A Novel on Film

Zeldovich (b. 1958) enrolled in the Higher Courses for Scriptwriters and Directors in 1985 as a student in Gleb Panfilov's workshop. From the beginning, his work has been deeply influenced by the Russian literary tradition. His 1986 diploma film was an adaptation of Nikolai Leskov's *Warrior Woman* (*Voditel'nitsa*, 1866), and his feature debut was the 1990 film *Sunset* (*Zakat*), based on the 1928 play by Isaac Babel. He wrote the screenplay for his second feature, *Moscow* (*Moskva*, 2000), also in collaboration with Vladimir Sorokin—a cultural and cinematic monument of the beginning of the twenty-first century, capturing the "godlessness" of the 1990s in Chekhovian fashion.[1] Barbara Wurm describes how the unintentional pacing of Zeldovich's films at approximately one per decade, together with his grand style, has meant that his films represent entire decades, each serving as a "quintessential resume" of their time.[2]

Target opens in Moscow in the year 2020. Set only nine years ahead of the film's release date, Russia's capital city is at once futuristic and familiar: computer-generated skyscrapers fill the spaces between historical landmarks, while Russian culture is paired with a cosmopolitan acceptance of the Chinese influence that permeates life in the metropole.[3] The film's five protagonists, each corresponding more or less to a hero or heroine in *Anna Karenina*, are attractive and wealthy, and determined to stay that way. Viktor, the Minister of Natural Resources, is at the peak of his career; his wife Zoia at the peak of her beauty. Both are preoccupied with the inevitability of extinction at multiple levels. Viktor is responsible for redirecting the troubled environmental and ethical trajectory of the Russian Federation, while his young wife is consumed by her own mortality and infertility, evident in her endless experimentation with anti-aging showers and rejuvenating face masks.

When Viktor hears of a "fountain of youth" tucked in the Altai mountains, he and Zoia make the journey with three others to a place the locals call "the target": an abandoned astrophysics station that siphons cosmic radiation and promises to halt aging indefinitely. Upon returning to Moscow, the group initially experiences an unparalleled sense of freedom. Within days, this feeling gives way to emptiness and terror. The characters begin slowly shedding their identities: the men—Viktor, Nikolai, and Mitia—are overcome by brutality and episodes of psychosis, becoming the perpetrators of sexual violence, public outbursts, and self-mutilation; the women, in turn, grow increasingly frail and hysterical, and Zoia and Taia (a former resident of the target) begin to dress and act increasingly similarly until even Viktor treats them as though they were indistinguishable. With the removal of death from the equation, their lives—and, by artistic extension, the narrative logic of the film—are stripped of order and motivation, sinking each character into a path of violence and irrationalism that culminates at the end of two weeks with the death or exile of all involved.

The five protagonists in *Target* are an anachronistic blending of the wealthy, self-indulgent new Russians of the 1990s and the social indifference and cult of glamour of the 2000s. Their trip to the target holds the promise of extending immortality from the personal to the imperial, freezing Russian culture at its most decadent and solipsistic post-Soviet moment—an imaginary composite of the past, present, and future, or what Mariia Kuvshinova refers to as "a genre palindrome, at once a utopia and an anti-utopia."[4] The disappearance of death from the narrative ushers in a new state in which "there should be no limitations," as Mitia puts it after returning from the target.

The search for youth that consumes Zeldovich's protagonists, in turn, is amplified in the resource crisis depicted in the film. Like the dissonance between physical beauty and existential turmoil that defines the personal lives of the characters, Russia's achievements too are only surface deep. With Chinese cultural practices having become a staple of daily life in Moscow, Russia is left to assert its imperial authority through control of a lengthy leg of the congested transcontinental trucking highway that cuts from Guangzhou to Paris. The country is sliced from east to west, a truck-stop in the transportation of goods and resources between the two continents it has historically straddled—both geographically and intellectually.

Meanwhile, the Ministry of Natural Resources has placed all its efforts in extracting a rare element, Runium, from volcanic gas on Kamchatka as a way to secure Russia's influence on the global stage. On the domestic front, the scramble for power and resources is inscribed on Zoia's body as a demographic crisis. In the opening scenes, her physical and psychological fragility, along with her infertility and desperation to preserve an irreparable younger self, captures the imperial body in acute crisis. Having swelled to its most expansive size and unable to regenerate further, the empire pauses for a moment before collapsing inward. Under a polished shell of skyscrapers, technology, and the soothing sounds of the Far East, an empire built on the extraction and exportation of its natural reserves, of its own body, is struggling to sustain itself.

At the level of aesthetics, the sterile melodrama and porcelain aesthetics of *Target* contrast starkly with the dark provincial melodramas set in the Russian heartland (*glubinka*) that were prevalent in Russian festival programming at the time of the film's release, to the point where *Target* was criticized for superficiality by several critics.⁵ The visual world of the film is an extension of the narrative disconnect between form and content, echoing the lack of meaning in the protagonists' search for physical perfection: the airy expanses of Altai, the glass and marble arcades of Moscow, the computer-generated city of the future, and Zoia's flawless features are all captured in an idealized state of frozen, pre-patina perfection. Zeldovich conducted a long search to fill the lead female role before settling on South African actress Justine Waddell, whose frailty and accented Russian (which she learned in several months for this role) contribute to the sense of estrangement depicted on screen. The flawless and sterile representation of Moscow's elite is enhanced by the film's original score, composed by former Bolshoi Theatre Music Director Leonid Desiatnikov. Ethereal swells are balanced by intervals of staccato and rest through which the sounds of the environment push, giving rise to a mood of suspense and awe that complements the stunning scenery of Altai.⁶ In her review of *Target*, Zara Abdullaeva argues that "style (interiors, costumes, set design, camera angles, props, and subject matter) becomes the film's primary content."⁷

Zeldovich has repeatedly stated that the goal of his film is to transgress genres, to engage with Russia's rich novelistic tradition in a cinematic medium. Reviewers of the film have gone as far as calling *Target* a "tracing" of *Anna Karenina*, while Zeldovich has spoken openly about "taking the entire plot concept—even the outlines of the characters— from *Anna Karenina* and simply transposing them [into the future]."⁸ Zeldovich describes the film as taking place "in a Russian novel" and indicates that he sees *Target* as the blending of the major genres of literature— the short story, the short novel (*povest'*), and the novel—in a "cinematic novel" lasting just under two and a half hours.⁹ "We made a novel," he said in a March 2001 interview.¹⁰

To add to the film's literary underpinnings, *Target* is deeply rooted in the futuristic world of Sorokin's 2006 dystopia, *Day of the Oprichnik* (*Den' oprichnika*).¹¹ In Sorokin's novel, set just under a decade ahead of *Target* in the year 2028, Russia has isolated itself from every country but China and the protagonist, a high-ranking *oprichnik*, channels the authoritarianism of Ivan the Terrible in his service to the Czar. *Target* and *Day of the Oprichnik* share clear narrative similarities, including the treatment of Chinese immigration, a blended Russian-Chinese culture of the future, and the depiction of a Guangzhou–Paris highway that stretches across the country. Sorokin's work in general is also known for its ambiguity in setting, both in place and time, including the way he mines literary motifs from the nineteenth-century canon and projects them into a future that is both familiar and not. Thus, *Target* is connected to literature on two temporal ends, reaching back to its narrative roots in Tolstoy, on the one, and sharing deep roots in Sorokin's historico-futuristic dystopia and postmodern approach to the classical Russian canon, on the other.

Zeldovich was a student of Mamardashvili's from 1984 to 1986, when Mamardashvili was teaching the required course in philosophy at the Higher Courses. In a 2015 interview, he describes how, after completing promotional work for *Target*, he bought several volumes of Mamardashvili's lectures and began reading. Like most directors who studied with Mamardashvili, including Alexander Sokurov, Zeldovich recalls feeling that he understood the full impact of the philosopher's influence only at a later point in his life—in Zeldovich's case, more than twenty years after his time at the Higher Courses, and by then an established filmmaker.[12] *Target* lends itself to dialogue with Mamardashvili's work, not only because of the direct connection between the director and the philosopher, but because the concepts of infinity and eternity had important philosophical implications for Mamardashvili's work as well. According to philosopher Erik Solovyov, in fact, the Tolstoy–Mamardashvili connection is less unexpected that one might think, and "Mamardashvili's comments at times resemble a categorical explication of Leo Tolstoy's revelations."[13] Mamardashvili himself argued that Tolstoy was neglected in the shadow of Dostoevsky's philosophy, and that Tolstoy "was not just a great writer but was actually a remarkable thinker."[14]

Tolstoy on the Infinite and the Eternal

Tolstoy's complex philosophy of death hinged on the way he understood immortality and, importantly, how he distinguished immortality from infinity. Infinity has been theorized in countless ways in the history of philosophy, including as potentiality without completion (Aristotle), as simultaneously incompatible and compatible with finitude (Zeno's paradoxes), and as the incomprehensible and the divine (e.g. the scholastics). Immortality is commonly understood as "cheating" the physical constraints of biological life (i.e. death) *within* the finitude of space and time, either by extending life indefinitely (e.g. in the case of the vampire myth), or by projecting the fruits of human activity forward in spite of human death (e.g. in the official Marxist-Leninist platform on the immortal material mark of human influence). The existential crises of countless Tolstoyan characters hinge on the difference between these two terms: Tolstoy's characters want immortality, but neglect infinity. In lamenting the loss of their corporeal selves and their consciousness, they fail to recognize the unsurpassed spiritual value of an existence directed towards infinity—or what Tolstoy called "true life." It is not only that in "true life" death should not be feared; for Tolstoy, the concept of death itself did not exist for the individual leading a "true life" guided by infinity.[15]

Collectivity played a crucial role in the achievement of "true life" for Tolstoy. While immortality involves the desire to preserve the individual human body (in *Target*) or the individual soul (in the Christian model), Tolstoy's view of infinity outside space and time in fact hinged on a collective spiritual union in the physical world. In "Three Deaths" ("Tri smerti," 1858/1859), life comes together to fill in the gaps that death leaves: grass grows over the grave of the deceased coachman and, when a tree is cut down, others extend their branches "joyously in the newly cleared space."[16] The desire for immortality among many of Tolstoy's characters, and also the protagonists of *Target*, is a symptom of a false value placed on individuality (*lichnost'*), and, as Vasilii Zenkovskii emphasized, the value of the individual was almost completely foreign to Tolstoy's philosophy.[17] If there was any escape from the pitfall of individuality, "it is certainly to be found in the renunciation of the welfare of the personality," Tolstoy expressed.[18] Communion with others through love, as he would argue in "The Law of Love and the Law of Violence" ("Zakon nasiliia i zakon liubvi," 1908), is the only way that "true life" can be achieved.

Here we run up against a paradox in Tolstoy's thought. While he was clear that "true life" exists outside the temporal and spatial constraints of the physical world, we have also seen from his philosophy's social component that "true life" must take place in *this* world. He was outright dismissive of the belief that corporeal life aims only to service an afterlife, and even in *On Life* (*O zhizni*, 1888), which counts among the author's most exhaustive philosophical investigations of the individual's relationship to death, he avoids speculating on the immortality of the soul or any possibility for posthumous redemption. For Tolstoy, in other words, the meaning of life is tethered firmly to the present. "A life with no other aim than a life beyond the grave . . . is an evil and an absurdity," he confirms.[19]

In the *Tractatus Logico-Philosophicus* (1921), written during a period when Ludwig Wittgenstein was highly influenced by Tolstoy's *The Gospel in Brief* (*Kratkoe izlozhenie Evangelii*, 1906), Wittgenstein offered a view that may, at least partially, resolve the Tolstoyan paradox between the social milieu and infinity. Speaking of the semantic relationship between time and timelessness, Wittgenstein wrote, "If we take eternity to mean not infinite temporal duration but timelessness, then eternal life belongs to those who live in the present. Our life has no end in just the way in which our visual field has no limits."[20] Although Tolstoy preferred a natural metaphor to describe "true life's" timelessness in time, the idea was remarkably similar: "Man will believe in his immortality only when he understands that his life is not a wave but an eternal movement, which shows itself only as a wave in this life."[21]

Even more controversial is Tolstoy's claim that the moment of death is not just the endpoint of physical life but is the source of meaning in that life. In *The Pathway of Life* (*Put' zhizni*), on which he worked for most of 1910, he asserted that the value of one's life increases as one draws closer to death. He then distilled his philosophical position on the value of death into a mathematical formula in prose: "the value of life is in inverse ratio to the square of the distance from death."[22] If we were to rewrite this statement in mathematical notation, we would arrive at the following formula, where V stands for the value of life and d for the distance from death:

$$V \sim \frac{1}{d^2}$$

Structurally, we see that Tolstoy's formula is modeled on Newton's Law of Universal Gravitation.[23] Newton's Law asserts that the force between two point masses is inversely proportional to the square of the distance between them. In other words, as two masses move closer together, so the force between them grows infinitely.

In the case of Tolstoy's formula, the variables in question are not celestial bodies but the individual and the endpoint of physical death. Like in Newton's Law, in Tolstoy's formula the closer d gets to 0 (i.e. the closer the individual gets to death), the higher the value for V. Thus, the value of one's life is at its highest in the moments directly before that life ends. Although Tolstoy had critiqued the scientific, or materialist (as opposed to theological), approach to life that had captivated many of the brightest Russian minds of the nineteenth century, Newton's Law offered a fruitful structure for expressing his position on the value of life in relation to death.[24] He would repeat the same formula in prose in several other works, including in a journal entry several years earlier, dated February 18, 1906.

We find Tolstoy's most complex use of this Newtonian metaphor in 1886 in *The Death of Ivan Ilych*, the author's first major fiction work following his conversion. Deteriorating in both body and mind, Ivan Ilych likens the progression of his terminal illness to "a stone falling downward with increasing velocity."[25] As the dying man looks back at his past, he notices that "[t]here's one bright spot there at the back, at the beginning of life . . . and afterwards all becomes blacker and blacker and proceeds more and more rapidly—*an inverse ratio to the square of the distance from death.*"[26]

However, unlike the formula's appearance in 1910 in *The Pathway of Life*, where life becomes *increasingly* valuable in the moments before death, Ivan Ilych sees his life as *decreasing* in value as his illness progresses. The onset of the protagonist's illness marks the moment at which the "blackness" increases "in inverse ratio to the square of the distance from death." Ivan Ilych has not yet come to appreciate his life or the value of his own death; he is formal, insular, and isolated, and he shudders as he "await[s] the dreadful fall and shock and destruction" he anticipates his impending death to be.[27] On the Tolstoyan path to infinity, in other words, he is still misguided, stagnant, and fearful of death, living his life by the wrong formula.

It is on the fourth day before his death, when he receives communion "with tears in his eyes," that Ivan Ilych is filled with the desire to live.[28] His final three days are consumed by pain, flailing, and a lingering refusal to submit. He recognizes that although his life had not been ideal, there had always been the hope to make it better. Things no longer appear "blacker and blacker." It is not that he wants to live; he wants to become better while he still lives. Upon this realization, "he looked for his former accustomed fear of death but did not find it . . . In place of death there was light."[29] Having transformed his protagonist, Tolstoy transfers the light Ivan Ilych saw at the *beginning* of his life to the *end*. As Ivan Ilych takes his final breaths, where he once saw a light in his memory he now sees it in his current condition, realizing the restorative and penitent force of what Tolstoy will later call in *The Pathway of Life* "that valuable final moment before death."[30] Vasily Brekhunov, the selfish landowner in "Master and Man" ("Khoziain i rabotnik," 1895), sees in the sky this same light, one that causes him to alter the course of his actions and sacrifice his life so that his peasant might live out the snowstorm under the warmth of his dying body.

For Tolstoy, an abstract experience of death was not enough to initiate a moral conversation: one must face death concretely and corporeally. For Brekhunov, it is only when he believes that he will freeze and hears his peasant pronounce the words "I'm dying" that he sees the error of his ways and commits to changing the course of his life in his final moments. Tolstoy's requirement for his characters to gain a palpable and personal, as opposed to abstract, experience of death is played out in perhaps the most famous of all of his near-death vignettes. As Prince Andrei Bolkonsky lies wounded on the battlefield, he sees nothing but the sky above and around him—an endless expanse of gray stretching into infinity.[31] Like both Ivan Ilych and Brekhunov, Prince Andrei's experience of death in *War and Peace* (*Voina i mir*, 1867) marks a complete break with his former self, as

Lev Shestov described it.[32] But it also marks his acceptance of infinity through the metaphor of the endless sky. "How was it I did not see that lofty sky before?," Andrei wonders. "And how happy I am to have found it at last! Yes! All is vanity, all falsehood, except that infinite sky. There is nothing, nothing, but that."[33] Andrei's brush with death allows him to reflect on his mortality and then think past it, unfolding before him the possibility of "true life" that had until then been closed.

In the final paragraphs of *A Confession* (*Ispoved'*), Tolstoy recalled a transformative dream not unlike Prince Andrei's rebirth on the battlefield. He recounted how he dreamt himself dangling over an abyss, "disgusted and horrified by infinity below, but drawn upwards and strengthened by infinity above."[34] A voice called to him to look up to the infinity above; the precipice below at once became a column that supported his torso in a noose "so that there is no possibility of falling."[35] For Tolstoy, faith was the only way out of the paralyzing paradox in which he had spent much of his life, caught between two contradictory approaches to infinity. To submit to the infinity below was to fear death and cling to the self; to embrace the infinity above was to accept death as the pillar that supports meaning in life.[36] "What am I?" Tolstoy asked in *A Confession*. "A part of infinity," was his answer.[37]

In preparing for a reading of Zeldovich's *Target*, it is also important to keep in mind that Tolstoy emphasized the role of active, lived moral progress. Although progress was crucial for his ethical philosophy, he emphasized that it is not the speed that one moves toward a good death that matters, but the fact that one reaches it at all. And indeed, pace or temporal length is not a variable that enters into the quantification of that life's value. "I don't dare to think that the one who moves [through life] slowly lives any more than the one who moves quickly," he confirmed.[38] Moreover, he went as far as to claim in *On Life* that time does not exist for the individual who lives a "true life," since that individual is guided only by the ideals on which his actions are modeled and not the earthly parameters of the real-life applications of those ideals. Just as individual lives move toward perfection mediated by death, "human life in its totality cannot but advance toward the eternal ideal of perfection."[39]

In *On Life* and *A Confession*, among other works, Tolstoy continuously characterized the meaning of life as continued movement from evil toward good. In other words, "true life" is motion. Ivan Ilych's mistaken conviction that his life had been a good one "held him fast and prevented his moving forward, and it caused him the most torment of all."[40] Even slow, and perhaps even belabored, progress along life's path is better than no progress. "Why speak?," Ivan Ilych thinks moments before his death.

"I must act."[41] As Scanlan points out, in Tolstoy's philosophy, "a person who is far from the moral ideal, but is striving to improve, is morally superior to a person who is closer to the ideal but is making no effort at improvement."[42] "Life is a blessing only when death is not considered to be evil," Tolstoy said in the May 12th entry in *A Cycle of Reading* (*Krug chteniia*, 1886–1910).[43] Like meaning, motion too is predicated mathematically on death. In another great irony, for Tolstoy there was no progress in life without death.

It is also important to remember that in Tolstoy's formula V is not connected to length of life. If we were to misread a longer life as a more valuable one, as his above-mentioned comment from *The Pathway of Life* suggests, then the characters of Zeldovich's film would have hit the Tolstoyan target. Having discovered the potential for eternal youth, their lives would grow increasingly meaningful with each passing decade. Rather than seek out meaning in the "perfect equilibrium" of faith and infinity of which Tolstoy spoke in *A Confession*, however, Zeldovich's characters initially represent the antithesis of his philosophical position by seeking to preserve the self through eternal youth.[44] It is in this way that I see *Target* as a cinematic case study of Tolstoy's philosophical position on death in the final third of his life. In viewing the film through a Tolstoyan lens and the characters of *Target* as stand-ins for the implied opponents of Tolstoy's later writings on death, we see how their devastating fates affirm the untenability of the anti-Tolstoyan utopia constructed in the film, as well as Tolstoy's belief that a world without death is a world without meaning.

Mamardashvili on the Infinite

Variations on the word "infinite" were among the more repeated terms in Mamardashvili's writing and lectures. Although his philosophical position on this question was nowhere near as developed as Tolstoy's, he referred to the concept of the infinite regularly, both as a noun and an adjective, as well as literally and metaphorically. When he used the term in adjectival form it was often a vehicle for hyperbole, especially with regards to Kant, whom he described as an "infinitely kind and delicate soul."[45] He also regularly spoke about falling into "infinite contradictions" in the study of consciousness and, ironically, in the study of the infinite itself.[46] In *Cartesian Meditations*, the Russian noun and adjectival variations for the concepts "infinite" or "infinity" appear nearly a hundred times in total; in *Kantian Variations*, the same terms receive over 150 mentions.

The infinite was not just a rhetorical device for Mamardashvili, but an integral component of the problem of human consciousness. He described consciousness as infinite: first, as a concept, since we cannot conceive of its beginning or end; second, as a function, since "human consciousness is constantly in the process of illuminating, making clear everything that already existed within it"; and third, as a continuousness of being, since consciousness does not have variations or gradations, but is always, in every case, just *consciousness*.[47] All three components of consciousness come together such that where there is no consciousness, there can be no being, and vice versa.

The infinite posed a particularly challenging philosophical problem for Mamardashvili. "The term 'infinity' in our language is just as indistinct and unclear . . . as the terms 'conscience,' 'God', or 'I,'" he argued in 1981.[48] Like consciousness, infinity can never "be taken as a given" and can never become the object of analysis, although we must always enter into it and must *think it*.[49] In other words, like our own faculty of consciousness, "infinity is only posed and never given—it is posed as a problem, as a question."[50] Mamardashvili took up the philosophical question of infinity in particular detail in his work on Descartes and Kant, where he distinguished between two kinds of infinity. There was the true infinite, which he saw as a sustaining necessity for human consciousness and reason, and which was transcendental in character. There was also the spurious infinite, which he described as a state of indefiniteness with no spatial or temporal progression, and where "no moment in time is indistinguishable from another."[51]

Although Mamardashvili did not elaborate on the difference between these two kinds of infinity in any sustained way, it is clear that here he was influenced by Hegel, for whom the true infinite, as Alper Türken perspicaciously articulates, described the move from consciousness to self-consciousness and ultimately to reason.[52] Hegel's true infinite was synonymous with continuous and uninterrupted being that includes the finite within its boundlessness. The concept of infinity was what, for Hegel, unified the recognitive relationship between individual self-consciousness and other, as well as two ways of being: being-in-itself and being-for-another. As Hegel put it, the true infinite was necessary for self-consciousness because "when infinity is finally an object for consciousness, and consciousness is aware of it as what it is, then consciousness is self-consciousness."[53]

Though the spurious infinite is one stage on the way to the true infinite, it falls short of the limitlessness of the true infinite in its relationship to finite things. The true infinite contains the finite as a component of its continuousness, while the spurious infinite stands in a negative relationship to the finite. As Türken describes it in his work on Hegel, "by differentiating itself and excluding the finite from itself, the [spurious] infinite obtains the determination of a finite being."[54] Mamardashvili too described the spurious infinite as a dialectical cycle, or "spurious eternity of repetition," in which new infinities emerge but are always limited by their negative relation to the finite, and thereby "always fall back to finitude."[55] Türken refers to the dialectic of the finite and infinite, whereby both concepts rely on reference to one another in order for the true infinite to exist, as "arguably one of the most important moves of Hegel's Logic."[56]

Like Hegel, Mamardashvili seemed to think that a proper understanding of the infinite was necessary for self-consciousness, for social relations, and for philosophical thinking to occur. He described the human being "as a small image of a larger infinity," and in this way he addressed, in his own terms, the Hegelian unity of being-in-itself and being-for-another. For Mamardashvili, the relationship of individual being and collective being mirrored the relationship of the finite to the infinite, in which each demands the sustaining force of the other and where every individual is "unique and at the same time universal."[57] The dialectical relationship between individual and collective being is apparent in his *Vilnius Lectures*, where he talked about how philosophy arises in social context but that its ultimate expression has a profoundly existential character: "nobody can understand something in place of you—it has to be you."[58]

For Mamardashvili, the tension between the finite and the infinite, or the concrete and the ideal, risked serving as a source of cultural and philosophical nihilism. In "Philosophy is Consciousness Aloud" ("Filosofiia – eto soznanie vslukh," 1988), he explained how humans crave concrete examples of the infinite—ideal governments, ideal laws, and ideal individuals. When these ideals do not and cannot materialize in concrete examples, those who seek them conclude that there is no truth at all and fall into nihilism. One of Mamardashvili's methodological goals was, thus, to neutralize nihilism by laying out the relationship of transcendent truths to the finitude of the lived world.

The relationship between truths and lived examples was also an important component for moral progress for Tolstoy. The categorical nature of his moral code (e.g. absolute non-violence, absolute love) was tempered by real-life examples of moral striving and failing, often in literary form. In Book XI, Chapter 1 of *War and Peace*, for instance, Tolstoy introduced Zeno's paradox of Achilles and the Tortoise to illustrate this very point: that the laws of motion are comprehensible to the human mind only if we focus on select, concrete instances of that motion in the physical world. James Scanlan argues the same of Tolstoy's doctrine of absolute non-violence, describing the "law of love" as "the distinction between an unattainable ideal and a practical precept. Christ's injunction to speak no ill of anyone, for example, Tolstoy called a feasible step in the direction of the not perfectly realizable ideal of loving all men."[59]

We see a similar distinction between the moral ideal and the concrete in Book III, Chapter 19 of *War and Peace*, in which Prince Andrei vacillates between appealing for mercy to an abstract God or his visual representation—between "a Power indefinable, incomprehensible, ... which [Andrei] not only cannot address but cannot even express in words" and "that God who has been sewn into this amulet by Mary."[60] For Tolstoy, "human life in its totality cannot but advance toward the eternal ideal of perfection," but moral and spiritual progress requires models on which we may base our behavior.[61] This at times causes a dissonance with Tolstoy's often uncompromising rhetorical adherence to non-violent action, in the vein of Kant's categorical imperative from "On A Supposed Right to Lie from Altruistic Motives," in which Kant asserted that lying is prohibited in all instances, even to a known murderer who knocks at the door and asks whether anyone is at home.

Like Tolstoy, Mamardashvili too relied on the Sermon on the Mount for guidance, but in his view

> the command to "turn the other cheek to your enemy" is not a prescription for our behavior. It is an abstracted spiritual prescription, which says to the individual: if you took offense to this, it means that in that offence there is some truth about you. And if you want to discover that truth, don't be timid, stop what you're doing, don't allow yourself to answer in such a way that you answer in turn to the one who slapped you.[62]

Here Mamardashvili called not for a moral imperative for social relations, but for us to turn inward and assess our own moral code. He argued that there exist "pure emotions," like pure faith or pure love, that are possible only as symbolic constructions and never "as a lived psychological condition of any human being."[63] He did not suggest we move toward a law of love, as Tolstoy did, but "an altogether different answer," which "assumes a literacy of the soul and the heart" in each individual, and which can be cultivated in one's character not only through love, but through "philosophy in praxis."[64] Film was an important component of such philosophical praxis, as film had the power to offer its viewers "a reality that is inaccessible by other paths, by other means."[65]

Mamardashvili entered into explicit dialogue with Tolstoy's philosophy of death in *The Aesthetics of Thinking*, where he argued: "In his day, Leo Tolstoy compared peasants' consciousness of their own death to that of contemporary urbanites, saying that for peasants, death had meaning precisely because life had meaning. In this respect, he meant that the urbanite conceives of life as a race, where they are rushing ahead."[66] Mamardashvili continued: "In this regard, Tolstoy was right: life had meaning only for those for whom death was not a meaningless coincidence."[67] While Mamardashvili does not appear here to fully appreciate the transformative role that death played in Tolstoy's philosophical position, in his lectures on Proust Mamardashvili did argue, along Tolstoyan lines, that "death does not come after life—it takes part in life itself."[68]

Tolstoyan Targets

Returning to Zeldovich's *Target* in light of our investigations into both Tolstoy's and Mamardashvili's views of infinity, it is telling that the closing scenes of the film offer redemption only for those characters who are willing to give up their immortality. *Target* does not end with Tolstoy's Anna, but with Zeldovich's: with Anna and Mitia, who met and fell in love on their trip to the target. Hours earlier, the couple decided to part ways and meet again in exactly twenty years—this on the advice of Taia, a resident of the target, who made the same decision decades earlier with her lover. In an episode reminiscent of *The Kreutzer Sonata* (*Kreitserova sonata*, 1890), Taia tells how her lover became consumed with jealously to the point of violence. In order to "break the habit," the pair agreed to meet in thirty years' time at the only cultural monument they were confident would still be standing: the Bolshoi Theatre. These self-imposed breaks serve as a stand-in for death in a world where the normal ends imposed by biological finitude no longer exist. And indeed, when the time comes to reunite with her lover, Taia leaves her glamorous Moscow attire behind and is reborn as a simpler, earlier version of herself, before her acquisition of eternal youth.

In the closing scene of the film, we see Anna following Taia's example, having returned to the target to work while she waits out her separation with Mitia. Anna is a particularly fitting candidate for redemption, as she has already had a brush with death in her past: as a child she suffered from a rare disease called "glass bones," which kept her indoors for much of her youth. In the film's final scene, Anna looks out over the target from above. Her view is flooded by otherworldly rays of light, a visual citation of an earlier scene in which the same light illuminated the landscape as Anna recited Lermontov's "I go out on the road alone" ("Vykhozhu odin ia na dorogu," 1841). Like Tolstoy's Dolly, here Anna is at once linked to nature, to Russianness, and to "true life," in a Tolstoyan sense, as she serves her twenty-year penance. Zeldovich's characters seek immortality and neglect infinity, while for Tolstoy "true life" is possible only because of the meaning bestowed to it by physical death.

The most anticipated moment of *Target* is bound to be its clearest homage to Tolstoy's novel: Anna's suicide. The image of the steam locomotive has become synonymous with the novel, with a recent reviewer quipping that the first adaptation of Tolstoy's novel was the first scene committed to celluloid: the Lumière brothers' *The Arrival of a Train at La Ciotat* (1895).[69] Anna's suicide, a morally unforgivable act according to Tolstoy's later writing (despite that it brings the perpetrator immediately to *d*), is foreshadowed in the novel's earliest episodes and has been foreboded in cinematic adaptations in a variety of ways, from close-ups of model trains to the distant sound of a steam engine. Tolstoy repeatedly used the train as the metaphor of life's journey, especially in *The Pathway of Life*. His family estate at Yasnaya Polyana was located close to a relatively new railway line from which passengers could catch a glimpse of the home. From his yard, Tolstoy could hear the trains passing; he could see the smoke, and probably smell it too. "Remember that you are not standing but passing by, that you are not in a house but on a train that is taking you to death," he wrote.[70]

Zoia too is thrown under a train, though her suicide is more than a nod to Anna's demise—it further enriches the dialogic relationship between texts and temporalities, reinforcing the fact that *Target* is much more than a tracing of the novel. Though Anna is condemned to the tracks for abandoning her son and husband in *Anna Karenina*, Zoia's suicide offers her a chance to regain what she gave up. If we are to continue to apply Tolstoy's formula to the film, death is the only way for Zoia to return meaning to her life and undo the damage she has done by exchanging "true life" for the wicked allure of eternal youth. Like Ivan Ilych, Brekhunov, and Prince Andrei, it is only after a concrete experience of death—witnessing her husband's murder—that she seeks to return meaning to her life. In an alternative reading, Zoia's leap from a bridge in front of a high-speed train is not an act of suicide but her second chance at the Tolstoyan train of true life, a ticket that gives her back death (and by extension—infinity) as quickly as she boards.

When Mamardashvili said that "the individual realizes his universality only within the conditions of a measurement," he was articulating the finite–infinite relationship in yet another way, arguing that the true finite, expressed here as universality, is only possible within the restrictions that go hand in hand with being in a finite world of limits and laws.[71] In this context, the concluding scenes of Zeldovich's *Target* bear a striking resemblance to my earlier Tolstoyan reading of the film. The characters in *Target* make a radical break with limitation in its most absolute form, transgressing biological finitude for eternal youth. Mamardashvili added that universality is only possible in the context of a shared community—or what he called "a universal humanness that is independent of geographical length and breadth."[72] His vision here is at least reminiscent of Tolstoy's vision of community, although certainly Tolstoy's Christian vision of love-based ethics is far from the cosmopolitan, humanist, and existential (insofar as consciousness is a shared function of being human) vision of humanity that Mamardashvili held.

By the finale of Zeldovich's *Target*, any communal bonds have been severed and all the main characters have fled or died. Viktor is murdered by an unruly gang; Nikolai and Mitia flee Moscow; Anna returns to the target to wait out her penance; and Zoia drives to an overpass and throws herself onto the railroad tracks below. The introduction of eternity in *Target* leads to moral collapse and a lapse in the inner logic of the narrative. Zoia and Nikolai's affair in particular, which was a direct result of their visit to the target, becomes increasingly consumed by violence and hysteria. The particularly brutal end to Nikolai and Zoia's romantic relationship occurs without warning, and its emotional and narrative abruptness is literalized visually. None of the film's violent episodes are particularly motivated, in fact; terror strips the protagonists' lives—and, in turn, the film—of a comfortable narrative logic. The glamorous utopia of Moscow without death quickly lapses into moral dystopia, culminating in a Rabelaisian party scene that acts as limbo-space for individuals whose lives have lost meaning. By the closing scenes, the frozen, youthful faces of the protagonists serve as anomalies against the horrific scenarios in which they find themselves, cursed like Lermontov's Demon to immortality, boundless power, and an existence that leaves no room for love.

Toward the end of *Target*, Viktor and Zoia host a party at their country home outside the city, a carnival fantasy space of disarray and vice. As the evening progresses the guests become increasingly disheveled, disrobed, and intoxicated, holding balloons, playing musical instruments, engaging in destructive actions and public sexual displays, and indulging in a grotesque assortment of food and drink. Earlier in the film, Zoia expressed fantasies of her husband being reduced to poverty, and of inflicting violence over the impoverished. In her social reading of *Target*, Irina Anisimova has highlighted the film's concern with the problem of inequality, imaged most explicitly in scenes where sexual arousal goes hand in hand with social and physical degradation.[73] Outside of this social lens, we can also read the grotesque nature of the party scene as a kind

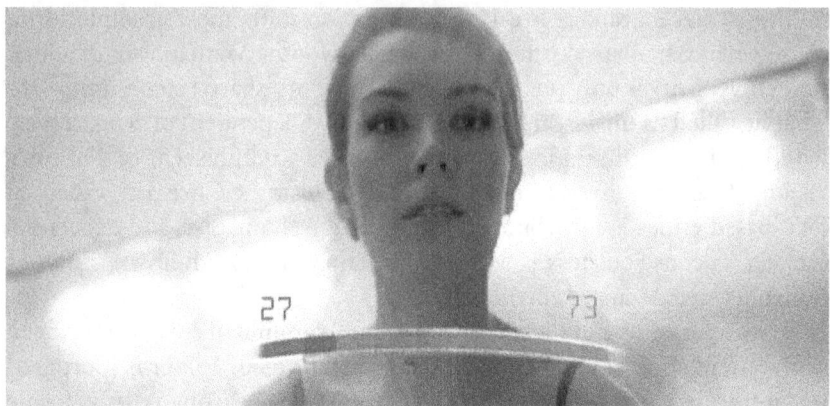

Figure 5.1 Before traveling to the target, Zoia is measured by Viktor at 27 percent evil and 73 percent good.

of performative rupture of normativity, where the rules of the finite no longer apply in predictable ways.

Neither does Viktor participate in the activities at the party scene, but instead watches the partygoers with special glasses that display the level of good and evil in individuals. In introducing this positivist tool for assessing the moral degeneration of Moscow's eternally young, we see how, after their return from the target, Viktor's glasses begin to read progressively higher levels of evil as he surveys his once-familiar world (see Figure 5.1). Zoia, who previously registered as being overwhelmingly good, measures at 97% evil and 3% good after returning from the target and beginning her affair with Nikolai. In the party scene, the glasses observe overwhelming evil in those in attendance at the *fête*.

For Mamardashvili, it was impossible to talk about good and evil in objective terms at the individual level, or to measure it at all. At times, he held an overly simplistic view of cultural subjectivity, for instance when he argued how "in one tribe they value their children, while in another tribe they kill them."[74] Moreover, a person can consider acts "50% or 60% good, or 50% bad, and everything good has another side and this is where we begin to lose our way," he continued.[75] At the very least, it is clear that he believed ethics cannot be articulated in absolute terms: "We can say 'I understand' or 'I believe,' but we cannot say 'this is.'"[76] Moreover, Mamardashvili argued that evil exists in every person and that, in particular, we are evil when we are not "masters of ourselves" (*vladet' soboi*).[77] "Moral law is a miracle," he said in "The Problem of Man in Philosophy" ("Problema cheloveka v filosofii," 1991).[78] The futuristic vision of ethical objectivity in Zeldovich's *Target*, or at least the ethical objectivity that Viktor claims to access with his special glasses, was pure fantasy for Mamardashvili.

It is no coincidence that Anna and Mitia are missing from the final party sequence in *Target*, having decided to impose temporal limits on their relationship in order to regain the limitations that they gave up at the target. Nikolai's flight from Moscow, however, is marked as a false search for infinity. He escapes his crimes under the cover of night by boarding one of the hundreds of thousands of trucks that pass through the Moscow stretch of the Paris–Guangzhou highway each day. Although Tolstoy was exceptionally fond of the image of the moving train as a metaphor for moral progress, there is no such potential for progress offered on this highway. Nikolai becomes just another nameless fugitive in a sea of nearly identical red-and-white trucks that are distinguishable, in many cases, only by large barcodes on their shipping containers. We might consider Nikolai's escape a visual representation of that "eternal repetition of the spurious" about which Mamardashvili spoke, where "no moment in time is indistinguishable from another" and which the philosopher likened to Nietzsche's philosophical mode of the eternal return.[79]

Almost two hours into the film, Viktor publicly reveals the secrets of his Ministry at a press conference, including his research into the concrete existence of good and evil, of depleted mines, and the existence of secret government spending. As he leaves the event, he walks with a sense of lightness through a marble arcade. Although Viktor has ostensibly done something good by revealing these secrets, his plan to control and ration morality mirrors the Ministry's control of natural resources in the "interest of the entire country," where morality is spoken about in industrial metaphors: "We must make it so that evil stays in the ground forever and only good is mined," he pontificates. Viktor's moment of catharsis at the press conference, and in the arcade, is in fact a false triumph. The colorless repetition of the arcade's columns is evocative of eternal life, but repetitive and without meaning—and therefore an encounter with the spurious infinite. Viktor will reinsert himself fully into infinity only during the party scene, when he is murdered while defending his wife against the realization of her earlier-expressed fantasies of violence at the hands of strangers.

Mamardashvili addressed the question of eternal life directly. In his lectures on Proust, he described Hell in opposite terms: as "eternal death," or "a death that continues constantly," as "death without an end."[80] Earlier in these lectures, he summarized Proust's view of eternal life as what is happening *right now*. Eternity does not come after this life, but it is a vertical cut in relation to the horizontal progression of our life, he explained.[81] Mamardashvili rarely quoted from the work of Russian or Soviet philosophers, neither from his contemporaries nor from Russia's philosophical past, and so it is interesting here that he cited Evgenii Trubetskoi's statement that "Hell is living forever."[82] Mamardashvili continued in his own words: "After all, we only die once, and forever by true death. But the kind of death where you are in an eternal process of dying but cannot die—then you are dying an eternal death."[83] For Mamardashvili, the concept of "eternal death" was just another way of describing the spurious infinite, "when everything spurious repeats itself over and over again in our lives, or while history repeats one and the same mistake."[84] The mistakes of Soviet history are among the topics of the next chapter, on Vadim Abdrashitov and Alexander Mindadze's 1982 film *The Train Stopped*.

Notes

1. Aleksandr Zel'dovich, "Bog i supermarket," *Rossiiskaia gazeta* (March 29, 2013), http://www.rg.ru/2013/03/28/d2b-zeldovich-intro.html.
2. Barbara Wurm, "Review of Aleksandr Zel'dovich: *The Target* (*Mishen'*, 2011)," *KinoKultura* 32 (2011), http://www.kinokultura.com/2011/32r-mishen.shtml#1.
3. The opening credits of the film are an early indication of this Chinese influence: the director's and actors' names are displayed with the letters superimposed over one another, thereby creating Hanzi-like characters from the Cyrillic.
4. Mariia Kuvshinova, "Mishen'," OpenSpace.ru (Feb. 15, 2011), http://os.colta.ru/cinema/events/details/20563/.
5. See, for instance, Oleg Aronson's comments on "Zakrytyi pokaz: 'Mishen','" Pervyi kanal, May 5, 2010.
6. On Desiatnikov's score for the film, see Dmitrii Renanskii, "Mishen' Desiatnikova," Openspace.ru (March 1, 2011), http://os.colta.ru/music_classic/events/details/20803/. Desiatnikov also composed the score for *Moscow*, which earned him the 2002 International Prize for Film and Media Music and a Golden Ram from the Russian Guild of Film Critics.
7. Zara Abdullaeva, "Roman-fantaziia, *Iskusstvo kino* 3 (March 2011), http://kinoart.ru/archive/2011/03/n3-article4. The primary cinematographer for *Target* was Alexander Ilkhovsky, who filmed three other screenplays by Sorokin: *Moscow* with Zeldovich, *Kopeck* (*Kopeika*, 2002) with Ivan Dykhovichnyi, and *4* (2004) with Ilya Khrzhanovsky.
8. Vladimir Gromkovskii, "Anna Karenina Mtsenskogo uezda: o fil'me 'Mishen',"" Snob.ru, June 27, 2011, http://www.snob.ru/profile/10951/blog/37490; Vladimir Liashchenko, "Svet narisovan, nebesa nastoiashchie: Interv'iu s Aleksandrom Zel'dovichem," *Gazeta.ru* (July 7, 2011), http://m.gazeta.ru/culture/2011/07/07/a_3689017.shtml.

9. Larisa Maliukova, "Aleksandr Zel'dovich: Neskol'ko knizhek – eto strana," *Novaia gazeta* (Feb. 10, 2011), also available at http://www.novayagazeta.ru/arts/7173.html; Andrei Plakhov. "Virtual'nyi proekt ideal'nogo budushchego, pridumannogo kremlevskimi polittekhnologami. Aleksandr Zel'dovich o fil'me 'Mishen'," *Kommersant* (Feb. 16, 2011), http://kommersant.ru/doc/1586065.
10. Elena Paisova, "Aleksandr Zel'dovich: Ne stat' geran'iu," *Iskusstvo kino* 3 (March 2011), http://kinoart.ru/archive/2011/03/n3-article5.
11. Sorokin also has a short story from 2005 by the name of "Target" ("Mishen'"), though the plot bears no direct similarities to the film script. See Plakhov on the collaboration between Sorokin and Zeldovich.
12. Zel'dovich, "Zel'dovich to DeBlasio."
13. Erik Solov'ev, "The Existential Soteriology of Merab Mamardashvili," *Russian Studies in Philosophy* 49, No. 1 (summer 2010), p. 61.
14. Lev Tolstoi, *Polnoe sobranie sochinenii (PSS)*. 90 Vols, ed. V. G. Chertkov (Liechtenstein: Nendeln, 1972), XXVI, pp. 398–401.
15. For instance, see *On Life* in Tolstoi, *PSS*, pp. 398–401.
16. *PSS*, V, pp. 64-5. Trans. from Leo Tolstoy, "Three Deaths," *Tolstoy's Short Fiction*, ed. Michael R. Katz, 2nd edn (New York: Norton, 2008), p. 56.
17. Vasilii Zen'kovskii, "Problema bessmertiia u L.N. Tolstogo," *L.N. Tolstoi. Pro et contra* (St Petersburg: Iz-vo RKhGI, 2000), p. 509.
18. *PSS*, XXVI, p. 379. Trans. taken from Leo Tolstoy, *On Life and Essays on Religion*, trans. Aylmer Maude (London: Oxford University Press, 1934), p. 87.
19. *PSS*, XXVI, p. 338. Trans. from *On Life*, p. 35. On Tolstoy's treatment of "the present," see: Sarah Hudspith, "Life in the Present: Time and Immortality in the Works of Tolstoy," *The Modern Language Review* 101.4. (Oct. 2006): p. 1055. Among the numerous works addressing the roles of death, infinity, and/or immortality in Tolstoy, most relevant to the argument here are Gary R. Jahn, "Tolstoj's Vision of the Power of Death and 'How Much Land Does a Man Need?'," *SEEJ* 22.4 (winter 1978): pp. 442–53; Natalie Repin, "*Being-Towards-Death* in Tolstoy's *The Death of Ivan Il'Ich*: Tolstoy and Heidegger," *Canadian-American Slavic Studies* 36.1–2 (2002): pp. 101–32; and Elizabeth Trahan, "The Divine and the Human, or Three More Deaths: A Late Chapter in Leo Tolstoy's Dialogue with Death," *Tolstoy Studies Journal* 3 (1990): pp. 33–48. Additionally, James P. Scanlan's "Tolstoy among the Philosophers" takes an in-depth look at how Tolstoy understood the term "life." Scanlan, "Tolstoy among the Philosophers: His Book *On Life* and its Critical Reception," *Tolstoy Studies Journal* XVIII (2006): pp. 52–69.
20. Ludwig Wittgenstein, *Tractatus Logic-Philosophicus*, trans. D. F. Pears and B. F. McGuinness (London and New York: Routledge, 2007), 6.4311.
21. *PSS*, XXVI, p. 417. Trans. from *On Life*, p. 137.
22. *PSS*, XLV, pp. 463–4.

23. For other scientific metaphors in Tolstoy, Valeria Sobol has written on the controversial contribution of Tolstoy's *Family Happiness* (*Semeinoe schast'e*, 1859) to psychological conceptions of love between the sexes. Sobol, "In Search of an Alternative Love Plot: Tolstoy, Science, and Post-Romantic Love Narratives," *Tolstoy Studies Journal* 19 (2007): pp. 54–75. Additionally, Edgerton looks at Tolstoy's concept of space and time in the context of the new physicists of the twentieth century. Neither Sobol nor Edgerton refer to Tolstoy's Newtonian metaphor on the value of death.
24. Tolstoy does not specify what he means by value (*tsennost'*), but given that his examples comprise both corporeal and metaphysical concerns, we might be safe to assume that he had both the living and the infinite in mind when contemplating value. Interestingly, the equation is only solvable when an individual is alive; once d is 0, the value of life (V) is undefined.
25. *PSS*, XXVI, p. 109. Trans. from Leo Tolstoy, *The Death of Ivan Il'ich*, *Tolstoy's Short Fiction*, ed. Michael R. Katz, p. 124. Gary Jahn has already pointed out that as Ivan's illness progresses the chapters decrease in page length, thereby literalizing the metaphor of a stone plummeting to the earth. See: Gary Jahn's "The Image of the Railroad in *Anna Karenina*," *SEEJ* 25.2 (1981): p. 20.
26. *PSS*, XXVI, pp. 108–9. Trans. from *The Death of Ivan Ilych*, p. 124. Emphasis mine.
27. Ibid.
28. *PSS*, XXVI, p. 111. Trans. from *The Death of Ivan Ilych*, p. 124.
29. *PSS*, XXVI, p. 113. Trans. from *The Death of Ivan Ilych*, p. 126.
30. *PSS*, XLV, p. 464. Incidentally, in his journal entry from September 2, 1906 on his wife's recent operation, Tolstoy quotes Ivan Ilych: "... when she dies [death] will be completely revealed to her. 'Ah, so that's what it is!' But we who are left behind can't yet see what has been revealed to the person dying." Trans. from *Tolstoy's Diaries*, 2 vols, ed. and trans. R. F. Christian (New York: Faber & Faber, 1985), pp. 555–6.
31. *PSS*, IX, p. 844. Trans. from *War and Peace*, trans. Louise and Aylmer Maude, ed. George Gibian (New York: Norton, 1966), p. 301.
32. Shestov, Leo, "The Last Judgment: Tolstoy's Last Works," *Tolstoy: A Collection of Critical Essays*, ed. Ralph E. Matlaw (Englewood Cliffs, NJ: Prentice Hall, 1967), p. 170.
33. *PSS*, IX, p. 844. Trans. from *War and Peace*, pp. 301–2.
34. *PSS*, XXIII, p. 58. Trans. from *A Confession*, trans. Anthony Briggs (London: Hesperus, 2010), p. 82.
35. *PSS*, XXIII, p. 59.
36. Tolstoy's dream recalls Timothy 3:15, which states that believers ought to recognize their faith in the church as "the pillar and foundation of the truth." Perhaps Pavel Florensky had Tolstoy's "pillar" in mind when between 1908 and 1912 he worked on *The Pillar and Ground of Truth* (*Stolp i utverzhdenie istiny*), which he defended in 1914 as his magistrate dissertation.

37. *PSS*, XXIII, p. 36. Trans. from *A Confession*, p. 50.
38. *PSS*, XLV, p. 448.
39. *PSS*, XXXVII, p. 205. Trans. from Leo Tolstoy, "The Law of Violence and the Law of Love," *Russian Philosophy*, Vol. II, ed. James M. Edie, James P. Scanlan, and Mary-Barbara Zeldin (Chicago: Quadrangle, 1965), p. 230.
40. *PSS*, XXVI, p. 112. Trans. from *The Death of Ivan Ilych*, p. 127.
41. *PSS*, XXVI, p. 113.
42. Scanlan, p. 6.
43. *PSS*, XLI, p. 319.
44. Tolstoy was sympathetic to this desire. In his journal entry for Oct. 6, 1863, before he wrote *A Confession*, he expressed his own longing for eternal life: "I'm sliding, sliding down the hill of death, and hardly feel I have the strength to stop. But I don't want death, I want and love immortality. I don't have to choose. The choice has been made long ago" (*PSS*, XLVIII, p. 57. Trans. from *Tolstoy's Diaries*, Vol. I, p. 180).
45. Mamardashvili, *Kantianskie variatsii*, p. 16.
46. "Problema soznaniia i filosofskoe prizvanie," p. 47.
47. *Kantianskie variatsii*, p. 71. For example, Mamardashvili described how "we cannot talk about clear consciousness or unclear consciousness—it is always consciousness" (Ibid.).
48. *Vil'niusskie lektsii*, pp. 34–5.
49. *Kantianskie variatsii*, p. 78.
50. Ibid., p. 119.
51. Mamardashvili, "D'iavol igraet nami, kogda my ne myslim tochno...," p. 137.
52. Alper Türken, "Hegel's Concept of the True Infinite and the Idea of a Post-Critical Metaphysics," in *Hegel and Metaphysics: On Logic and Ontology in the System*, ed. Allegra de Laurentiis (Berlin: De Gruyter, 2016), p. 12.
53. Qtd Ibid., p. 12.
54. Ibid., p. 16.
55. Mamardashvili, "O filosofii," *Voprosy filosofii*, No. 5 (1991): pp. 3–25; Türken, p. 16.
56. Ibid.
57. *Kartezianskie razmyshleniia*, p. 81.
58. *Vil'niusskie lektsii*, p. 258.
59. Scanlan, p. 7.
60. *PSS*, IX, p. 359. Trans. from *War and Peace*, pp. 314–15.
61. *PSS*, XXXVII, p. 205. Trans. from "The Law of Violence and the Law of Love," p. 230.
62. "Problema cheloveka v filosofii," pp. 237–8.
63. Mamardashvili, "Fenomenologiia – soputstvuiushchii moment vsiakoi filosofii," in *Kak ia ponimaiu filosofiiu*, ed. Iu. P. Senokosov, 2nd edn (Moscow: Progress – Kul'tura, 1992), pp. 105–6.
64. "Problema cheloveka v filosofii," p. 238.
65. Mamardashvili, "Besedy o myshlenii."

66. *Estetika myshleniia*, p. 106.
67. Ibid.
68. *Psikhologicheskaia topologiia puti*, p. 14.
69. Boris Lokshin, "Igraem v Kareninu," *Iskusstvo kino* (Nov. 2, 2012), http://www.kinoart.ru/blogs/igraem-v-kareninu.
70. *PSS*, XLV, p. 449. Much has been written on Tolstoy's use of train imagery and language (e.g. rails, railroads), including Jahn's "The Image of the Railroad in *Anna Karenina*"; Henry W. Pickford, "Of Rules and Rails: On a Motif in Tolstoy and Wittgenstein," *Tolstoy Studies Journal* XXII (2010): pp. 39–53; and M. S. Al'tman, "Zheleznaia doroga," in *Chitaia Tolstogo* (Tula: Priokskoe knizhnoe izdatel'stvo, 1966), p. 111.
71. "Drugoe nebo," p. 334.
72. Ibid., 334.
73. Irina Anisimova, "Heterotopia in Contemporary Russian Fiction," PhD diss. (University of Pittsburgh, 2014).
74. Merab Mamardashvili and Natan Eidel'man, "O dobre i zle," in *Professiia – kinematografist*, ed. P. D. Volkova, A. N. Gerasimov, and V. I. Sumenova (Ekaterinburg: U-Faktoriia, 2004), pp. 285 and 289.
75. Ibid., p. 286.
76. Ibid., pp. 286–7.
77. "Drugoe nebo," p. 332.
78. "Problema cheloveka v filosofii," p. 238.
79. "D'iavol igraet nami, kogda my ne myslim tochno ...," p. 137.
80. *Psikhologicheskaia topologiia puti*, p. 27.
81. Ibid., p. 162.
82. "Problema cheloveka v filosofii," p. 235. On the way that Mamardashvili distanced himself from the historical tradition of "Russian philosophy," see Igor' Evlampiev, *Russkaia filosofiia v evropeiskom kontekste* (St Petersburg: Izd-vo RKhGA, 2017), pp. 416–34.
83. Ibid., p. 235.
84. *Psikhologicheskaia topologiia puti*, p. 27.

CHAPTER 6

Vadim Abdrashitov and Alexander Mindadze's *The Train Stopped* (1982): Film as a Metaphor for Consciousness

Merab Mamardashvili had well-documented personal ties to the Soviet film industry and led courses in philosophy to cinema students between 1977 and 1990, but in his own work he made only occasional references to cinema and did not undertake film analysis in any holistic or sustained way. He was a "philosopher who loved film," but he was not a philosopher of film.[1] His references were mostly general reflections at the level of plot or reception, mainly as examples to reiterate philosophical positions to which he was already committed, and he did not delve into the technical elements of film like montage, sound, or camera movement. Neither did he engage with film criticism, with a few exceptions, most notably his discussions of the films and theory of Jean-Luc Godard. The comparatively sparse inclusion of film analysis in Mamardashvili's work stands out especially when we consider the influential role that literature played in his philosophy, in particular the novels of Marcel Proust, to whom the philosopher dedicated two full cycles of lectures at Tbilisi State University in 1982 and 1984–5.

When Mamardashvili did turn to film in his lectures and writing, it was often in service of the guiding questions of his philosophical work. Specifically, he engaged film art and the phenomenology of film spectatorship as a metaphor for consciousness and its analysis. He argued that cinema could construct an extended, empirical, and psychological reality—"a different regime of life than the one to which we are accustomed, that is in the flow of empirical, or real, or physical, or mental space and time (because mental reactions are also subject to temporal and spatial definitions)."[2] While Godard attempted to show how a cinematic landscape could be a state of mind, for Mamardashvili cinema signaled the potential for a new space–time axis originating in itself, opening a door for reflection upon the defining paradox of his philosophical project: the dually constituted nature of human conscious experience.[3] The cinematic examples scattered throughout his lecture cycles offered support for philosophical ideas he was expounding and helped contextualize ongoing arguments for students in a new light, much in the way that Godard argued that "cinema makes reality specific."[4]

Most of Mamardashvili's direct commentary on film came not from the lectures he delivered at the Higher Courses in the 1980s, nor from his time on the faculty of VGIK as Professor of Philosophy and Scientific Communism, a post he held between 1976 and 1980. We find his lengthiest reflections on cinema in *The Aesthetics of Thinking* (*Estetika myshleniia*), a lecture series he gave to students at Tbilisi State University during the 1986–7 academic year. Most of Mamardashvili's specific cinematic examples, in turn, came primarily from two Soviet films: (1) Georgian director Tengiz Abuladze's *Repentance* (*Monanieba* in Georgian; *Pokoianie* in Russian, 1984), which was shelved by Soviet authorities until 1987; and (2) *The Train Stopped* (*Ostanovilsia poezd*, 1982), director-writer team Vadim Abdrashitov (b. 1945) and Alexander Mindadze's (b. 1949) fourth film, which earned them a USSR State Prize the year of its release. The preceding chapters have looked at films where we find the mark of Mamardashvili's influence, ranging from direct connections to philosophical affinity across the genres of literature, philosophy, and film. This chapter is a study in a different kind of affinity: Mamardashvili's use of film metaphors to describe contemporary problems of consciousness.

Near the beginning of the eleventh lecture of *The Aesthetics of Thinking*, Mamardashvili referred to having recently seen *The Train Stopped* for the first time. The film tells the story of a train driver who loses his life in a railroad accident and is posthumously declared a hero by the residents of Ensk—an unremarkable "town called N," in the nineteenth-century tradition, and a Soviet *anyplace* in the film. The railroad crash that opens *The Train Stopped* becomes the subject of a dual investigation: a criminal investigation, which seeks to establish fault for a series of procedural mistakes that may have caused the crash, and a journalistic investigation, which seeks to confirm in the eyes of the townspeople "the conductor's heroic act" (*podvig mashinista*) in sacrificing his life for his passengers. For Vladimir Padunov, "in pursuing the cause of the train accident, the investigator finds that the truth is irrelevant to the train-working community, even though it is the only relevant fact in his own life."[5]

As the epistemological confrontation of the film unfolds—the rift between investigator and journalist, and between outsider and insider—the everyday assumptions and realities of the townspeople's *Soviet habitus* are laid bare. The film closes with the dedication of a new monument to the fallen conductor-hero, the investigator having been ostracized from the community. After seeing *The Train Stopped*, Mamardashvili returned to his class at Tbilisi State University and described it as "perhaps one of the simplest and most vivid illustrations of *what I was telling you*" [emphasis added].[6] Later, in an essay from the late 1980s, he recalled: "I could have only dreamed of such an illustration of what I had been telling my students."[7]

Here, the *what I was telling you* refers to the content of Mamardashvili's previous lecture, in which he described the mysterious quality of human thought—that "to think is to stand face to face with something foreign."[8] Before looking at his analysis of *The Train Stopped*, it is important that we first examine more closely the concepts of *thought* (*mysl'*) and *thinking* (*myshlenie*) in his work. We have seen how Mamardashvili very often appealed to metaphor and analogy as a mode of philosophical explication, and his work on *thought* and *thinking* was no different in this regard. He described the process of *thought* as a moment of philosophical genesis, "insofar as according to the well-known paradox of antiquity, a thought cannot flow from another thought."[9] He also highlighted its subjective and individual quality, whereby its subjectivity and individuality are "the existential ground of thought," as Van der Zweerde puts it.[10] *Thought* also has an unknowable quality, which Mamardashvili likened to a theater where the "heart of the matter is concealed off-stage, and on stage there are masks and marionettes."[11] Van der Zweerde summarizes the philosopher's understanding of *thought* as a reality "in which there is full adequacy of form and content," but that is also inaccessible to the thinker except in the very moment of its thinking.[12] For Mamardashvili, thought was a condition of conscious experience and a necessary matter (methodological, or otherwise) of any philosophical investigation.[13]

If thought is a genesis moment that is both individual and irretrievable, *thinking* is the process of thought extended over time—the ongoing stream of thoughts and ideas within conscious experience. To "reside in thought as a philosophical subject requires effort [*usilie*]," he argued, and "in a fundamental sense, the word *thinking* is not only a human faculty but a faculty and condition of that type of field. And in that case, we are able to exist *in thought*, and not 'a thought came to my mind'" [emphasis added].[14]

Insofar as both *thought* and *thinking* are the business of consciousness, Mamardashvili argued that we cannot extricate ourselves from either, in the same way that we are bound to consciousness by virtue of our humanness. "Thought is the impossibility of renouncing consciousness," he argued, and both categories had existential implications: "When we are not afraid of death is when we find ourselves at the point where a thought begins."[15] Moreover, he argued that thought forms the basis for a cognitive network connecting human thinkers in a shared community of thought and ideas.

To the question of whether there is any higher meaning to human life, Mamardashvili answered in the affirmative in large part due to the power of thought: we reach immortality not according to our goodness or because we are beings endowed with souls, but by participating in the eternal and communal process of shared human thought. It is by engaging thought in our lives and in culture, he argued, that the individual "will exist everywhere where the other exists, as if [that individual] . . . entered into these thoughts and feelings."[16] Mamardashvili continued: "Thus, when I am no longer here and everything ends, this does not end. If I am part of this then . . . I am immortal and I possess an absolute, obvious consciousness of immortality itself."[17] One way to understand the distinction between thought and thinking in Mamardashvili's work is to conceptualize them as two interconnected forces: while *thought* is a single act of consciousness within the broad cache of human creativity and ideas, *thinking* is the process of thought extended over time, and can be traced and analyzed in a literary or cinematic text.[18]

The investigation of the accident in *The Train Stopped* was, for Mamardashvili, a narrative representation of the unknowability of thought and, by extension, of other minds. The action of the film is predicated on the train conductor's motivations, about which we have no narrative or psychological insight: we do not know what he was thinking or how he acted in those final moments, yet his status as hero goes unquestioned by the townspeople. In other words, the townspeople claim access to the driver's thoughts, joining together in their

> struggle for survival . . . as a collective organism, a collective body, a corresponding colony of mutually parasitic polyps. They are all connected to each other in order to join together in that body and in their struggle for survival, connected with what I would call the garrote [*udavka*] noose of humanity.[19]

Their commitment to this version of truth leads to a situation in which "nobody takes any action whatsoever, since action is always by an individual and to an individual, unlike reactions, which act 'according to a mask.'"[20]

For Mamardashvili, the guiding epistemological tension of *The Train Stopped*, and ultimately the cause of the investigator's disillusionment and departure, is the townspeople's claim to "that unique experience that belongs to [the experiencer] alone, and from which he alone can derive meaning."[21] Visually, the film highlights this *inability to know* by showing the train and its passengers, but never the driver. In the opening sequence, we see only darkened shots of the train rushing down the tracks at night, the camera settling on the faces of sleeping passengers soon to be jolted awake from the force of impact—the same passengers who will later draw collective conclusions about an event they slept through.

In the tenth installment of *The Aesthetics of Thinking*, Mamardashvili drew a parallel between *The Train Stopped* and the Chernobyl disaster, which had occurred only months earlier. He described the clean-up efforts at the disaster site as a situation in which "we find ourselves in an impassable place, in the sense that we have already been pressed into the image of a hero and we cannot escape it."[22] The political message of his argument is amplified as he condemned the media response surrounding the event, which focused on the "heroism" of the response rather than the social and political neglect underlying the disaster. He wrote: "[Man] must carry out actions that have already been designated as heroic, although knowing, possibly, that it is all the result of crimes committed by different people at different times, but he must sacrifice his life already carrying in advance the designation of 'hero.'"[23]

When the investigator arrives on the scene in *The Train Stopped* in search of explanations and causes, he too begins to discover a string of underlying crimes. The crash was precipitated by a series of human choices and oversights, all rationalized within the context of the Soviet system: the railway engineer, for instance, set up only one terminal block and not two, not because he failed to remember the procedure, but because he had been setting up only one for the entirety of his career on the railroad. The exasperated director who oversaw the production of the train's broken speedometer defends his actions in the name of efficiency, exclaiming that "if [he] were to do everything by the book, it would basically shut down rail traffic for the summer!"

The "collective organism" of the townspeople is most clearly represented in the character of the journalist, also a passenger on the train, who decides to write a story on "The Conductor's Heroic Act." As a former resident of Ensk, he chastises the inspector for his faith in truth and positivism, and for failing to side with the collective: "Haven't we had enough victims?" he asks. Nancy Condee describes how *The Train Stopped* presents the positions of the inspector and the journalist with a balance that was unsettling to Soviet censors, resulting in limited screenings of the film.[24] The three epistemological positions it raises—the investigator's commitment to objective truth, the public's satisfaction with a story that protects the social order, and the experience accessible only to the now-deceased conductor—are set against one another as the main confrontation of the film.

We can see how Mamardashvili might have been drawn to *The Train Stopped* for its emphasis on dialogue, rather than action or resolution. Critics have noted that the film is a series of dialogues, primarily between the investigator and the journalist. While equal weight is initially afforded to both sides, at the film's close it is the inspector who is cast out.[25] This point was raised by M. Vlasov on the film's release, and he noted that the working title for this and several other of Abdrashitov-Mindadze's films was in fact *Dialogues* (*Dialogi*).[26] Mamardashvili's own interest in dialogue is present not only in his preference for the spoken over the written genre, but in his comments on philosophy as a public practice in the Socratic tradition, "best understood by those who know nothing about it and are encountering it for the first time."[27] Godard described filmmaking (in the context of Ingmar Bergman's work) as a process of identifying and answering questions, much the same way Mamardashvili saw philosophy as the continuation of the Socratic tradition of dialogue, debate, and dialectics.[28]

Godard was born in 1930, the same year as Mamardashvili, and was a pioneering figure in the European new wave cinema that Mamardashvili so admired during his travels abroad in Prague in the 1950s and 1960s. With their radical aesthetics and Marxist influence, Godard's early films bridged the political, the philosophical, and the experimental. For both Mamardashvili and Godard, the power of cinema was bound up in its dialectical potential; not just in what it could show, but in *how* it could show—in the robust aesthetic possibilities of the new medium. Mikhail Iampolski describes Godard in terms that nearly mimic Mamardashvili, when he writes that "for Godard, representation is thought [*myshlenie*]."[29] Moreover, Godard employed what he called "a continuity between all forms of expression," including novels, non-fiction, and cinema, which offers yet another description of the confluences of genres, texts, and methodologies present in Mamardashvili's own work on aesthetics and the history of philosophy.[30]

These and other lines of comparison make it even more puzzling that Mamardashvili wrote so little about film, referenced only a small number of films at any length, and did not refer to those Russian and Soviet classics that he would have surely seen: the films of Sergei Eisenstein, Andrei Tarkovsky, and others. Eisenstein, in particular, developed the idea of film as a form of thought through his use of what he called "intellectual montage": the arrangement of shots through editing could produce new meaning, in a dialectical sense, in the mind of the viewer. Filmmakers, critics, and philosophers since Eisenstein have worked through a variety of mechanical and conceptual techniques to, as Christopher Pavsek puts it, "raise cinema to a level of discourse equivalent to that of philosophy or theory."[31]

Mamardashvili too saw film as an experiment through which we could see an alternative model of thought at work. By presenting opposing positions in one narrative, film art presents a challenge to the mind's relationship to its own sense data. For Mamardashvili, it challenged what he called "a kind of complete and absolute regard for what you see ... without leaving any space for free interpretation."[32] It was in this vein that Mamardashvili distinguished *thought* from *ideology*. "A thought is not an ideology, which we may accept or not. Ideology is something that we always accept through reasons and motivations that are external to thought ... but the question of whether to accept or not accept a thought will never come up."[33] The act of thought, however, he argued, is metaphysical. "Why have I called thought metaphysics? For one simple reason: ... I called thought that which is impossible to define in a positive way. Thought is without content."[34]

In his brief writing on *The Train Stopped*, Mamardashvili identified the character of the inspector as occupying the position of *thought*. He wrote: "[The inspector] is completely removed from everything that people usually think; they think according to the laws of what I have called the garrote of humanity, while he is on the border—and that is where *thought* is."[35] If the townspeople and the journalist represent the social ills of Soviet collectivity and its attitude toward the mind, the inspector embodies that genesis moment of thought: independent, experimental, and often isolated.

Mamardashvili continued by arguing that the film raises for us the question of the mind's reception of its own thoughts, in the way that the human thought process "does not leave any room for free interpretation and non-conformist intellectualizing."[36] Here I take Mamardashvili to be arguing that the human mind consists of one indivisible "voice" (a single consciousness), and while that voice may reflect on or challenge itself (thinking about thought), it is by nature unified and not a sphere of epistemological competition. Cinema, like literature, has the ability to challenge the structure of human experience through counterfactual fictionalization, through presenting multiple voices at once as "true." Within our own minds, however, we are by virtue of our design unable to ignore or reject the genesis moment of our own consciousness. We are unable to say "no" to a thought except after it has appeared; we are unable to free ourselves from that unified voice by which thought is given to us, except as a response to thought as meta-reflection. In this and other instances, Mamardashvili's use of film metaphors brings together the guiding philosophical topics this book has addressed: questions of consciousness, thinking (vs. thought), language, the absurd, and the concept of indivisibility.

Mamardashvili also referred to Abuladze's *Repentance* as an example of the impassable distance among individuals on civic issues, and on the impossibility of connections among discrete minds. In 1987 Mamardashvili served on the jury of the Tbilisi International Film Festival, where he was charged with deciding which shelved film should be awarded the Grand Prix: Kira Muratova's *Long Farewells* (*Dolgie provody*, 1971), which had been shelved by Soviet authorities for more than fifteen years before its release, or Tengiz Abuladze's *Repentance*, which had also been censored. The screenplay for the former was written by Mamardashvili's romantic partner, Nataliia Riazantseva, while the latter was awarded the prize for best film at that year's festival. Mamardashvili argued that *Repentance* could be especially instructive for dealing with contentious moral and political issues facing Soviet citizens in the perestroika era.

In his analysis of *Repentance* in *The Aesthetics of Thinking*, Mamardashvili said that "when discussing this film, you have surely noticed that no arguments or explanations will help those who don't understand it . . . Here there is no middle ground, nothing intermediary or mediated—it's a sheer drop."[37] Elsewhere, he described how "Abuladze was faced with a difficult question, one that opened up the problem of the absurd: how to depict the nonsense that is not only a part of life, but that almost takes the place of life itself."[38] Although it is up for debate whether Mamardashvili and Abuladze ever met, Abuladze was an avid reader of philosophy and seems to have been aware of Mamardashvili's writing on the distinction between a thought (*mysl'*) and thinking (*myshlenie*).[39]

Just as the concepts of *thought* and *thinking* were, for Mamardashvili, profoundly paradoxical and multifaceted components of human conscious experience, so was the nature of the human condition guided by the classical logic of aporia. He saw human experience as dually constituted: there are those universal patterns of human cognition that structure conscious experience, on the one hand, and there is the singular, subjective nature of each individual experience, on the other. Each threatens to obscure the other. "Let's take [the example of] love, the rules of which are known to all," Mamardashvili proposed to his audience in Tbilisi in 1986. "If millions of people have already loved, then what is [love] good for? What meaning does it have?"[40] The philosophical paradox between the particular and the universal, the subjective and the objective, and the unknown and the known—Mamardashvili called this the "knot" (*uzel*) of the human condition, and also the "garrote of humanness."[41] To be human was to engage all these levels at once, but at the level of the absurd: "The human being recognizes himself as a living and undisputed condition for himself, and for this reason he is superfluous in the world."[42]

We have already seen how Mamardashvili's attraction to the trope of the unknowable is evident in the many philosophical issues to which he assigned a paradoxical or evasive quality. This is especially present in his essays and interviews from the second half of the 1980s, when he began to take up political and anthropological concerns more explicitly, in large part thanks to the freedoms allowed by the perestroika and glasnost reforms. The unknown side of human experience, which Mamardashvili referred to as the "third" in "The 'Third' Condition" and which we discussed in detail in Chapter Three, was critical for clarifying the role of the absurd in his philosophy. Mamardashvili addressed the problem of the absurd most extensively in an earlier essay, "Consciousness and Civilization," in which he defined the condition of the absurd as embodied by Kafka's literary mode: "that which cannot be, which doesn't exist, which is nothing, and which cannot exist according to our understanding."[43]

Alongside his use of the trope of the absurd and the image of the zombie to describe the philosophical problem of the unknowable, Mamardashvili also turned to the example of the Greek aporia, whereby he described the unknown as the logical puzzle of "impassable space."[44] Once again, this description includes both a metaphysical and a physical component: it is both conceptual, as a logical puzzle or impasse, and physical, since "it is precisely [the concept of] 'place' that figures in the word 'aporia.'"[45] The notion of the absurd and the trope of aporia was not just a poetic approach to the unknown for Mamardashvili, but it contextualized a fundamental phenomenological component of human experience. In the same way, *The Train Stopped* was not merely a commentary on the nature and paradox of thought, but on the human condition more broadly—the idea that "to think is to stand face to face with something foreign."[46] In this vein, we might read the epistemological conundrum in *The Train Stopped* as a metaphor for "that unknown condition that we try to define, to feel, to define as thought and to understand what the mind is."[47] Both at the level of mind and at the level of world, that condition is best described within the mode of the absurd.

It is a challenge to impose the form of linear argument and explication on a thinker like Mamardashvili, who often spoke evocatively, metaphorically, and associatively. These same challenges hold true for his work on cinema, though we have already seen how film might serve as: (1) a window into specific philosophical problems (e.g. *thought* and *thinking*); (2) a metaphor for the human condition; and (3) an entry point for political and social commentary. What is more, Mamardashvili extended his commitment to the philosophical potential of the cinematic image to the very act of viewership itself, considering the dialectical moment where viewer, film, and mind/interpretation meet. During a lecture cycle on contemporary European philosophy, which he delivered to a full auditorium of film students and members of the public at VGIK in the late 1970s, Mamardashvili relayed to his audience a hypothetical scenario in a movie theatre:

> Let's recall the simple act of exiting the movie theatre. True, we don't make it there often, but when we do, presumably we leave knowing distinctly that there are some things about which it is pointless to speak, argue, or discuss. If somebody didn't understand, well, then they didn't understand and that's that. After all, we know, if only in the genius of our language, that the act of understanding is an absolutely concrete and at the same time undisputed act. In other words, as humans we are faced with things that are simultaneously undisputed and also seem to not exist (and for this reason we try to talk about them).[48]

For Mamardashvili, the movie theatre represented a conceptual space in which the dually constituted nature of human experience and its associated layers could be visualized. While all viewers in the audience see the same film and therefore share a common experience, they also each live through their own subjective and exclusive experiences of viewership. The movie theatre was also an apt metaphor for consciousness and the human condition, in that it was not only a conceptual space for philosophical praxis, but a physical one. Indeed, Mamardashvili emphasized the physical extension of aporia not only as a puzzle or moment of logical paradox, but as a spatial configuration. Film art could also serve as a window for the phenomenological analysis of consciousness by constructing an empirical and psychological reality, a new space and time that, if only for a couple of hours, allows us to experience ourselves from the outside.

As we have seen in *The Aesthetics of Thinking* and elsewhere, for Mamardashvili the act of thought and the process of thinking had potent creative and existential power. By broaching difficult topics on screen, films like *The Train Stopped* and *Repentance* served as starting points for reflection on contentious questions in the contemporary era. On resistance to the film *Repentance*, Mamardashvili wrote:

> People who [oppose the film] aren't engaged in the act of thought, because for the act of thought the gates and doors are open when you look at yourself, into the depths of the foundation of your existence and death. And we become frustrated: well he's just stupid. No, in fact, he's not stupid, he's just not thinking [*ne myslit*].[49]

Indeed, Mamardashvili's reformulation of the Cartesian *cogito* reads, "I think, I exist, *I can*,"[50] whereby the act of thought was imbued with the power to forge new philosophical beginnings, to "do everything over, from the beginning."[51] The philosophical investigation of cinema was one way to better understand the human mind and human responsibility in the world.[52] Moreover, in the case of *Repentence*, Mamardashvili felt it was not enough to consider the film according to artistic or cinematic criteria—it must be viewed as a "civic act" (*postupok grazhdanskii*).[53]

When discussing politically charged films like *Repentance*, Mamardashvili believed that there is no use avoiding sensitive topics by appealing to the fictional nature of film (it's only fiction, after all!), or the counterfactual possibility of a cinematic narrative to have "happened another way."[54] Cinema does not distance us from reality but brings us closer to it. Just as we cannot dismiss cinema that addresses controversial and sensitive issues as "mere fiction," nor can we reason away our responsibility to others by imagining the course of history as a plot line that could have gone another way. In his references to cinema in *The Aesthetics of Thinking* and elsewhere, Mamardashvili reimagined Godard's vision of art, of "revealing our most secret self."[55] He argued that in order to open the "gates and doors . . . to yourself"—to set yourself to the work of philosophy—you must engage in aesthetic dialogue, cinema being one way of achieving this.[56]

Notes

1. Dularidze, "Stranstvuiushchii filosof."
2. Mamardashvili, "Vremia i prostranstvo."
3. Jean-Luc Godard, *Godard on Godard. Critical Writings by Jean-Luc Godard*, ed. Jean Narboni and Tom Milne (Da Capo Press, 1986), p. 31.
4. Ibid., p. 21.
5. Vladimir Padunov, "Alienation and the Everyday: The Films of Aleksandr Mindadze and Vadim Abdrashitov," *Newsletter. Institute of Current World Affairs*, March 19, 1987, p. 6.
6. *Estetika myshleniia*, p. 80.
7. "Esli osmelit'sia byt'," p. 192.
8. *Estetika myshleniia*, p. 52.
9. Ibid.
10. Van der Zweerde, p. 187.
11. "Esli osmelit'sia byt'," p. 192.
12. Van der Zweerde, pp. 4, 8, 11, 13, and 84.
13. *Estetika myshleniia*, p. 74.
14. Ibid., p. 52.
15. Ibid., pp. 74–5.
16. Ibid.

17. Ibid., p. 82.
18. For another discussion of *thought* and *thinking* in Mamardashvili, see: Van der Zweerde.
19. *Estetika myshleniia*, p. 80. Mamardashvili used the same word, struggle (*bor'ba*), to describe the meta-theory of consciousness, which he referred to as "a struggle with consciousness" (Mamardashvili and Piatigorskii, pp. 29–37).
20. "Esli osmelit'sia byt'," p. 192.
21. *Estetika myshleniia*, p. 89.
22. Ibid., p. 71.
23. Ibid., p. 72.
24. Condee, *The Imperial Trace*, p. 156 and n. 23.
25. See: Padunov, "Alienation and the Everyday," pp. 3–4; Vladimir Padunov and Nancy Condee, "Recent Soviet Cinema and Public Responses: Abdrashitov and German," *Framework* (Jan. 1, 1985), p. 47.
26. M. Vlasov, "Vysokaia tsena istiny," *Iskusstvo kino* 1 (1983): pp. 22–35.
27. "Esli osmelit'sia byt'," p. 198.
28. Godard discusses Ingmar Bergman's filmmaking as a process of answering questions. See: Godard, p. 76.
29. Mikhail Iampol'skii, "Chitaia Godara. Zametki na poliakh Godarovskikh tekstov," in *Zhan-Liuk Godar. Strast'. Mezhdu chernym i belym* (n.p., 1997), p. 54.
30. Godard, p. 171.
31. Christopher Pavsek, *The Utopia of Film: Cinema and Its Futures in Godard, Kluge, and Tahimik* (New York: Columbia University Press, 2013), p. 15.
32. *Estetika myshleniia*, pp. 80–1.
33. Ibid., p. 81.
34. Ibid.
35. Ibid., p. 89. Emphasis added.
36. Ibid., p. 81.
37. Ibid., p. 91.
38. "D'iavol igraet nami, kogda my ne myslim tochno …," p. 139.
39. In an interview from 1980, Abuladze speaks about *thought* and *thinking* in a way that suggests he has encountered Mamardashvili's distinctive philosophical language on these same topics. Thank you to Olga Kim for sharing this reference with me. See: Alla Gerber, "Tengiz Abuladze: 'Liubov' rozhaet poznanie,'" in *Ekran* (Moscow: Iskusstvo, 1980), p. 110.
40. *Estetika myshleniia*, p. 71.
41. Ibid., pp. 71, 88, 89, and 140.
42. Ibid., p. 71.
43. "Soznanie i tsivilizatsiia," p. 162.
44. *Estetika myshleniia*, p. 71.
45. Ibid.
46. "Esli osmelit'sia byt'," p. 182.
47. *Estetika myshleniia*, p. 80.

48. *Ocherk sovremennoi evropeiskoi filosofii*, p. 260.
49. *Besedy o myshlenii*, p. 67.
50. "Soznanie i tsivilizatsiia," p. 14.
51. *Kartezianskie razmyshleniia*, p. 49.
52. In *Sketch of Contemporary European Philosophy*, Mamardashvili identified the aesthetic question (artistic and textual analysis, in particular) as one of the main topics that philosophy must address. *Ocherk sovremennoi evropeiskoi filosofii*, p. 12.
53. Margarita Kvasnetskaia, *Tengiz Abuladze. Put' k "Pokoianiiu"* (Kul'turnaia revoliutsiia, 2009), p. 187.
54. *Besedy o myshlenii*, p. 67.
55. Godard, p. 31.
56. *Estetika myshleniia*, p. 67.

CONCLUSION

Andrey Zvyagintsev's *Loveless* (2017): The Philosophical Image and the Possibilities of Film

> Camera operators loved [Mamardashvili] because he was more expressive than any movie star.
> Filmmakers loved him because there was no better viewer.
> Intelligent people loved him because in his company, they became brilliant.
> Tamara Dularidze, filmmaker[1]

Between his arrival at VGIK in 1976 and his death in 1990, Mamardashvili taught and worked alongside a generation of internationally prolific film directors, including Alexander Sokurov, Alexei Balabanov, Ivan Dykhovichnyi, Alexander Zeldovich, Dmitry Mamuliya, and Yuri Norshtein. These names, when considered together as a group, have little in common; they do not share obvious thematic interests, nor can we identify any common directorial style or visual language among them, as Vlad Strukov has argued about recent Russian cinema on the whole.[2] We have seen, however, how Mamardashvili's influence on Russian-Soviet filmmaking forms the basis of an *intellectual* affinity among these disparate directors, one that translates into meaningful philosophical synapses across the Russian cinematic canon. The commonality among directors of the Mamardashvili generation exists not in any individual unit of their filmmaking, but in their attention to questions of the boundaries of form (philosophy, film, literature), and in the ways that they engage the construct of the philosophical image to define the boundaries of the human mind.

In his essays on the form of the novel, Milan Kundera argues that the adaptation of a novel to film results in the destruction of the artistic quality of the original composition, "reducing it to just its 'story'" and "renouncing its form."[3] For Kundera, a great novel transposed to celluloid was no more a work of novelistic art than a film stripped of images could remain a film.[4] The same questions of interplay among genres become all the more complex when directed toward the practice of moving among literature, philosophy, and film. Though the work of Martha Nussbaum and others in recent decades has reestablished that philosophy cannot be reduced to one rhetorical mode and that novels can indeed embody philosophical problems, it is still very much up for debate how to categorize the relationship between philosophy and film. What form does philosophy take on film, and what does philosophical influence look like on film? How can we track the influence of Mamardashvili's philosophy, which was delivered in primarily oral form, as it moves from the word to the screen? We have added the question of literature to the discussion in Chapters Two, Four, and Five, where filmmakers of the Mamardashvili generation have taken cinematic inspiration from literary texts. In this concluding chapter, we will consider the methodological and conceptual possibilities that the Mamardashvili case opens up for the philosophy of film, and investigate how this knowledge might offer us a new way to think about recent Russian film.

An excellent case study in this regard is the work of Andrey Zvyagintsev—Golden Globe winner, two-time Academy Award nominee (2015 and 2018), and the most internationally acclaimed Russian director of the early twenty-first century. Zvyagintsev never studied with Mamardashvili, but has referenced Mamardashvili's philosophical output on several occasions, and at different stages in his career. What is more, Zvyagintsev's incorporation of Mamardashvili's aphorisms into his own artistic position suggests how philosophical influence lends itself especially well to adaptation to the moving image—a conclusion shared by Dmitry Mamuliya, and which Mamardashvili's own lectures on aesthetics support.[5] Zvyagintsev's references to Mamardashvili also open up new ways of interpreting his cinematic vision, in particular where his 2017 film *Loveless* (*Neliubov'*) is concerned.

Film as a Kind of Thinking

Andrey Zvyagintsev (b. 1964), who was in his mid-twenties when the Soviet Union dissolved, did not find his way to the director's chair via the typical path of a Soviet-trained director. He began studying acting in his hometown of Novosibirsk in the early 1980s and then moved to Moscow in 1986, where he graduated from the State Academy of Theatre Arts in 1990. Before beginning his directing career in television, he held jobs in children's theatre, as an army entertainer, and as a groundskeeper, and acted several roles in stage plays and soap operas.

In 2003 Zvyagintsev released his feature-length debut, *The Return* (*Vozvrashchenie*), which received sensational praise at the Venice International Film Festival and earned him two Golden Lion awards. *The*

Return is both a religious and a folk allegory that explores the theme of fatherlessness in post-Soviet Russia. Zvyagintsev's first film established his trademark, theatrical-inspired style of deliberate and introspective takes, and its release catapulted him from obscurity into the international ranks of the most promising new directors of the twenty-first century. His second feature, *Banishment* (*Izgnanie*, 2007), is also a spiritual allegory and was shot in the same meditative, tableau style as *The Return*, though *Banishment* was generally dismissed by critics as a weak follow-up to his award-winning debut.[6]

Among Russian critics, Zvyagintsev's early films earned him the title of the "new Tarkovsky," an association that Elena Stishova finds in the "profound existential longing (*toska*)" in the films of both directors, "the source of which is concealed from [the viewer]."[7] The association of Zvyagintsev with Russia's archetypal "philosophical director" would hold until his third film, *Elena* (2011), an existential drama about family bonds and class conflict in two distinct neighborhoods of contemporary Moscow. Zvyagintsev's next film, *Leviathan* (*Leviafan*, 2014), was an even bigger and bolder family drama set in the Russian far north, and once again he earned international repute when the film was refused domestic screenings for its pointed critique of state and church corruption in Putin-era Russia.

All Zvyagintsev's films, including *Loveless*, center around the violent death or disappearance of a family member. In *Loveless*, a young boy flees home when he overhears his parents arguing over who should take him, with neither wanting custody of him after their divorce. The parents' lengthy search for their missing son ultimately turns up a disfigured body that neither can positively or negatively identify as the boy. The family in crisis, and orphaned or neglected children in particular, serves as an allegoric axis in the director's work for the representation of trauma and crisis in Russian society on the whole.

Zvyagintsev is a classical filmmaker, in the sense that his approach to mise-en-scène and art direction is highly informed by his theatrical background. His camera is slow and intentional, often pausing on architectural scenes framed as compositions would be arranged on a stage—the bones of neglected buildings, tableau-style shots of decorated rooms, scenes of families at the table, and bare tree branches in the snow. Zvyagintsev's role as director for several episodes of the television series *Black Room* (*Chernaia komnata*, 2000) marked the beginning of a long relationship with cinematographer Mikhail Kritchman, known for extended, atmospheric takes and regular use of a wide lens.[8] In Zvyagintsev's films, the combination of long, wide takes and meditative montage conjures a nostalgia for an idealized Russian cinema of the past, a reaction rooted both in the stylization of the films themselves and in the critical acclaim of Zvyagintsev's cinema, including the many early associations of his work with the films of Tarkovsky.

Like Mamuliya's *Another Sky* (2010), Zvyagintsev chose to film *Elena* and *Loveless* in Moscow, but without showing the landmarks and skylines generally associated with the Russian capital. In both films, nature surrounds the edifices of human civilization, often in secret and subliminal ways. The introduction of unexpected, natural spaces struggling against human habitation adds to a sense of alienation while also constructing a dual picture of Moscow on-screen, one in which the city is both artificial and wild. Characters are separated from untamed spaces by glass and are framed by windows and doors like animals in captivity, gazing at a lost freedom they seek to regain. At the same time, nature is a vicious space where bodies are destroyed by the elements and where babies, once they are no longer restrained in the cages of their cribs, teeter precariously on the precipice of danger. Familial bonds do not offer love or protection, but instead it is often parents and caregivers who are responsible for placing the children of Zvyagintsev's films in harm's way. Moreover, the same mistakes are repeated by different characters across the canon of his work, whereby adult protagonists torment the younger generation in ways that reinforce the trauma they themselves have suffered.

Zvyagintsev's reliance in all his films on the juxtaposition between urban (or populated) and natural settings indicates a connection to some instinctual, and even predatory truths, a nature shared among characters and audience alike. In *Loveless*, the liminal meeting point between the competing forces of "inhabited" and "uninhabited" is the abandoned Soviet-era House of Culture where the missing boy hides, a cultural palace that neglect and time have transformed into an ambiguous zone that is neither human nor wild. The cultural and political symbolism of this ruin site encourage the viewer to participate in the film's sense of shared memory, and to *think* together with Zvyagintsev's film in an intentional way. If Zvyagintsev shares anything with Alexei Balabanov, it is that we can view the work of both directors as a kind of disaster tourism, not only to the forsaken spaces of Russia's back alleys and provincial towns, but to those same shared dark spaces in the human mind.

When taken together as a body of work, Zvyagintsev's films share many aesthetic and narrative similarities. These commonalities lend a sense of universalism to his filmmaking, and it is easy to discuss ways in which all his films address more or less the same thing. On the one hand, the commonalities among his work appear in his choice to repeat actors, themes, and mise-en-scène across films.[9] On the other hand, the sense of universalism his films impart clearly transcends individual choices and can be attributed to a broader mood emanating from his cinematic grammar and, more specifically, to the way he presents a certain way of thinking through film.

For Stanley Cavell, who approaches the philosophy of film by way of Ludwig Wittgenstein and the philosophy of language, film art has the potential to reproduce many of the hallmarks of human thought. It reproduces intention in its multi-layered apparatus (e.g. image, editing, sound), self-reflexivity in the way it reflects back on itself and its medium, and spontaneity in its ability to engage with philosophical problems by rediscovering them ad infinitum.[10] In this way, Cavell maintains that we can speak about film as a kind of thinking, and that as engaged viewers we are encouraged by films to *think along with them*; one of the ways that a film can *think*, Cavell continues, is that it aids us in the process of self-discovery.[11] When John Carvalho says that "an artwork is thinking," he has in mind not only that art forces us to grapple with uncertainty in our own thought processes, but that the works of art themselves become sites for thought; more radically stated, that "the artwork is thinking when it moves us to think."[12] To consider Zvyagintsev's aesthetics in this vein would be to see him as presenting a particular way of thinking about the world and oneself through the consistency of his cinematic vision, in which each film in his *oeuvre* is a successive step in the same cognitive direction.

Zvyagintsev regularly refers to Mamardashvili by name when describing his personal stance on his filmmaking and on society more broadly. In one such interview from 2009, he said:

> I want to believe, perhaps naively, that it's still possible to fight for mankind. I am sympathetic with the position of some of the representatives from the older generation, which is literally disappearing before our eyes—the position that Merab Mamardashvili formulated when he said that "The human being is the effort to become human."[13]

Zvyagintsev would go on to quote that line from Mamardashvili's 1988 essay "European Responsibility" several more times in the decade that followed, sometimes attributing the line to Mamardashvili directly and other times paraphrasing it and assimilating the idea into his own words.[14] In 2017, after the premiere of *Loveless*, he cited the line twice, paraphrasing Mamardashvili's concept of the human being as "a measure [*mera*] of humanity . . . defined only by our own inner efforts to become a human being, and not by any external forces, be it another person, authority, or any external conditions."[15]

Zvyagintsev's films, and especially *Elena*, *Leviathan*, and *Loveless*, are about characters who are failing in that process of striving toward self-improvement. Failures in communication make up a significant narrative force in all his films. Family dramas are often predicated upon, or extended by, the failure to communicate on topics of real significance: in *The Return*, the mystery surrounding the father's disappearance is never revealed; the parallel families in *Elena* do not converse, except through the performance of domestic rituals; in *Leviathan*, both Roma and Liliia leave without saying goodbye, with Roma fleeing to Moscow and Liliia throwing herself into the water. The failure to communicate in *Loveless* is passed down from each generation to its offspring; just as Zhenia remembers the birth of her son in terms of the trauma of labor, so does her own mother perform a laborious display of disgust toward her daughter.

For Zvyagintsev, technology plays an important role in those ruptures in communication. In another paraphrase of Mamardashvili's idea that "the human being is the effort to become human," Zvyagintsev cites the corrupting role of television and how the internet focuses attention away from the inner drive for moral improvement.[16] His inclusion of news sound bites in *Elena* and *Loveless*, as Mamuliya also chose to do in *Another Sky*, employs media as a monologic intrusion that comments on the narrative from outside. Characters are reduced to their psychological defenses and autonomic bodily functions, a narrative choice that Mikhail Epstein likens to the process of chewing: human relationships in the film are reduced "to mastication, the mechanical process of chewing up and eliminating time."[17]

News reporting in *Loveless* about Mayan prophecy also lends an apocalyptic tone to the film, much in the spirit of Mamardashvili's own work on the "sickness of consciousness" of the contemporary age, whereby he warned that communication had failed, and that an impassable epistemological rift had developed between the individual and the community—an "anthropological disaster" that aroused "a sense of horror" in him.[18] Alena Solntseva argues that Zvyagintsev's choice of television clips in *Loveless* sets up an explicit stance against Russian authoritarianism and, more specifically, Putin-era politics, though in a more subtle way than in *Leviathan*, where the protagonists practice their marksmanship against portraits of Soviet leaders.[19] For Mamardashvili, however, even film was incapable of making strides toward building a functional civil society in Russia. Any notion of open discourse, he argued, was erased with the Bolshevik Revolution "like a black hole in the universe, so dense that it collapsed in on itself."[20]

Figure C.1 Zhenia runs on the treadmill in the snow.

Characters in Zvyagintsev's films, and in *Loveless* in particular, expend significant effort on the opposite of understanding, on the act of being inhumane. This behavior is at the root of the Russian title of Zvyagintsev's most recent film, which refers not to the absence of love, as Solntseva points out, but to the opposite of love—to the effort to push love away and negate it.[21] In the extent to which its lead protagonists are so successful in this act, *Loveless* emphasizes better than all the director's previous films that it is hard to be human and that attempts at community can easily be misdirected toward harm and spite. Neither do new surroundings or circumstances negate the need for that "internal work" of being a human being. At the end of *Loveless*, both husband and wife find themselves in old patterns with new partners: while Boris is trapped in an overcrowded middle-class apartment and burdened by the same parental duties he sought to escape, the film ends with Zhenia back in motion but without progress, separated by a glass wall from her new life (See Figure C.1).

In *The Aesthetics of Thinking* lecture cycle, which he delivered to students at Tbilisi State University during the 1986–7 academic year, Mamardashvili spoke about the idea of "lovelessness" (*neliubov'*) and its relationship to consciousness. He suggested that the act of "lovelessness" is incompatible with an awareness of one's own consciousness; that to be "loveless" is to be in a state in which one is alienated from one's own mind and, by extension, from society.[22] In Chapter Six we saw how Mamardashvili referred to a similar formula in his work on the idea of "non-thinking" (*ne myslit'*), which he described as a state when individuals are not actively engaged in the process of thought.[23] In the case of much of Mamardashvili's work, there was also an alternative side to his reading of "non-thinking," which described the fact that thought is essentially impossible to articulate. Thoughts can only be fully expressed in the form in which they are originally experienced, he argued, yet we know from our look at his work on consciousness in Chapter One that Mamardashvili also considered thoughts irretrievable after the moment of their inception in the mind of the thinker.

At the level of corpus, the consistency among Zvyagintsev's films lends itself to a Cavellian reading as "a body that thinks," as a group of cinematic texts contributing to the same conversation. Here Zvyagintsev's repetition of places, character types, and scenarios highlights the cyclical and unescapable work of humanness—a return to the existential conundrum that Camus faced, that one must either kill oneself or do the work of living. In Zvyagintsev's films, variations of the same mistakes are repeated in different scenarios, over and over, and one imagines that eventually the director will have to make a film in which the characters *get it right*. Perhaps it was in response to this kind of claim that in 2017 Zvyagintsev again paraphrased Mamardashvili, noting that

> if the effort [to become human] is being undertaken or, conversely, not undertaken, it nonetheless defines us here and now. The human being is in an eternal search for himself. It is us, and not God, who are responsible for what happens to us.[24]

Later he added that "the proverbial 'happy end' should occur in your own life, and not on the screen."[25] These and other comments by Zvyagintsev suggest that he sees film as a place to observe, or even play out, mistakes, and that he intends his own films to be instructive and effect change in the lives of his viewers.[26] Perhaps his work seeks to overcome failures in communication precisely by creating a common language among viewers. In such a reading, to be frustrated, troubled, or moved at all by this kind of cinema would be already to enter into a kind of dialogue, one that originates in the cinematic form.

Film as Philosophical Image

Mamardashvili talked and wrote a lot about thought. It is not surprising, thus, that he viewed cinema as an experiment through which we might see an alternative model of thought at work. In his reading of Abdrashitov-Mindadze's *The Train Stopped*, he described how the train conductor represented the role of thought in a contested event, and how the other characters in the film negotiated varying relationships to an event about which they had no subjective experience. Although Mamardashvili used film examples as starting points for philosophical reflection and rarely engaged in extended cinematic analysis, his work on film can nonetheless be productively viewed in the tradition of philosophers like Stanley Cavell, Jim Conant, and Robert Pippen, who all argue for a more robust relationship between the disciplines of philosophy and film art.

For Robert Pippen, who is mostly known for his work on German philosophy but who published a philosophical study of Alfred Hitchcock in 2017, the contentious question at hand in the philosophy of film is the argument from Cavell we considered earlier—whether film can itself "be understood as a form of thought, especially a form of philosophical thought."[27] What Pippen fails to mention, however, is the fact that this question is only contentious in the immediate disciplinary context in which he raises it. Philosophers in the European-grown traditions of existentialism, structuralism, postmodernism, and post-structuralism regularly took aesthetic texts with the utmost philosophical seriousness, while thinkers like Hegel, Kierkegaard, Nietzsche, Wittgenstein, Dostoevsky, Tolstoy, Sartre, and countless other philosophers, including among them many Russian thinkers, all engaged with literature and the arts as forms of philosophical inquiry. For many, philosophical ideas were best expressed through indirect and/or poetic forms of communication (e.g. the structure of the Socratic dialogue, Kierkegaard's use of literary devices in *Either/Or*, or Nietzsche's aphorisms); for others, and in particular among Russian thinkers, literature and the arts were among the many ways that human beings could engage the metaphysical realm.

From its inception, Russian cinema has been deeply invested in the literary canon, both as a way of building viewership and of continuing the ongoing renegotiation (in the Russian tradition) of the dialectical relationship between text and image, as established by Plato. Among the filmmakers discussed in this book, most of them have taken inspiration from literary texts: *Faust* in the case of Sokurov; Chekhov for Dykhovichnyi; Beckett and Kafka for Balabanov; Chekhov and Tolstoy for Zeldovich; and William Saroyan in the case of Zvyagintsev's second film, *The Banishment*. In the case of the Mamardashvili generation, we might consider how the established presence of the text and word, and even the *logos* to some degree, in the Russian film industry has meant that Russian and Soviet directors have long been grappling with questions of cross-disciplinary form and representation. Within this long-standing tradition, one as old in Russia as cinema itself, the question of how to adapt philosophical ideas to film is just one part of that process.

If the history of European philosophy has established the medium of cinema as having philosophical potential, the question remains open as to the nature of the relationship between the two. Popular approaches to the philosophy of film have generally taken one of two forms. The first approach has been to read a cinematic text according to the work of a particular philosopher (Lacan and Foucault are especially popular in this regard), resulting in, for example, a Lacanian or Foucauldian reading of a film. A modification of this approach is to read a film according to thinkers like André Bazin, Gilles Deleuze, or Jean-Luc Godard, only some of whom were philosophers, but all of whom wrote explicitly on film. Simon Critchley, Cavell, and others have argued for the limitations of this approach, warning that "application" readings silence a film's internal philosophical voice, and that "a philosophical reading of film should not be concerned with ideas about the thing, but with the thing itself," as Critchley puts it.[28] Carvalho has also pointed out that one of the blind spots of philosophical criticism of art is what he calls the risk of "leaving the materiality of the work of art behind."[29] Philosophical "application" readings of films from the Mamardashvili generation risk not only losing the voice of the film in the process, but risk ignoring the very real intellectual and historical ties between Mamardashvili and cinema that have made up the main content of this book.

A second approach to the philosophy of film has been to treat a filmmaker as philosopher, mainly by synthesizing their work in order to make claims about what positions they did hold or might have held, had they been writing philosophy and not making films. This position has been especially popular as an approach to the work of leading auteurs, for instance Terrence Malick or Andrei Tarkovsky.[30] While this method can indeed lead to philosophical insights, in particular in the case of directors who have established themselves as "philosophical filmmakers," it places too much emphasis on the director as philosophical author and again neglects the role of the film as the "thinking body." This approach to film philosophy also tends to neglect questions of transposition and transmutation that go hand in hand with a movement from rhetorical/argumentative forms (philosophy) to cinematic form.

In the case of Malick, for example, Critchley describes how we must resist the temptation to read Malick's work through the lens of Cavell, who was his teacher in philosophy at Harvard, or through the lens of Heidegger, whom Malick taught to undergraduate students as a philosophy instructor at MIT.[31] In doing so, Critchley continues, we ignore the voice of the film. Here again, we see how calls to increase the application of theory where film philosophy is concerned risk limiting the philosophical spontaneity of cinema. A more "bare bones" approach to criticism forms the basis of Ludwig Wittgenstein's own philosophical method, which emphasized the values of observation, simplification, and the reduction of theory in order that we might see philosophical problems more clearly—a revolutionary approach to the philosophy of language in which Cavell found inspiration for his work in the philosophy of film.

One productive model for considering the interplay between Mamardashvili's philosophy and Zvyagintsev's films, or between philosophy and film more broadly, is through the notion of the dialectical image. For Walter Benjamin, the dialectical image captured a space between meanings; it harnessed the relationship of the past to the present, not as a progression but as an "explosion" that was "not temporal in nature, but figural."[32] Benjamin took hold of the important role of the dream state in the young Marx and reconfigured the act of critical reading as awakening, as the rupture moment between "the synthesis of dream consciousness [as thesis] and waking consciousness [as antithesis]."[33] In fact, the genealogy of the dialectical image takes us back further, to Kant, for whom image was limited as an object of experience, except when considered in its pure form as expressing the abstract notions of both space and time.[34]

Benjamin's notion of the dialectical image transcends both time and space in its moment of rupture: it is "dialectics at a standstill," and provides a critical moment for reflection, thereby constituting "the only genuine image."[35] Susan Buck-Morss and others have looked at Benjamin's use of modern technological metaphors, like the camera flash and the cutting mechanisms of montage, as new possibilities for bringing forth the dialectical image and the "cognitive explosiveness," to use Buck-Morss' term, that it entailed.[36] The dialectical image is likewise the genesis of critical reading in the Marxist tradition, according to Benjamin's assertion that the dialectical image "bears to the highest degree the imprint of the perilous critical moment on which all reading is founded."[37] Important for our purposes is that the Benjaminian vision of the dialectical image does not turn us toward theory for interpreting films, but allows the cinematic moment to retain its interpretive internal potency as a guiding force. The dialectical image is only completed, in other words, at the moment when past, present, and viewer engage the voice of the film.

Mamardashvili did not harness the language of Benjamin or of the dialectical image in his work. He did, however, agree that the literary or cinematic image could capture a moment of thought. Unlike Plato, Mamardashvili saw the image as containing a kind of truth that the philosophical word did not. Mike Wayne, by way of Buck-Morss, describes the tradition out of which the dialectical image emerges as precisely this "cross-fertilization between the Word and Image, one in which the Word returns to the *aesthetic* Image as a source for revivifying its own formulations, questioning its own assumptions, or even circumnavigating the aporias in its own philosophical structures."[38] We can trace Mamardashvili's receptivity to the status of the image to the phenomenological foundation of his philosophical method, and perhaps in particular to his take on Husserl's "eidetic reduction," or the imaginative, image-based process by which the phenomenologist tries to reduce a phenomenon to its necessary essences. For Mamardashvili, this took the form of visualizing the unity of consciousness by finding features of consciousness in literary and cinematic images.

Mamardashvili briefly addressed the question of adaptation between genres and forms of representation, including between a literary text and a script, between a script and celluloid, and between a literary text and a philosophical work. In *Conversations About Thought* (*Besedy o myshlenii*), a lecture series he delivered at Tbilisi State University between 1986 and 1987, he recounted an interview in which Jean-Luc Godard argued that there is no single "truthful" or "right" image that the filmmaker must achieve when moving from script to film.[39] For Mamardashvili, the true image comes only after the cinematic image has been constructed: the truth comes from the completed form. Where film viewership was concerned, the movie theatre could serve as a conceptual space for producing the dialectical charge about which Benjamin spoke, in which the dually constituted nature of human experience and its associated layers could be visualized and interrogated. Film is not just another kind of artistic text to which we might apply the methods of philosophy, in this reading, but a new philosophical possibility in its own right, providing new ways for self-reflection and moral reasoning.

The same force behind Benjamin's dialectical image also appears to be at play in Mamardashvili's method of reading literary texts through phenomenological means. Even the earlier idea that Zvyagintsev returns to, in which Mamardashvili expressed that humanness consists in "the effort to be human," was inspired by Marcel Proust, to whom Mamardashvili dedicated two lecture series at Tbilisi State University in the 1980s. He quoted Proust's description of life as "effort in time" and described how acts of existential effort move the individual along one's existential way, from "me to me," as he put it.[40] We might consider this rupture in the face of sameness, the act of effort that effects a shift in the seemingly unchanged "me," not only in light of Proust's unfinished *In Search of Lost Time*, but in terms of Benjamin's description of the dialectical image as a "caesura in the movement of thought."[41] The idea of the dialectical image can help us account for questions that arise in the process of adaptation, where two genres come together not as a seamless transition from one form to another, but as a moment of critical rupture that can only be resolved in its being "read," as Benjamin argued.

In the context of Mamardashvili's influence, we must ask ourselves another question: not just whether philosophy and film share any conceptual territory and what that territory is, but why his philosophy was so influential on cinema but not on other areas. Mamardashvili lectured at the Institute of Psychology, the Institute of Pedagogical Sciences, and the Institute of Philosophy, yet he has a comparatively small following among professionals in disciplines outside of film; we find no Mamardashvili generation of psychologists or pedagogues, and even among philosophers he has a comparatively small following, localized primarily within the department that employed him at the Institute of Philosophy in Moscow.

His legacy is most acutely felt in film, even among directors with diverse professional backgrounds: Zeldovich was a psychologist before hearing Mamardashvili lecture at the Higher Courses; Mamuliya was a philosophy student at Tbilisi before turning to film; Alexander Arkhangelsky attended Mamardashvili's lectures at the Institute of Psychology before establishing himself as one of contemporary Russia's leading TV journalists and cultural commentators. Maurice Merleau-Ponty asserted that "the philosopher and the filmmaker share a certain way of being, a certain view of the world that belongs to a generation."[42] The concept of generation is important in Mamardashvili's case, but to a significant degree his influence appears also to be a historical accident, a confluence of cultural and institutional forces unlikely to be repeated.

Thinking about Mamardashvili's influence in terms of generation helps explain how directors as disparate as Sokurov, Zeldovich, Balabanov, and Zvyagintsev could see themselves as having been influenced by the same person, as participants in the same intellectual (but not cinematic) tradition. This model of influence should remind us very much of the Soviet tradition of intellectual training, whereby affiliation is consolidated around an intellectual figurehead and lines of influence run from individuals to the teacher, but not necessarily from student to student.[43] In this centripetal model, members of a school can associate themselves with the teacher, but not necessarily with each other. For Karl Mannheim, teachers cannot pass the "mental climate" of their generation down to their pupils because the effectiveness of the teacher–student relationship hinges on the meeting of two discrete modes of consciousness.[44] When Mamardashvili's students stop making films, in other words, the Mamardashvili generation will end. The generational markers are already apparent in the ages of his students, spanning almost two decades: Sokurov is the oldest, born in 1951; Dmitry Mamuliya is the youngest, born in 1969.

Keeping in mind Mannheim's claim, it is important to note that the filmmakers of the Mamardashvili generation do not represent Mamardashvili's own generation, but a "mental climate" that formed under his influence. And just as the image contained a special truth in Mamardashvili's philosophy, so was it his image that influenced the directors with whom he worked and taught. In 2018 Mamuliya emphasized the power of the image over the word in his memories of Mamardashvili from his student years:

> Merab cannot be reduced to his speech, his lectures, or his philosophy. His texts give birth to a sense of simulated connectivity to the things about which he spoke. In order to understand what he said you must climb out from the bonds of that connectivity, which is quite difficult. It's not just about the nimble metaphors that were a part of his thought, but his tonal wizardry, comprising several dozen elements and with a chemistry that is impossible to discern. In this way, his philosophy is akin to poetry or to life itself. I tried to look for one of the phrases by Merab that had vanished from my mind but was unable to find it. I am citing here from memory ... "A thinker can look like anything except Rodin's 'The Thinker.'" This is that truth that has proven foundational for me—not only in my life, but in film. I came to understand what a false image looks like. Falsity is when an image is reduced to itself. When a thinker looks like a thinker, a poet looks like a poet, a lover like a lover, and a thief like a thief, then they can hardly be a thinker, a poet, a lover, and a thief. This simple thought turned out to be revolutionary for me in comprehending not only life, but also film.[45]

Zeldovich utilized a similar metaphor, when he remarked that "Mamardashvili stayed in [his] mind more as an image than as a thought."[46]

Although the word *image* denotes an idea or representation of a thing rather than the thing itself, the image of Mamardashvili (as described by his colleagues and students) is often bound to both memory and materiality: his canary yellow sweater, the smell of his pipe, the sound of his voice. In the case of Mamuliya and Zvyagintsev, we see how a faithful reproduction of the semantic content of Mamardashvili's speech was less important than the general impression his words imparted, a representation that went on to underpin the relationship between word and image for both directors. In Arkhangelsky's eight-episode television miniseries, *The Department* (*Otdel*, 2010), Mamardashvili's legacy is signaled through repeated close-ups of his portrait hanging on the wall of the Institute of Philosophy in Moscow, where an audio recording of his voice is superimposed over his image. In Sokurov's *The Demoted*, the inclusion of a rare recording of Mamardashvili's voice is dominated by the absent image, by the movement of the camera as it zooms in on the radio in search for the physical source of the sound.

Mamardashvili's own method, in turn, privileged the role of image. He embellished the philosophical positions of Descartes and Kant with biographical details he inferred from paintings, and merged his own positions with the prose of Proust and Chekhov and the cinema of Abuladze and Abdrashitov-Mindadze. The visualization of the invisible—through performance, through literary description, through metaphors and paradox, through film—was not only a question of representation for Mamardashvili. The act of reading across genres and engaging the explosive potential of the image comprised for him the very essence of what it was to be a free, thinking human being—to be a human being at all. The profoundly visual component to his thinking perhaps explains why his philosophical influence took its most enduring shape on film.

Notes

1. Dularidze, "Stranstvuiushchii filosof."
2. Strukov, p. 9.
3. Milan Kundera, *The Curtain. An Essay in Seven Parts*, trans. Linda Asher (HarperCollins, 2006), p. 155.
4. In the ontology of film as it relates to questions of adaptation and literary and/or philosophical inspiration, see: Gregory Currie, *Image and Mind: Film, Philosophy and Cognitive Science* (New York: Cambridge University Press, 1995), p. 1; Trevor Ponech, "The Substance of Cinema," in *Thinking Through Cinema. Film as Philosophy* (Hoboken, NJ: Blackwell Publishers, 2006), p. 196.
5. Mamuliia, "Mamuliia to DeBlasio."
6. For in-depth biographical background on Zvyagintsev and his rise to fame, see: Nancy Condee, "Knowledge (Imperfective): Andrei Zviagintsev and Contemporary Cinema," in *A Companion to Russian Cinema*, ed. Birgit Beumers (Hoboken, NJ: Wiley-Blackwell, 2016), pp. 565–84.
7. Elena Stishova, "Na glubine. 'Vozvrashchenie,' rezhisser Andrei Zviagintsev," *Iskusstvo kino* 1 (January 2004).
8. Kritchman was awarded a prize at the 2010 Venice International Film Festival for his cinematography on Aleksei Fedorchenko's *Silent Souls* (*Ovsianki*, 2010).
9. Condee has discussed Zvyagintsev's universalizing tendencies in the creation, production, and marketing of his films as well in Condee, "Knowledge (Imperfective)," p. 573.
10. Cavell, p. 190.
11. The same argument has been waged in favor of the role of literature in self-reflection, although proponents of film philosophy often turn to the sensory density inherent to the medium of film as a way to support its distinctive role in "carving new paths for our own modes of thought." See: Hunter Vaughan, *Where Film Meets Philosophy. Godard, Resnais, and Experiments in Cinematic Thinking* (New York: Columbia University Press, 2013), p. 2.
12. John Carvalho, *Thinking with Images: An Enactivist Aesthetics* (New York: Routledge, 2019), p. 14.

13. Viktor Matizen, "Rezhisser Andrei Zviagintsev," *Novye izvestiia* (Aug. 14, 2009), https://newizv.ru/news/culture/14-08-2009/113243-rezhisser-and rej-zvjagincev.
14. See, for instance: Andrei Zviagintsev, "'Chitaia proizvedenie, smotria fil'm, nuzhno iskat' svoi portret, chtoby uzhasnut'sia samomu sebe." Interview by Kira Al'tman,'" *BFM* (May 19, 2017), https://www.bfm.ru/news/354871.
15. Ibid.
16. Andrei Zviagintsev, "Bez vertikali nel'zia nichego postroit'," *AZ Film* (May 26, 2011), http://az-film.com/ru/Publications/52-Bez-vertikali-nelzja-nichego-postroit.html.
17. Mikhail Epstein, "Zhizn' kak zhov," *Chastnyi korrespondent* (Nov. 30, 2011), http://www.chaskor.ru/article/zhizn_kak_zhov_25908.
18. "Soznanie i tsivilizatsiia," p. 7.
19. Alena Solntseva, "Introduction to Zvyagintsev's *Loveless*" (20th Russian Film Symposium, Pittsburgh, May 2, 2018).
20. "The Civil Society," p. 6.
21. Solntseva, "Introduction to Zvyagintsev's *Loveless*."
22. *Estetika myshleniia*, p. 69.
23. *Besedy o myshlenii*, p. 67.
24. Andrei Zviagintsev, "Rezhisser Andrei Zviagintsev na vstreche so zriteliami v Iaroslave: preslovutyi 'kheppi end' dolzhen sluchit'sia v vashei zhizni, a ne na ekrane," *Iaroslavskaia oblast'* (Aug. 8, 2017), https://7x7-journal.ru/item/97457.
25. Ibid.
26. Zvyagintsev has said on several occasions that the primary goal behind filming *Loveless* was that viewers would "go home and hug their loved ones." See, for instance: Andrei Zviagintsev, "Zviagintsev: My snimali 'Neliubov',' chtoby zriteli obniali svoikh blizkikh," *Argumenty i fakty* (May 31, 2017), http://www.aif.ru/culture/movie/zvyagincev_my_snimali_nelyubov_chtoby_zriteli_obnyali_svoih_blizkih.
27. Robert B. Pippen, *The Philosophical Hitchcock: "Vertigo" and the Anxieties of Unknowingness* (Chicago: University of Chicago Press, 2017), p. 3.
28. Simon Critchley, "Calm: On Terrence Malick's *The Thin Red Line*," in *Film as Philosophy. Essays in Cinema after Wittgenstein and Cavell*, ed. Rupert Read and Jerry Goodenough (New York: Palgrave Macmillan, 2005), p. 139.
29. Carvalho, p. 21.
30. For one such study on Tarkovsky, see: Igor' Evlampiev, *Khudozhestvennaia filosofiia Andreia Tarkovskogo* (St Petersburg: Aleteiia, 2001).
31. Critchley, p. 138.
32. Walter Benjamin, *The Arcades Project*, trans. Howard Eiland and Kevin McLaughlin (Cambridge, MA: Belknap Press of Harvard University Press, 2002), p. 463, N3,1.
33. Ibid., p. 463, N3a,3.
34. Kant, *Critique of Pure Reason*, p. 273, A140.

35. *The Arcades Project*, p. 462, N2a,3.
36. Susan Buck-Morss, *The Dialectics of Seeing: Walter Benjamin and the Arcades Project* (Cambridge, MA: MIT Press, 1991), p. 251.
37. *The Arcades Project*, p. 463, N3,1.
38. Mike Wayne and Ewa Mazierska, "The Dialectical Image: Kant, Marx, and Adorno," in *Marx at the Movies: Revisiting History, Theory, and Practice* (New York: Palgrave Macmillan, 2014), p. 28.
39. *Besedy o myshlenii*.
40. *Psikhologicheskaia topologiia puti*, pp. 7 and 218–19.
41. *The Arcades Project*, p. 475, N10a,3.
42. Maurice Merleau-Ponty, *Sens et Non-Sens* (Paris: Gallimard, 1945), p. 74.
43. Natalia Kovalyova's work has described the effects of this centripetal system of influence on scholarly engagement in Russian academic journals. See: Kovalyova, "The Interplay of the Material and the Discursive in Russian Academic Prose (1980–2010)," ed. Alyssa DeBlasio and Maxim Demin, *Russian Journal of Communication. Special Issue on The Scholarly Journal as a Form of Communication* 6, No. 1 (2014): pp. 6–19.
44. Mannheim, p. 301.
45. Mamuliia, "Mamuliia to DeBlasio."
46. Zel'dovich, "Zel'dovich to DeBlasio." In the extra footage to the 2007 film *Georgian Kant* (*Gruzinskii Kant*), Erik Solovyov describes how his memories of Mamardashvili as a philosopher have already faded, and how he now remembers Mamardashvili primarily as a person and as a friend.

Appendix

Films Discussed in this Book, in Order of Presentation

Demoted / Razzhalovannyi (Russia, 1980)
b&w, 31 minutes
Director: Aleksandr Sokurov
Screenplay: Aleksandr Sokurov, based on a story by Grigorii Baklanov
Cinematography: Sergei Iurizditskii
Cast: Il'ia Rivin, Sergei Koshonin, Anatolii Petrov, Stanislav Sokolov, Irina Sokolova
Producer: Boris Krishtul
Studio: Lenfil'm, EMTO "Debut"

The Black Monk / Chernyi monakh (Russia, 1988)
color, 83 minutes
Director: Ivan Dykhovichnyi
Screenplay: Ivan Dykhovichnyi and Sergei Solov'ev, based on the novella by Anton Chekhov
Cinematography: Vadim Iusov
Music: Teimuraz Bakuradze and the Georgian National Quartet
Sound: Aleksandr Nekhoroshev
Cast: Tat'iana Drubich, Stanislav Liubshin, Petr Fomenko
Studio: Kul'tura Channel, Mosfil'm, RITM

Another Sky / Drugoe nebo (Russia, 2010)
color, 86 minutes
Director: Dmitrii Mamuliia
Screenplay: Dmitrii Mamuliia and Leonid Sitov
Cinematography: Alisher Khamidkhodzhaev
Music: Anna Muzychenko
Sound: Marina Nigmatulina

Cast: Habib Boufares, Amirza Mukhamadi, Mitra Zakhedi
Producer: Arsen Gotlib
Production: Metronomfil'm

The Castle/Zamok (Russia, 1994)
color, 107 minutes
Director: Aleksei Balabanov
Screenplay: Aleksei Balabanov and Sergei Sel'ianov, based on the novel by Franz Kafka
Cinematography: Sergei Iurizditskii
Music: Sergei Kurekhin
Editing: Tamara Lipartiia
Cast: Nikolai Stotskii, Svetlana Pis'michenko, Viktor Sukhorukov
Studio: 2P and K, Orient Express, Lenfil'm, Bioskop Film, and the Filmmaking Committee of the Russian Federation

Me Too/Ia tozhe khochu (Russia, 2012)
color, 89 minutes
Director: Aleksei Balabanov
Screenplay: Aleksei Balabanov
Cinematography: Aleksandr Simonov
Music: Leonid Fedorov
Editing: Tat'iana Kuzmicheva
Cast: Aleksandr Mosin, Iurii Matveev, Oleg Garkusha, Alisa Shitikova, Viktor Gorbunov, Petr Balabanov
Producer: Sergei Sel'ianov
Production: CTB Film Company

Target/Mishen' (Russia, 2011)
color, 158 minutes
Director: Aleksandr Zel'dovich
Screenplay: Aleksandr Zel'dovich and Vladimir Sorokin
Cinematography: Aleksandr Il'khovskii
Music: Leonid Desiatnikov
Cast: Maksim Sukhanov, Justine Waddell, Danila Kozlovskii, Daniela Stoianovich, Vitalii Kishchenko, Nina Loshchinina,
Producer: Dmitrii Lesnevskii
Studio: Renfil'm

The Train Stopped/Ostanovilsia poezd (Russia; Soviet Union, 1982)
color, 90 minutes
Director: Vadim Abdrashitov
Screenplay: Aleksandr Mindadze
Cinematography: Iurii Nevskii
Cast: Oleg Borisov, Anatolii Solonitsyn, Mikhail Gluzskii, Nina Ruslanova, Liudmila Zaitseva, Nikolai Skorobogatov, Petr Kolbasin, Iosif Rylkin
Production: Mosfil'm

Repentance/Pokoianie/Monanieba (Georgia; Soviet Union, 1984/1987)
color, 153 minutes
Director: Tengiz Abuladze
Screenplay: Nana Dzhanelidze and Tengiz Abuladze
Cinematography: Mikhail Agranovich
Cast: Avtandil Makharadze, Iia Ninidze, Zeinab Botsvadze, Ketevan Abuladze
Production: Gruziia-fil'm

Loveless/Neliubov' (Russia/Belgium/Germany/France, 2017)
color, 127 minutes
Director: Andrei Zviagintsev
Screenplay: Andrei Zviagintsev and Oleg Nemin
Cinematography: Mikhail Krichman
Music: Evgenii Galperin, Sasha Galperin
Editor: Anna Mass
Cast: Mar'iana Spivak, Aleksei Rozin, Matvei Novikov, Marina Vasil'eva, Andris Keiss, Aleksei Fateev, Sergei Borisov
Producer: Aleksandr Rodnianskii, Sergei Mel'kumov, Gleb Fetisov
Production: Nonstop Production, Fetisov Illuzion, Why Not Productions, Les Films du Fleuve, Senator Film, Arte France Cinema

Films About or Including Merab Mamardashvili, in Chronological Order

VGIK student film about the Decembrists; unfinished (Russia, mid-1970s)
Director: Vladimir Tret'iakov

Demoted/Razzhalovannyi (Russia, 1980)
Director: Aleksandr Sokurov

Should the Sighted Lead the Blind?/ V otvete l' zriachii za sleptsa . . . (Russia, 1989)
Director: Vladimir Bondarev

The Interpretation of Dreams – Merab Mamardashvili and Mark Zakharov/ Tolkovanie snovidenii – Merab Mamardashvili i Mark Zakharov (TV broadcast; Russia, late 1980s)
Host: Mark Zakharov

The Road Home/ Put' domoi (two parts; Georgia, 1990)
Director: Nikolai Drozdov

Socrates at the Duel/ Sokrat na dueli (Georgia, 1991)
Director: Tamara Dularidze

The Time of Merab/ Vremia Meraba (Russia, 1993)
Director: Olesia Fokina

Islands. Merab Mamardashvili/ Ostrova. Merab Mamardashvili (Russia, 2005)
Director: Valerii Balaian

The Philosopher Ran Away/ Filosof sbezhal (Latvia, 2005)
Director: Uldis Tirons

Georgian Kant/ Gruzinskii Kant (Russia, 2007)
Director: Ol'ga Rolengof
In collaboration with Nabi Balaev

The Department/ Otdel (eight episodes; Russia, 2010)
Director: Aleksandr Arkhangel'skii

The *Lecture/ Lektsiia* (Georgia, 2016)
Director: Beso Odishariia

Bibliography

Abdullaeva, Zara. "Roman-fantaziia." *Iskusstvo kino* 3 (March 2011). http://kinoart.ru/archive/2011/03/n3-article4 (accessed Sept. 4, 2018).
Akhutin, Anatolii. "In Mamardashvili's Country." *Russian Studies in Philosophy* 49, No. 1 (summer 2010): pp. 20–52.
"Aleksei Balabanov byl tiazhelo bolen i zhdal smerti." NTV (May 18, 2013). http://www.ntv.ru/novosti/596097/ (accessed Oct. 10, 2018).
Al'tman, M. S. "Zheleznaia doroga." In *Chitaia Tolstogo*. Tula: Priokskoe knizhnoe izdatel'stvo, 1966: p. 111.
Anisimova, Irina. "Aleksei Balabanov: *Me Too (Ia tozhe khochu*, 2012)." *KinoKultura* 30 (2013). http://www.kinokultura.com/2013/40r-ya-tozhe-khochu.shtml (accessed Sept. 4, 2018).
———. "Heterotopia in Contemporary Russian Fiction." PhD diss., University of Pittsburgh, 2014.
Anninskii, Lev. "The Sixties Generation, the Seventies Generation, the Eighties Generation …: Toward a Dialectic of Generations in Russian Literature." Trans. Nancy Condee and Vladimir Padunov. *Soviet Studies in Literature* 27, No. 4 (1991): pp. 10–14.
Aristotle. *Poetics*. Trans. S. H. Butcher. 3rd edn. London: Macmillan & Co., 1902.
Arkhangel'skii, Aleksandr. "Istoriia sil'nee vozhdia." Arzamas Academy. Course No. 9. https://arzamas.academy/materials/260 (accessed Oct. 10, 2018).
———. *Otdel* (2010). Eight series. Russia K.
Arkus, Liubov'. "Balabanov kak poslednii modernist." St Petersburg and Moscow: Seans, 2015. http://seance.ru/balabanov/2015/conference/abstracts/arkus/ (accessed Sept. 17, 2018).
Aronson, Oleg. "Neumestnoe bytie." In *Vil'niusskie lektsii po sotsial'noi filosofii (Opyt fizicheskoi metafiziki)*. St Petersburg: Azbuka, 2012: pp. 291–302.
———. "Zakrytyi pokaz: "Mishen'," Pervyi kanal, May 5, 2010.
Avtonomova, Nataliia. "Letter to M. Mamardashvili," Feb. 3, 1978.
Balabanov, Aleksei. "Aleksei Balabanov: Ia ubil slishkom mnogo liudei v kino." RIA Novosti (Sept. 8, 2012). https://ria.ru/interview/20120908/745890762.html (accessed May 14, 2018).

———. "Balabanov o Balabanove." *Seans*, No. 17/18. http://seance.ru/n/17-18/portret-4/balabanov-o-balabanove/ (accessed May 14, 2018).

———. "Moe kino – eto novyi zhanr, fantasticheskii realizm. Vse igraiut sami sebia." Tass.ru (Sept. 10, 2012). http://tass.ru/opinions/interviews/1599012 (accessed Sept. 4, 2018).

Balabanova, Irina. "Byvshaia zhena Balabanova rasskazala o schast'e i tragediiakh v zhizni rezhissera." 7days.Ru. http://7days.ru/caravan-collection/2013/9/byvshaya-zhena-balabanova-rasskazala-o-schaste-i-tragediyakh-v-zhizni-rezhissera.htm (accessed Aug. 30, 2018).

Balaian, Valerii. "Fil'm o Merabe, sniatyi ego uchenikom." Ed. Aleksandr Arkhangel'skii. Arzamas Academy, no. Course No. 9. http://arzamas.academy/materials/334 (accessed April 17, 2015).

Bartlett, Rosamund. "Sonata Form in Chekhov's 'The Black Monk.'" *Intersections and Transpositions: Russian Music, Literature and Society*. Ed. Andrew Wachtel. Evanston: Northwestern University Press, 1998: pp. 58–72.

Bellefroid, Pierre. "Prazhskie gody. Merab Mamardashvili." Mamardashvili.ru, 2008. http://mamardashvili.com/about/bellefroid/1.html (accessed Sept. 17, 2018).

Benjamin, Walter. *The Arcades Project*. Trans. Howard Eiland and Kevin McLaughlin. Cambridge, MA: Belknap Press of Harvard University Press, 2002.

———. "Theses on the Philosophy of History." In *Illuminations. Essays and Reflections*. Trans. Harry Zohn. New York: Schoken Books, 1968: pp. 254–64.

Bernet, Rudolf, Iso Kern, and Eduard Marbach. *An Introduction to Husserlian Phenomenology*. Evanston, IL: Northwestern University Press, 1993.

Bondarev, Sergei and Dar'ia Goriacheva. "Kinobizon pogovoril s Dmitriem Mamuliem i Gennadiem Kostrovym o shkole i industrii." Moskovskaia shkola novogo kino. http://www.newcinemaschool.com/kinobizon-pogovoril-o-shkole-s-dmitriem-mamuliev-i-gennadiev-kostrovyim/ (accessed May 23, 2018).

Brashinskii, Mikhail. "Portret. Aleksei Balabanov." *Seans* No. 17/18. http://seance.ru/n/17-18/portret-4/2505/ (accessed Oct. 6, 2017).

Bykova, Marina F. "The Georgian Socrates." *Russian Studies in Philosophy* 49.1 (2010): pp. 3–6.

Buck-Morss, Susan. *Dreamworld and Catastrophe: The Passing of Mass Utopia in East and West*. Cambridge, MA: MIT Press, 2000.

———. *The Dialectics of Seeing: Walter Benjamin and the Arcades Project*. Cambridge, MA: MIT Press, 1991.

Camus, Albert. *The Myth of Sisyphus*. New York: Alfred A. Knopf, 1983.

Carvalho, John. *Thinking with Images: An Enactivist Aesthetics*. New York: Routledge, 2019.

Cavell, Stanley. "'What Becomes of Thinking on Film?' (Stanley Cavell in Conversation with Andrew Klevan)." In *Film as Philosophy. Essays in Cinema after Wittgenstein and Cavell*. Ed. Rupert Read and Jerry Goodenough. New York: Palgrave Macmillan, 2005: pp. 167–209.

Chalmers, David J. "Facing Up to the Problem of Consciousness." *Journal of Consciousness Studies* 2, No. 3 (1995): pp. 200–19.
Chapman, Andrew. "The Stoker." Program Notes. University of Pittsburgh Russian Film Symposium, 2011. http://www.rusfilm.pitt.edu/2011/thestoker.html (accessed May 1, 2018).
Chechot, Aglaia. "Pozovi menia, nebo." *Seans* (March 15, 2012). http://seance.ru/blog/call-me-sky/ (accessed Sept. 4, 2018).
Chekhov, Anton. "Chernyi monakh." Lib.ru, ed. Aleksei Komarov, n.d. http://www.ilibrary.ru/text/985/index.html (accessed Sept. 3, 2018).
———. *Polnoe sobranie sochinenii i pisem v tridtsati tomakh.* Moscow, 1974–83, Vol. 8, pp. 488–9.
Condee, Nancy. "Knowledge (Imperfective): Andrei Zviagintsev and Contemporary Cinema." In *A Companion to Russian Cinema.* Ed. Birgit Beumers. Hoboken, NJ: Wiley-Blackwell, 2016: pp. 565–84.
———. *The Imperial Trace: Recent Russian Cinema.* Oxford: Oxford University Press, 2009.
———. *The Stoker:* "Aleksei Balabanov: *Stoker (Kochegar,* 2010)." *KinoKultura* 32 (2011). http://www.kinokultura.com/2011/32r-kochegar.shtml (accessed Oct. 30, 2018).
Cornwell, Neil. *The Absurd in Literature.* Manchester: Manchester University Press, 2006.
Critchley, Simon. "Calm: On Terrence Malick's *The Thin Red Line.*" In *Film as Philosophy. Essays in Cinema after Wittgenstein and Cavell.* Ed. Rupert Read and Jerry Goodenough. New York: Palgrave Macmillan, 2005: pp. 133–48.
Currie, Gregory. *Image and Mind: Film, Philosophy and Cognitive Science.* New York: Cambridge University Press, 1995.
Danilov, Dennis. "'V chem sila, brat?'. Piat' luchshikh fil'mov rezhissera Alekseia Balabanova." *Argumenty i fakty* (Feb. 25, 2016). http://www.spb.aif.ru/culture/person/v_chem_sila_brat_pyat_luchshih_filmov_rezhissera_alekseya_balabanova (accessed May 14, 2018).
DeBlasio, Alyssa. "'Nothing in Life but Death': Aleksandr Zel'dovich's *Target* in Conversation with Tolstoy's Philosophy on the Value of Death.'" *The Russian Review* 73, No. 3 (2014): pp. 2–21.
Degutis, Algirdas. "Vospominaniia o Vil'niusskikh lektsiiakh Meraba Mamardashvili." In *Vil'niusskie lektsii po sotsial'noi filosofii (Opyt fizicheskoi metafiziki).* St Petersburg: Azbuka, 2012: pp. 303–6.
Dennett, Daniel. "The Unimagined Preposterousness of Zombies." *Journal of Consciousness Studies* 2.4 (1995): pp. 322–6.
Descartes, René. *Principles of Philosophy.* Trans. Valentine Roger Miller and Reese P. Miller. Dordrecht, Holland: D. Reidel Publishing Company, 1983.
Dobrokhotov, Aleksandr. "Traditsiia bessmertiia: Mamardashvili kak filosof kul'tury." In *Izbrannoe.* Moscow: Territoriia budushchego, 2008: pp. 357–78.
Dragunskii, Denis. "Filosofiia bez trepa." *Russkii zhurnal* (Oct. 6, 2010). http://

www.russ.ru/layout/set/print/Mirovaya-povestka/Filosofiya-bez-trepa (accessed April 20, 2015).

Dularidze, Tamara. "Merab Mamardashvili segodnia." Fond Meraba Mamardashvili, 1997. https://www.mamardashvili.com/ru/merab-mamardashvili/pamyati-m.m/tamara-dularidze/merab-mamardashvili-segodnya (accessed June 29, 2018).

———. "Stranstvuiushchii filosof, kotoryi liubil kino," 1991. https://www.mamardashvili.com/ru/merab-mamardashvili/pamyati-m.m/tamara-dularidze/my-vse-ego-tak-lyubili-vspominaya-meraba-mamardashvili (accessed Aug. 30, 2018).

Dykhovichnyi, Ivan. "Ty beresh' tam sily." In *Professiia – kinematografist*. Ed. P. D. Volkova, A. N. Gerasimov, and V. I. Sumenova. Ekaterinburg: U-Faktoriia, 2004: pp. 389–429.

Epelboin, Annie. "The Crossed Destinies or Two Philosophers: Louis Althusser and Merab Mamardashvili." *Transcultural Studies* 5 (2009): pp. 1–16.

———. "Annie Epelboin. "Perepiska Meraba Mamardashvili s Lui Al'tiusserom." In *Vstrecha: Meraba Mamardashvili i Lui Al'tiusser*. Moscow: Fond Meraba Mamardashvili, 2016: pp. 57–73.

Epstein, Mikhail. "Zhizn' kak zhov." *Chastnyi korrespondent* (Nov. 30, 2011). http://www.chaskor.ru/article/zhizn_kak_zhov_25908 (accessed Sept. 4, 2018).

Ermakova, Valeriia. "Balabanov, Poslednii modernist." *Medium* (April 6, 2015). https://medium.com/@epinevalery/последний-модернист-2b5872f91383 accessed Oct. 22, 2018).

Evlampiev, Igor'. *Khudozhestvennaia filosofiia Andreia Tarkovskogo*. St Petersburg: Aleteiia, 2001.

———. *Russkaia filosofiia v evropeiskom kontekste*. St Petersburg: Izd-vo RKhGA, 2017.

Ezerova, Dar'ia. "'Ia tozhe khochu': mezhdu fantasticheskim i magicheskim realizmom." In *Balabanov. Perekrestki*. Ed. A. Artamonov and V. Stepanov. St Petersburg: Seans, 2017: pp. 53–62.

Faibyshenko, Viktoriia. "Istoriia poznanie, ili poznanie kak istoriia." In *Formy i soderzhanie myshleniia*. St Petersburg: Azbuka, 2011: pp. 265–83.

Fokina, Olesia. *Vremia Meraba*, 1993.

Frierson, Patrick. "Kant on Mental Disorder." *History of Psychiatry* 20, No. 3 (2009): pp. 1–23.

Diana Gasparian, *Filosofiia soznaniia Meraba Mamardashvili*. Moscow: Kanon+, 2013.

Gasparyan, Diana. *Merab Mamardashvili's Philosophy of Consciousness*. Takoma Park, MD: PhotoPressArt, 2012.

Gerber, Alla. "Tengiz Abuladze: 'Liubov' rozhaet poznanie." In *Ekran*. Moscow: Iskusstvo, 1980: pp. 106–10.

Gessen, Masha. *Words Will Break Cement: The Passion of Pussy Riot*. New York: Riverhead, 2014.

Godard, Jean-Luc. *Godard on Godard. Critical Writings by Jean-Luc Godard*. Ed. Jean Narboni and Tom Milne. Cambridge, MA: Da Capo Press, 1986.

Golubitskaia, Anna. "'Vnutrennii sad' Meraba Mamardashvili." *Otrok* 2, No. 80 (2017). http://otrok-ua.ru/ru/sections/art/show/vnutrennii_sad_meraba_mamardashvili.html (accessed May 14, 2018).

Gordon, Peter E. "What Is Intellectual History? A Frankly Partisan Introduction to a Frequently Misunderstood Field," 2012. http://projects.iq.harvard.edu/files/history/files/what_is_intell_history_pgordon_mar2012.pdf (accessed May 3, 2018).

Gromkovskii, Vladimir. "Anna Karenina Mtsenskogo uezda: o fil'me 'Mishen'." Snob.ru (June 27, 2011). http://www.snob.ru/profile/10951/blog/37490 (accessed Sept. 4, 2018).

Gubin, V. D., T. Iu. Sidorina, and V. P. Filatov (eds). *Uchebnik filosofiia*. 2nd edn. Moscow: TON- Ostozh'e, 2001.

Gusiatinskii, Evgenii. "Aleksei Balabanov: 'Vsegda zhivem v Rossii.'" *Iskusstvo kino* 7 (July 2007). http://kinoart.ru/archive/2007/07/n7-article2 (accessed May 14, 2018).

———. "Bol'no, bystro." *Seans* (May 22, 2007). https://seance.ru/blog/reviews/ya-hochu-balabanov/ (accessed Jan. 14, 2019).

Hicks, Jeremy. "Sokurov's Documentaries." In *The Cinema of Alexander Sokurov*. Ed. Birgit Beumers and Nancy Condee. London: I. B. Tauris, 2011: pp. 13–27.

Hudspith, Sarah. "Life in the Present: Time and Immortality in the Works of Tolstoy." *The Modern Language Review* 101.4. (Oct. 2006): pp. 1055–67.

Iakovleva, Elena. "Otkroi okno v ogon'. Rezhisser Konstantin Lopushanskii khochet byt' uslyshannym v svoei strane." *Rossiiskaia gazeta* (March 23, 2012). https://rg.ru/2012/03/23/lopushanskiy.html (accessed Aug. 30, 2018).

Iampol'skii, Mikhail. "Chitaia Godara. Zametki na poliakh godarovskikh tekstov." In *Zhan-Liuk Godar. Strast'. Mezhdu chernym i belym*. N.p., 1997: pp. 54–61.

Iulina, Nina. "Taking in the Past at a Glance. An Interview with N.S. Iulina." *Russian Studies in Philosophy* 48, No. 1 (summer 2009): pp. 56–67.

Iurchak, Aleksei. "Rossiiskoe obshchestvo ne delitsia na bol'shuiu 'vatu' i malen'kuiu 'svobodu.'" *Gor'kii* (Nov. 30, 2016). https://gorky.media/intervyu/rossijskoe-obshhestvo-ne-delitsya-na-bolshuyu-vatu-i-malenkuyu-svobodu/ (accessed Aug. 30, 2018).

Jahn, Gary R. "The Image of the Railroad in *Anna Karenina*." *SEEJ* 25.2 (1981): pp. 1–10.

———. "Tolstoj's Vision of the Power of Death and 'How Much Land Does a Man Need?'" In *SEEJ* 22.4 (winter 1978): pp. 442–53.

Kafka, Franz. "The Bachelor's Unhappiness." In *The Metamorphosis, the Penal Colony, and Other Stories*. Trans. Joachim Neugroschel. New York: Simon & Schuster, 1995: p. 33.

Kakabadze, Irakli Zurab. "I Am with Chubik: Faces of Georgian AlterModernity, Modernity and Anti-Modernity." *Arcade* (Jan. 31, 2013). http://arcade.

stanford.edu/blogs/i-am-chubik-faces-georgian-altermodernity-modernity-and-anti-modernity (accessed Aug. 30, 2018).

Kant, Immanuel. *Critique of Pure Reason*. Trans. by Paul Guyer and Allen W. Wood. Cambridge: Cambridge University Press, 1998.

———. *Gesammelte Schriften*. Ed. DeGruyter. Berlin: Reimer, 1910.

Karst, Roman. "Kafka and the Russians." In *Perspectives and Personalities. Studies in Modern German Literature Honoring Claude Hill*. Ed. Ralph Ley, Maria Wagner, Joanna M. Ratych, and Kenneth Hughes. Heidelberg: Carl Winter Universitatsverlag, 1978: pp. 181–97.

Khotinenko, Vladimir. "Maksimal'no ispol'zovat' vremia, predostavlennoe sud'boi." In *Professiia – kinematografist*. Ed. P. D. Volkova, A. N. Gerasimov, and V. I. Sumenova. Ekaterinburg: U-Faktoriia, 2004: pp. 441–56.

Konstantinov, F. B. (ed.). "Soznanie." In *Filosofskaia entsiklopediia*, Vol. 5. Moscow: Iz-vo "Sovetskaia entsiklopediia," 1962: pp. 43–8.

Kovalov, Oleg. "We in The Lonely Voice." In *The Cinema of Alexander Sokurov*. Ed. Birgit Beumers and Nancy Condee. London: I. B. Tauris, 2011: pp. 216–19.

Kovalyova, Natalia. "The Interplay of the Material and the Discursive in Russian Academic Prose (1980–2010)." Ed. Alyssa DeBlasio and Maxim Demin. *Russian Journal of Communication. Special Issue on The Scholarly Journal as a Form of Communication* 6, No. 1 (2014): pp. 6–19.

Kundera, Milan. *The Curtain. An Essay in Seven Parts*. Trans. Linda Asher. London: HarperCollins, 2006.

Kuvshinova, Mariia. "Aleksei Balabanov: Tak okazalos', chto ia zdes' zhivu." *Seans* (Feb. 25, 2014). http://seance.ru/blog/chtenie/balabanov_book_intrvw/ (accessed May 14, 2018).

———. *Balabanov*. St Petersburg: Seans, 2015.

———. "Mishen'." OpenSpace.ru (Feb. 15, 2011). http://os.colta.ru/cinema/events/details/20563/ (accessed Sept. 4, 2018).

———. "Nakrylis' elkami." Colta.ru (Dec. 20, 2010). http://os.colta.ru/cinema/events/details/19391/ (accessed Aug. 30, 2018).

———. "Piat' let bez Balabanova." *Takie dela* (May 18, 2018). https://takiedela.ru/2018/05/pyat-let-bez-balabanova/ (accessed Oct. 16, 2018).

Kuzmicheva, Tatiana. "Interview with the Film Editor Tat'iana Kuz'micheva by Anna Nieman." *KinoKultura* 59 (2018). http://www.kinokultura.com/2018/59i-kuzmicheva_nieman.shtml (accessed Sept. 4, 2018).

Kvasnetskaia, Margarita. *Tengiz Abuladze. Put' k "Pokoianiiu."* Moscow: Kul'turnaia revoliutsiia, 2009.

Leontiev, Dmitry. "Life as Heroic Effort: Merab Mamardashvili's *Psychological Topology of the Way*." *Transcultural Studies* 5 (2009): pp. 74–91.

Liashchenko, Vladimir. "Svet narisovan, nebesa nastoiashchie: Interv'iu s Aleksandrom Zel'dovichem." Gazeta.ru (July 7, 2011). http://m.gazeta.ru/culture/2011/07/07/a_3689017.shtml (accessed Sept. 4, 2018).

Lokshin, Boris. "Igraem v Kareninu." *Iskusstvo kino* (Nov. 2, 2012). http://www.kinoart.ru/blogs/igraem-v-kareninu (accessed Sept. 4, 2018).
Longuenesse, Béatrice. "Kant's 'I Think' versus Descartes' 'I Am a Thing That Thinks.'" In *Kant and the Early Moderns*. Ed. Daniel Garber and Béatrice Longuenesse. Princeton, NJ: Princeton University Press, 2008: pp. 9–31.
Lotman, Iurii. "Ritorika." In *Ob iskusstve*. Ed. Grigor'ev. Iskusstvo-SPb, 1998: pp. 404–22.
MacIntyre, Alasdair. *After Virtue. A Study in Moral Theory*. 3rd edn. South Bend, IN: University of Notre Dame Press, 2007.
Maliukova, Larisa. "Aleksandr Zel'dovich: neskol'ko knizhek – eto strana." *Novaia gazeta* (Feb. 10, 2011). http://www.novayagazeta.ru/arts/7173.html (accessed Sept. 4, 2018).
Mamardashvili, Alena. "Alena Mamardashvili: 'Eto v pervuiu ochered' reaktsiia udivlennogo cheloveka, kotoryi v izumenii podnial brovi ...'" *Chastnyi korrespondent* (Sept. 17, 2010). http://www.chaskor.ru/article/alena_mamardashvili__eto_v_pervuyu_ochered__reaktsiya_udivlennogo_cheloveka_kotoryj_v_izumlenii_podnyal_brovi_20497 (accessed April 17, 2015).
———. "A. Mamardashvili to DeBlasio," Sept. 27, 2018.
Mamardashvili, Elena (ed.). *Vstrecha. Merab Mamardashvili – Lui Al'tiusser*. Fond Meraba Mamardashvili, 2016.
Mamardashvili, Merab. "Besedy o myshlenii." Mamardashvili.com No. 7. http://mamardashvili.com/archive/lectures/thinking/bm07.html (accessed May 7, 2017).
———. "Byt' filosofom – eto sud'ba." In *Kak ia ponimaiu filosofiiu*. Ed. Iu. P. Senokosov. 2nd edn. Moscow: Progress – Kul'tura, 1992: pp. 27–40.
———. "D'iavol igraet nami, kogda my ne myslim tochno ..." In *Kak ia ponimaiu filosofiiu*. Ed. Iu. P. Senokosov. 2nd edn. Moscow: Progress – Kul'tura, 1992: pp. 126–42.
———. "Drugoe nebo." In *Kak ia ponimaiu filosofiiu*. Ed. Iu. P. Senokosov. 2nd edn. Moscow: Progress – Kul'tura, 1992: pp. 320–39.
———. "Esli osmelit'sia byt'." In *Kak ia ponimaiu filosofiiu*. Ed. Iu. P. Senokosov. 2nd edn. Moscow: Progress – Kul'tura, 1992: pp. 172–200.
———. *Estetika myshleniia*. Ed. Iu. P. Senokosov. Moscow: Moskovskaia shkola politicheskikh issledovanii, 2000. http://rumol.ru/files/library/books/mamardashvili/m.mamardashvili_estetika%20mishleniya.pdf (accessed Sept. 17, 2018).
———. "Evropeiskaia otvetstvennost'." In *Soznanie i tsivilizatsiia*. St Petersburg: Lenizdat, 2013: pp. 36–42.
———. "Fenomenologiia – soputstvuiushchii moment vsiakoi filosofii." In *Kak ia ponimaiu filosofiiu*. Ed. Iu. P. Senokosov. 2nd edn. Moscow: Progress – Kul'tura, 1992: pp. 100–6.
———. "Filosofiia – eto soznanie vslukh." In *Kak ia ponimaiu filosofiiu*. Ed. Iu. P. Senokosov. 2nd edn. Moscow: Progress – Kul'tura, 1992: pp. 14–26.
———. "Filosofiia i lichnost'." *Chelovek* 5 (1994): pp. 5–19.

———. *Formy i soderzhanie myshleniia*. St Petersburg: Azbuka, 2011.
———. "Kak ia ponimaiu filosofiiu." In *Kak ia ponimaiu filosofiiu*. Ed. Iu. P. Senokosov. 2nd edn. Moscow: Progress – Kul'tura, 1992: pp. 114–26.
———. *Kantianskie variatsii. Put' k ochevidnosti*. Moscow: Agraf, 2002.
———. *Kartezianskie razmyshleniia*. Ed. Iurii Senokosov. Moscow: Progress – Kul'tura, 1993.
———. *Lektsii o Pruste (Psikhologicheskaia topologiia puti)*. Ed. E. B. Oznobkina, I. K. Mamardashvili, and Iu. P. Senokosov. Moscow: Ad Marginem, 1995.
———. Merab Mamardashvili Personnel File. 1976. Fond No. 1, Inventory No. 8-L, Storage No. 223. Archives of the Gerasimov Institute of Cinematography.
———. "Moi opyt ne tipichen." In *Kak ia ponimaiu filosofiiu*. Ed. Iu. P. Senokosov. 2nd edn. Moscow: Progress – Kul'tura, 1992: pp. 356–64.
———. *Neobkhodimost' sebia*. Moscow: Labarint, 1996.
———. "O filosofii." *Voprosy filosofii* 5 (1991): pp. 3–25.
———. *Ocherk sovremennoi evropeiskoi filosofii*. Moscow: Azbuka-Attikus, 2012.
———. "Odinochestvo – moia professiia. Interv'iu Uldisa Tironsa." Mamardashvili.com. https://mamardashvili.com/files/pdf/euro/28%20Одиночество%20-%20моя%20профессия....pdf (accessed June 5, 2017).
———. "Problema cheloveka v filosofii." *Silentium* 1 (1991): pp. 231–41.
———. "Problema soznaniia i filosofskoe prizvanie." In *Kak ia ponimaiu filosofiiu*. Ed. Iu. P. Senokosov. 2nd edn. Moscow: Progress – Kul'tura, 1992: pp. 41–56.
———. "Problemy analiza soznaniia." Mamardashvili.com, Lecture No. 10. http://www.mamardashvili.com/archive/lectures/consciousness/10.html (accessed Sept. 4, 2018).
———. *Psikhologicheskaia topologiia puti. M. Prust: "V poiskakh utrachennogo vremeni."* Ed. Elena Mamardashvili. Moscow: Fond Meraba Mamardashvili, 2014.
———. "Soznanie – eto paradoksal'nost', k kotoroi nevozmozhno privyknut'." In *Kak ia ponimaiu filosofiiu*. Ed. Iu. P. Senokosov. 2nd edn. Moscow: Progress – Kul'tura, 1992: pp. 72–85.
———. "Soznanie i tsivilizatsiia." In *Soznanie i tsivilizatsiia*. St Petersburg: Lenizdat, 2013: pp. 7–35.
———. "The Civil Society. A Conversation with Merab Mamardashvili." *The Civic Arts Review* (summer 1989): pp. 4–8.
———. "'Tret'e' sostoianie." In *Kak ia ponimaiu filosofiiu*. Ed. Iu. P. Senokosov. 2nd edn. Moscow: Progress – Kul'tura, 1992: pp. 163–71.
———. "Veriu v zdravyi smysl." Mamardashvili.com. https://www.mamardashvili.com/archive/interviews/common_sense.html (accessed Sept. 4, 2018).
———. *Vil'niusskie lektsii po sotsial'noi filosofii (Opyt fizicheskoi metafiziki)*. St Petersburg: Azbuka, 2012.
———. "Vremia i prostranstvo." Mamardashvili.com. https://mamardashvili.com/archive/interviews/timespace.html (accessed Aug. 4, 2017).
———. *Vvedenie v filosofiiu*. http://psylib.org.ua/books/mamar02/index.htm (accessed May 23, 2017).

Mamardashvili, Merab and Aleksandr Piatigorskii. *Simvol i soznanie. Metafizicheskie rassuzhdeniia o soznanii, simvolike i iazyke.* Moscow: Shkola "Iazyki russkoi kul'tury," 1999.

Mamardashvili, Merab and Natan Eidel'man. "O dobre i zle." In *Professiia – kinematografist.* Ed. P. D. Volkova, A. N. Gerasimov, and V. I. Sumenova. Ekaterinburg: U-Faktoriia, 2004: pp. 283–310.

Mamuliia, Dmitrii. "Dmitrii Mamuliia: 'My zhivem v strashnoe vremia.' Interview with Maria Baker," Kinote.info (Dec. 7, 2010). http://kinote.info/articles/4063-dmitriy-mamuliya-my-zhivem-v-strashnoe-vremya (accessed Dec. 7, 2010).

———. "Dmitrii Mamuliia: 'Neponimanie – samyi vazhnyi organ'" *Seans* (June 11, 2010). http://seance.ru/blog/dmitriy-mamuliya-neponimanie-samyiy-vazhnyiy-organ/ (accessed Sept. 17, 2018).

———. "Dmitrii Mamuliia: Nikto ne ponimaet, gde nakhoditsia i zachem." Interview with Larisa Maliukova. *Novaia gazeta* (July 7, 2015). http://www.novayagazeta.ru/arts/2805.html.

———. "Mamuliia to DeBlasio." May 23, 2017.

———. "Shpion, osedlavshii tigra. Dmitrii Mamuliia i ego fil'm 'Drugoe nebo.'" Interview with Dmitrii Volchek. Svoboda.org (July 15, 2016). http://www.svoboda.org/content/transcript/2100742.html (accessed Sept. 4, 2018).

———. "Situatsiia Ivana Il'icha." *Seans* (September 22, 2010). http://seance.ru/blog/ivan-ilyich-situation/ (January 20, 2019).

Mannheim, Karl. "The Problem of Generations." In *Karl Mannheim: Essays.* Ed. Paul Kecskemeti. New York: Routledge, 1972: pp. 276–322.

Marx, Karl. "Preface." In *A Contribution to the Critique of Political Economy.* Moscow: Progress, 1977. https://www.marxists.org/archive/marx/works/1859/critique-pol-economy/preface.htm (accessed Aug. 30, 2018).

Matizen, Viktor. "Rezhisser Andrei Zviagintsev." *Novye izvestiia* (Aug. 14, 2009). https://newizv.ru/news/culture/14-08-2009/113243-rezhisser-andrej-zvjagincev (accessed Sept. 4, 2018).

Medvedev, Aleksei. "Zhanr kak metafora." In *Balabanov. Perekrestki.* Ed. A. Artamonov and V. Stepanov. St Petersburg: Seans, 2017: pp. 79–90.

Merleau-Ponty, Maurice. *Sens et non-sens.* Paris: Gallimard, 1945.

Mezhuev, Boris. "Dekart v mire Kafki." *Russkii zhurnal* (Nov. 24, 2010). http://www.russ.ru/layout/set/print/pole/Dekart-v-mire-Kafki (accessed May 12, 2018).

Mitta, Aleksandr. "Gamburgskaia shkola rodilas' u menia na kukhne." Interview with Vlad Vasiukhin. Kinoshkola Aleksandra Mitty, 1999. http://mitta.ru/otzyvy/statji-i-publikacii/36-a-mitta-gamburgskaya-shkola-rodilas-u-menya-na-kukhne (accessed May 23, 2016).

"*Morphia* [*Morfii*]." Program Notes. University of Pittsburgh Russian Film Symposium, 2011. http://www.rusfilm.pitt.edu/2009/morphia.php (accessed Oct. 11, 2018).

Motroshilova, Nelli. *Merab Mamardashvili. Filosofskoe razmyshlenie i lichnostnyi opyt*. Moscow: Kanon+, 2007.
Nenashev, Mikhail. "O Merabe Mamardashvili." *Binokl'*. http://binokl-vyatka.narod.ru/B12/nenash.htm (accessed May 3, 2018).
Neugroschel, Joachim. "Introduction." In *The Metamorphosis, In the Penal Colony, and Other Stories*. Trans. Joachim Neugroschel. New York: Simon & Schuster, 1995: pp viii–xxiii.
Nieman, Anna. "A Picnic on the Road to the Temple." *KinoKultura* 40 (2013). http://www.kinokultura.com/2013/40-nieman.shtml (accessed May 4, 2018).
Nikolchina, Miglena. "Inverted Forms and Heterotopian Homonymy: Althusser, Mamardashvili, and the Problem of 'Man.'" *boundary 2* 41, No. 1 (2014): pp. 79–100.
Nizhnikov, S. A. "M. K. Mamardashvili ob osobennostiakh funktsionirovaniia religioznogo soznaniia." *Ezhegodnaia bogoslovskaia konferentsiia Pravoslavnogo Sviato-Tikhonovskogo Gumanitarnogo Universiteta* 25: pp. 172–5.
Nodia, Giorgi. "'Back to the Man Himself': The Philosophical Inspiration of Zurab Kakabadze." Ed. A. T. Tymieniecka. *Analecta Husserliana* XXVII (1989): pp. 1–7.
Orlova, Alisa. "'*Faust*' Aleksandra Sokurova: kreditnaia istoriia d'iavola." *Tat'ianin den'* (Jan. 30, 2012). http://www.taday.ru/text/1445414.html (Sept. 4, 2018).
Padunov, Vladimir. "Alienation and the Everyday: The Films of Aleksandr Mindadze and Vadim Abdrashitov." *Newsletter. Institute of Current World Affairs* (March 19, 1987): pp. 1–9.
Padunov, Vladimir and Nancy Condee. "Recent Soviet Cinema and Public Responses: Abdrashitov and German." *Framework* (Jan. 1, 1985): pp. 0–29.
Paisova, Elena. "Aleksandr Zel'dovich: Ne stat' geran'iu." *Iskusstvo kino* 3 (March 2011). http://kinoart.ru/archive/2011/03/n3-article5 (accessed Sept. 4, 2018).
Paramonov, Andrei. "Svobodnaia mysl' Meraba Mamardashvili: Interv'iu s issledovateliem filosofa." *Sputnik* (Sept. 15, 2017). https://sputnik-georgia.ru/interview/20170915/237345280/Svobodnaja-mysl-Meraba-Mamardashvili-intervju-s-issledovatelem-filosofa.html (accessed Sept. 17, 2018).
Pavsek, Christopher. *The Utopia of Film: Cinema and Its Futures in Godard, Kluge, and Tahimik*. New York: Columbia University Press, 2013.
Phillips, Brian. Interview with Iurii Norshtein. Trans. Alyssa DeBlasio, May 2016.
Pickford, Henry W. "Of Rules and Rails: On a Motif in Tolstoy and Wittgenstein." In *Tolstoy Studies Journal* XXII (2010): pp. 39–53.
Pippen, Robert B. *The Philosophical Hitchcock: Vertigo and the Anxieties of Unknowingness*. Chicago: University of Chicago Press, 2017.
Plakhov, Andrei. "Balabanov kak prokliatyi poet." In *Balabanov. Perekrestki*. Ed. A. Artamonov and V. Stepanov. St Petersburg: Seans, 2017: pp. 7–12.

———. "Virtual'nyi proekt ideal'nogo budushchego, pridumannogo kremlevskimi politekhnologami. Aleksandr Zel'dovich o fil'me 'Mishen'.'" *Kommersant'* (Feb. 16, 2011). http://kommersant.ru/doc/1586065 (accessed Sept. 4, 2018).

Plato. "Letter 7." *Plato, Letters*. Trans. R. G. Bury. Cambridge, MA.http://www.perseus.tufts.edu/hopper/text?doc=Perseus%3atext%3a1999.01.0164 (accessed Sept. 17, 2018).

———. *Timaeus and Critias*. Trans. Robin Waterfield. New York: Oxford University Press, 2008.

Platonov, Andrei. *Kotlovan*. St Petersburg: Lenizdat, 2014.

Ponech, Trevor. "The Substance of Cinema." In *Thinking Through Cinema. Film as Philosophy*. Ed. Murray Smith and Thomas E. Wartenberg. Hoboken, NJ: Blackwell Publishers, 2006: pp. 187–98.

Pontini, Elisa. "The Aesthetic Import of the Act of Knowledge and Its European Roots in Merab Mamardašvili." *Studies in East European Thought* 58 (2006), pp. 161–78.

Prokhorov, Alexander. "The Unknown New Wave: Soviet Cinema of the Sixties." In *Springtime for Soviet Cinema. Re/Viewing the 1960s*. Ed. Alexander Prokhorov. Pittsburgh, 2001. http://www.rusfilm.pitt.edu/booklets/Thaw.pdf. pp. 7–28 (accessed April 17, 2015).

Rayfield, Donald. "Orchards and Gardens in Chekhov." *The Slavonic and East European Review* 67.4 (Oct. 1989): pp. 530–45.

Renanskii, Dmitrii. "*Mishen'* Desiatnikova." Openspace.ru (March 1, 2011). http://os.colta.ru/music_classic/events/details/20803/ (accessed Sept. 4, 2018).

Repin, Natalie. "*Being-Towards-Death* in Tolstoy's *The Death of Ivan Il'Ich*: Tolstoy and Heidegger." *Canadian-American Slavic Studies* 36.1–2 (2002): pp. 101–32.

Riazantseva, Nataliia. "Adresa i daty." *Znamia* 11 (2011). http://magazines.russ.ru/znamia/2011/11/ra4.html (accessed Aug. 30, 2018).

Rivin, Il'ia. "Razzhalovannyi. Iz pis'ma ispolniteliu glavnoi roli I. Rivinu." In *Sokurov. Chasti rechi*. St Petersburg: Seans, 2011: pp. 475–6.

Rolengof, Ol'ga and Nabi Balaev. *Besedy o gruzinskom Kante*. Video material. 2007.

Savel'ev, Dmitrii. "Krugi Razzhalovannogo." In *Sokurov. Chasti rechi*. St Petersburg: Seans, 2011: pp. 37–43.

Scanlan, James P. "Tolstoy among the Philosophers: His Book *On Life* and its Critical Reception." In *Tolstoy Studies Journal* XVIII (2006): pp. 52–69.

Sedakova, Ol'ga. "Zhertvy veka ili samouchki 'predatel'stva sebia': k analizu 1970-x godov." Gefter.ru (Jan. 1, 2014). http://gefter.ru/archive/11164 (accessed Aug. 30, 2018).

Sel'ianov, Sergei. "Skazki, siuzhety i stsenarii sovremennoi Rossii." Polit.ru (May 1, 2004). http://polit.ru/article/2004/05/01/selianov/ (accessed Aug. 30, 2018).

Selivanov, Timur. "Svobodnaia mysl' Meraba Mamardashvili: Interv'iu s issledovatelem filosofa." *Svobodnaia Gruziia*. http://svobodnaya.info/ru/society/1620-svobodnaya-mysl-meraba-mamardashvili-intervyu-s-issledovatelem-filosofa (accessed Sept. 4, 2018).

Senokosov, Iurii. "Merab Mamardashvili: vekhi tvorchestva." Po kom zvonit kolokol (July 6, 2009). https://www.mgarsky-monastery.org/kolokol.php?id=1104 (accessed Sept. 4, 2018).

———. "Vstrecha Meraba Mamardashvili s otsom Aleksandrom Menem." *Vestnik Moskovskoi Shkoly Grazhdanskogo Prosveshcheniia* 68 (2015): pp. 2–3.

———. "Vstupitel'noe slovo." In *Kongenial'nost' mysli. O filosofe Merabe Mamardashvili*. Moscow: Progress – Kul'tura, 1994: pp. 9–13.

Shchedrovitskii, Georgii. *Ia vsegda byl idealistom*. Moscow: Put', 2001.

Shestov, Leo, "The Last Judgment: Tolstoy's Last Works." In *Tolstoy: A Collection of Critical Essays*. Ed. Ralph E. Matlaw. Prentice Hall: Englewood Cliffs, NJ, 1967: pp. 157–72.

Shilova, Irina. *. . . i moe kino*. Moscow: NII Kinoiskusstva/Kinovedcheskie zapiski, 1993.

Shklovskii, Viktor. *O teorii prozy*. Moscow: Sovetskii pisatel', 1983.

Sobol, Valeria. "In Search of an Alternative Love Plot: Tolstoy, Science, and Post-Romantic Love Narratives." *Tolstoy Studies Journal* 19 (2007): pp. 54–75.

Sokurov, Aleksandr. "Pamiati Meraba Mamardashvili." *Seans* 3 (July 1991). http://seance.ru/n/3/mamard_sokurov/ (accessed Sept. 4, 2018).

———. *Razzhalovannyi*. Mosfil'm, 1980.

———. *V tsentre okeana*. St Petersburg: Amfora, 2011.

Solntseva, Alena. "Govoriat, chto schast'e gde-to est'." Stengazeta.net (Oct. 3, 2012). https://stengazeta.net/?p=10008810 (accessed May 14, 2018).

———. "Introduction to Zvyagintsev's *Loveless*." Presented at the 20th Russian Film Symposium, Pittsburgh, May 2, 2018.

———. "Ten' Gastarbaitera." *Seans* 43/44 (2010). http://seance.ru/n/43-44/novyiy-geroy-gastarbayter/ten-gastarbaytera/ (accessed Aug. 15, 2018).

Solov'ev, Erik. "Filosofiia kak kritika ideologii. Chast' II." *Filosofskii zhurnal* 10, No. 3: pp. 5–31.

———. "Prostornoe slovo avtoritetov. Beseda T. A. Umanskoi i E. Iu. Solov'ev." In *Kak eto bylo. Vosponinaniia i razmyshleniia*. Ed. V. A. Lektorskii. Moscow: ROSSPEN, 2010.

———. "The Existential Soteriology of Merab Mamardashvili." *Russian Studies in Philosophy* 49, No. 1 (summer 2010): pp. 53–73.

Stam, Robert. "Beyond Fidelity: The Dialogics of Adaptation." In *Film Adaptation*. Ed. James Naremore. New Brunswick, NJ: Rutgers University Press, 2000: pp. 54–76.

Stishova, Elena. "Ekh, dorogi . . ." *Iskusstvo kino* 10 (Oct. 10, 2001). http://old.kinoart.ru/archive/2001/10/n10-article19 (accessed Jan. 31, 2019).

———. "Na glubine. 'Vozvrashchenie,' rezhisser Andrei Zviagintsev." *Iskusstvo kino* 1 (Jan. 2004). http://www.kinoart.ru/archive/2004/01/n1-article4 (accessed Sept. 17, 2018).

Strukov, Vlad. *Contemporary Russian Cinema. Symbols of a New Era*. Edinburgh: Edinburgh University Press, 2016.

Sukhorukov, Viktor. "Portret. Aleksei Balabanov." *Seans* 17/18. http://seance.ru/n/17-18/portret-4/2505/ (accessed Oct. 6, 2017).

Suny, Ronald Grigor. *The Making of the Georgian Nation*. 2nd edn. Bloomington: Indiana University Press, 1994.

Sychev, Sergei. "Balabanov snimaet fil'm 'Ia tozhe khochu' v ekstremal'nykh usloviiakh." Filmpro.ru (March 22, 2012). https://www.filmpro.ru/materials/16286 (accessed May 14, 2018).

Tirons, Uldis. "I Come to You from My Solitude." *Eurozine* (June 2006). http://www.eurozine.com/articles/2006-06-22-tirons-en.html (accessed Sept. 4, 2018).

Tolstoi, Lev. *Polnoe sobranie sochinenii*. 90 vols. Ed. V. G. Chertkov. Liechtenstein: Nendeln, 1972.

Tolstoy, Leo. *A Confession*. Trans. Anthony Briggs. London: Hesperus, 2010: p. 82.

———. *On Life and Essays on Religion*. Trans. Aylmer Maude. London: Oxford University Press, 1934.

———. *The Death of Ivan Il'ich, Tolstoy's Short Fiction*. Ed. Michael R. Katz. 2nd edn. New York: Norton, 2008: pp. 83–128.

———. "The Law of Violence and the Law of Love." In *Russian Philosophy*. Vol. II. Ed. James M. Edie, James P. Scanlan, and Mary-Barbara Zeldin. Chicago: Quadrangle, 1965: pp. 213–34.

———. "Three Deaths." In *Tolstoy's Short Fiction*. Ed. Michael R. Katz. 2nd edn. New York: Norton, 2008: pp. 45–56.

———. *Tolstoy's Diaries*. 2 vols. Ed. and trans. R. F. Christian. New York City: Faber & Faber, 1985.

———. *War and Peace*. Trans. Louise and Aylmer Maude. Ed. George Gibian. New York: Norton, 1966.

Trahan, Elizabeth. "The Divine and the Human, or Three More Deaths: A Late Chapter in Leo Tolstoy's Dialogue with Death." In *Tolstoy Studies Journal* 3 (1990): pp. 33–48.

Tsyrkun, Nina. "Seansu otvechaiut: pro urodov i liudei." *Seans* 17/18 (May 1999). http://seance.ru/n/17-18/rezhisser-film-kritik-2/pro-urodov-i-lyudey/pro-urodov-i-lyudey-2/ (accessed Sept. 4, 2018).

Tuchinskaia, Aleksandra. "Annotatsiia." In *Ostrov Sokurova*. http://sokurov.spb.ru/isle_ru/feature_films.html?num=4 (accessed April 20, 2015).

Türken, Alper. "Hegel's Concept of the True Infinite and the Idea of a Post-Critical Metaphysics." In *Hegel and Metaphysics: On Logic and Ontology in the System*. Ed. Allegra de Laurentiis. Berlin: De Gruyter, 2016: pp. 9–25.

Vagina, Mariia. "Shestidesiatnikam zdes' ne mesto." Mnenie.ru (Dec. 24, 2012). http://mnenia.ru/rubric/culture/shestidesyatnikam-zdes-ne-mesto/ (accessed March 2, 2015).

Van der Zweerde, Evert. "Philosophy in the Act: The Socio-Political Relevance of Mamardašvili's Philosophizing." *Studies in East European Thought* 58 (2006): pp. 179–203.

Vaughan, Hunter. *Where Film Meets Philosophy. Godard, Resnais, and Experiments in Cinematic Thinking*. New York: Columbia University Press, 2013.

Vernant, J. P. "Georgian Socrates." Trans. M. Kharbedia. *Arili* 14 (2000): pp. 6–8.

Vizgin, Viktor. "My vse ego tak liubili: vspominaia Meraba Mamardashvili." Mamardashvili.com, 2009. http://mamardashvili.com/about/vizgin/2.html (accessed May 23, 2017).

Vladiv-Glover, Slobodanka. "Poststructuralism in Georgia. The Phenomenology of the 'Objects-Centaurs' of Merab Mamardashvili." *Angelaki: Journal of the Theoretical Humanities* 15, No. 3 (Dec. 2010): pp. 27–39.

Vlasov, M. "Vysokaia tsena istiny." *Iskusstvo kino* 1 (1983): pp. 22–35.

Volkov, Aleksandr. "Redaktsiia zhurnala 'Problemy mira i sotsializma' 1958–1990. Vospominaniia sotrudnikov i sovremennikov. Chast' I." *Russkii zhurnal* (Oct. 9, 2013). http://russ.ru/pole/Redakciya-zhurnala-Problemy-mira-i-socializma-1958-1990 (accessed Aug. 3, 2018).

Volkova, Paola. "Merab na vysshikh kursakh," In *Merab Mamardashvili: "Byt' filosofom – eto sud'ba ..."* Ed. N. V. Motroshilova, A. A. Paramonov, and E. V. Petrovskaia. Moscow: Progress-Traditsiia, 2013: pp. 278–91.

———. "Ob"iasnenie neob"iasnimogo." In *Professiia – kinematografist*. Ed. P. D. Volkova, A. N. Gerasimov, and V. I. Sumenova. Ekaterinburg: U-Faktoriia, 2004: pp. 207–82.

———. "Paola Volkova o Merabe Mamardashvili." Youtube.com, March 18, 2015. https://www.youtube.com/watch?v=vW-fEGo2b4k (accessed May 23, 2018).

———. "Paola Volkova o tom, chto bol'she ne povtoritsia." Arzamas Academy. Course No. 9. http://arzamas.academy/materials/217 (accessed Aug. 3, 2018).

Wayne, Mike and Ewa Mazierska. "The Dialectical Image: Kant, Marx, and Adorno." In *Marx at the Movies: Revisiting History, Theory, and Practice*. New York: Palgrave Macmillan, 2014: pp. 27–45.

Weckowicz, T. E. and H. P. Liebel-Weckowicz. *A History of Great Ideas in Abnormal Psychology*. Vol. 66. Amsterdam: Elsevier, 1990.

White, Frederick H. "Aleksei Balabanov's 'Cinema About Cinema.'" *Essays in Honor of Alexander Zholkovsky*. Ed. Dennis Ioffe, Marcus Levitt, Joe Peschio, and Igor Pilshchikov. Boston: Academic Studies Press, 2018: pp. 621–41.

Whitehead, Claire. "Anton Chekhov's 'The Black Monk': An Example of the Fantastic?" *The Slavonic and East European Review* 85.4 (Oct. 2007): pp. 601–28.

Wilmes, Justin. "From *Tikhie* to *Gromkie*: The Discursive Strategies of the Putin-Era Auteurs," *Russian Literature* 96–8 (2018): pp. 297–327.
Wittgenstein, Ludwig. *Tractatus Logic-Philosophicus*. Trans. D. F. Pears and B. F. McGuinness. London and New York: Routledge, 2007.
Wurm, Barbara. "Review of Aleksandr Zel'dovich: *The Target* (*Mishen'*, 2011)." *KinoKultura* 32 (2011). http://www.kinokultura.com/2011/32r-mishen.shtml#1 (accessed Sept. 4, 2018).
Zaloutkha, Valerii. "My nazyvali kursy litseem." In *Professiia – kinematografist*. Ed. P. D. Volkova, A. N. Gerasimov, and V. I. Sumenova. Ekaterinburg: U-Faktoriia, 2004.
Zaozerskaia, Anzhelika. "Aleksei Balabanov: Ia khochu v rai, chtoby vstretit'sia so svoim papoi," (May 18, 2013). http://vm.ru/news/2013/05/18/aleksej-bababanov-ya-hochu-v-raj-chtobi-vstretitsya-so-svoim-papoj-196790.html (accessed Sept. 4, 2018).
Zel'dovich, Aleksandr. "Bog i supermarket." *Rossiiskaia gazeta* (March 29, 2013). http://www.rg.ru/2013/03/28/d2b-zeldovich-intro.html (accessed May 2, 2017).
———. "Zel'dovich to DeBlasio." Sept. 8, 2014.
Zen'kovskii, Vasilii. "Problema bessmertiia u L. N. Tolstogo." In *L.N. Tolstoi. Pro et contra*. SPb: Iz-vo RKhGI, 2000: pp. 509–24.
Zviagintsev, Andrei. "Bez vertikali nel'zia nichego postroit'." AZ Film (May 26, 2011). http://az-film.com/ru/Publications/52-Bez-vertikali-nelzja-nichego-postroit.html (accessed Sept. 4, 2018).
———. "'Chitaia proizvedenie, smotria fil'm, nuzhno iskat' svoi portret, chtoby uzhasnut'sia samomu sebe. Interview by Kira Al'tman." *BFM* (May 19, 2017). https://www.bfm.ru/news/354871 (accessed Sept. 10, 2018).
———. "Rezhisser Andrei Zviagintsev na vstreche so zriteliami v Iaroslave: preslovutyi 'kheppiend' dolzhen sluchit'sia v vashei zhizni, a ne na ekrane." *Iaroslavskaia oblast'* (Aug. 8, 2017). https://7x7-journal.ru/item/97457 (accessed Sept. 4, 2018).
———. "Zviagintsev: My snimali 'Neliubov',' chtoby zriteli obniali svoikh blizkikh."*Argumentyifakty*(May31,2017).http://www.aif.ru/culture/movie/zvyagincev_my_snimali_nelyubov_chtoby_zriteli_obnyali_svoih_blizkih (accessed Sept. 4, 2018).

Index

Abdrashitov, Vadim, 147
absurd
   contrasted with nihilism, 107
   the human condition and, 108–9, 154–5
   illusion of choice in, 112–13
   lack of pity in, 105–6
   literary mode of, 106
   literature of the absurd in Balabanov's work, 102, 105–6, 109, 116
   as narrative and aesthetic mode for Balabanov, 103–7, 114
   political dimension of, 112–13
   in relationship to faith, 110–12
   "The 'Third' Condition," 108, 155
   zombie image, 109–10, 155
   see also Kafka, Franz
Abuladaze, Tengiz, 153, 154, 156–7
The Aesthetics of Thinking, 42–3, 147, 151, 154, 156, 157, 166
Akhutin, Anatolii, 12, 21, 39
All-Union State Institute of Cinematography (VGIK), 2, 45, 57
   Mamardashvili's tenure at, 30, 31, 35–6, 48, 113
Althusser, Louis, 34, 84, 85, 86
Ambartsumov, Evgenii, 33
Anisimova, Irina, 139
Another Sky (Mamuliya)
   absence of consciousness in, 92
   absence of language in, 80, 90–1, 92, 94
   critical recognition, 80
   inaccessibility of individuals, 90
   Kazakh New Wave elements in, 80
   liminality in, 93–4
   narrative, 79, 81, 91
   national identity in, 92
   news soundbites, 91, 165
   silence as symptom of crisis, 80–1, 82
   sounds of Moscow, 91–2
   title of, 95
aporia
   and the human condition, 154
   as an impassable space, 42–3, 155, 156
   of philosophical dilemmas, 67
Arabov, Yuri, 100
Arkhangelsky, Alexander, 2
Aronson, Oleg, 9
Avtonomova, Nataliia, 35

Baklanov, Grigorii, 46, 47, 48
Balabanov, Alexei
   the absurd as narrative and aesthetic mode, 103–7, 114
   anti-heroes, 106
   Brother, 102, 103, 114, 115
   career of, 57, 101–2
   The Castle, 103, 114, 117–18
   cinematic style, 102–3, 115–16
   exploitation of actors' pain, 115–16
   fantastical realism of, 106–7
   Happy Days, 102, 115
   interactions with Mamardashvili, 2, 3, 160
   literature of the absurd in the work of, 102, 105–6, 109, 116
   Me Too, 102, 103, 104–5, 107–8, 115–17, 118–19
   modernism of, 101
   Morphia, 102, 103, 104, 107, 114
   as Soviet-trained director, 100–1, 114
   spiritual symbolism, 104–5, 107
   The Stoker, 103, 104
   style indirect libre, 115, 117, 118–19
   theme of journey in, 102–5
   Trofim, 102–3
   unifying themes in this work, 114–15
   use of the absurd, 114
Balaian, Valerii, 6, 31
Bartlett, Rosamund, 59, 70
Beckett, Samuel, 101, 116
behaviorism, 36
Bellefroid, Pierre, 33–4
Benjamin, Walter, 85, 86, 170–1

The Black Monk (Chekhov)
  the figure of the monk, 73
  narrative, 58–9, 61, 62
  Pesotsky's gardens and Kovrin's mental state, 70–1
The Black Monk (Dykhovichnyi)
  cinematography in, 58, 60–2, 72
  the figure of the monk, 73
  fragility of identity in, 64
  Kovrin's hallucinations and agency, 62–3
  landscape and topology in, 71–2
  mental illness and personal creativity, 64, 65, 66–7, 68–9
  screenplay, 59
  shifts in perspective, 60–2
  water/weather imagery, 72
Bondarev, Vladimir, 85
Brezhnev, Leonid, 34
Buck-Morss, Susan, 170

Camus, Albert, 103, 116, 167
Cavell, Stanley, 5, 31, 164, 168, 169
Chalmers, David, 30
Chekhov, Anton
  The Black Monk, 58–9, 61, 62, 70–1, 73
  consciousness in literature, 58
  mental illness in the works of, 59
  use of horticultural imagery, 70–1, 73
Cherniaev, Anatolii, 33
Chernobyl disaster, 151
chimera of idleness, 74–5
civil death concept, 95
Communist Party (USSR), 33
Condee, Nancy, 48, 151
consciousness
  access to through philosophy, 43, 88
  the act of lovelessness and, 166
  behaviorist approaches to, 36
  cinema as means for exploration of, 147–8
  as connection to others, 38, 90
  consciousness as witness, 38–9
  empirical analysis of, 42
  as fleeting, 41
  as the greatest unknown, 69, 73, 110
  higher dimension of, 44
  and the human mind, 45
  indivisibility of, 64–5, 67
  as infinite, 134
  inner garden metaphor, 73–4
  language of, 87–90, 95
  Mamardashvili's philosophy of, 4, 37–41
  meta-theory of consciousness, 38
  mind/external world relationship, 37–8, 44
  mirror metaphor and, 40
  non-physicalist reading of, 69
  paradox of, 30, 36, 40–1, 42–3, 44, 64, 108
  phenomenological approaches, 36–7, 39
  as a place, 42–3
  primacy of, 21
  and the process of thought, 149–50
  recording of, 43–5, 88
  relationship with text, 69–70
  self-consciousness as madness in *The Black Monk*, 62–3
  sick consciousness, 83, 90–1, 109, 165
  Soviet dialectical materialism and, 42, 44
  Soviet-Marxist approaches to, 37, 38
  thought as the voice of, 43–4, 70, 149–50
  unified voice of, 153–4
  unity of, 64–5
"Consciousness and Civilization" (lecture), 82–3
Critchley, Simon, 169
Czechoslovak New Wave, 33

death
  civil death concept, 95
  Tolstoy's philosophical position on, 128–9, 130–2, 136–7
defamiliarization, 40
Degutis, Algirdas, 8
Demoted (Sokurov)
  authentic human interactions, 47–8
  cinematic style, 46, 47, 49
  day in the life-style portrait, 46
  the driver's logic of consciousness, 49–50, 92
  fragment of a lecture by Merab Mamardashvili, 48, 49–50, 51–2
  The Lonely Voice of Man in, 50
  overview of, 45–6
  power-shifts within, 46
  water imagery, 50–1
Descartes, René
  Cartesian *cogito*, 17, 18, 19, 21, 110, 156–7
  consciousness as thought, 43

Descartes, René (*cont.*)
  consciousness/being relationship, 38, 115
  the Ego, 42
  "I," 18–19
  infinity and, 134
  Mamardashvili's philosophical roots in, 16–17, 21
  philosophy of freedom, 17–18
dialectical image
  cinema's dialectical potential, 152–3
  as space between meanings, 170–1
dialectical materialism, 14, 21, 32, 42, 86
Dostoevsky, Fedor, 68, 106–7, 168
Dularidze, Tamara, 6, 160
Dykhovichnyi, Ivan
  cinematic postmodernism and, 59
  early career, 58
  Europe-Asia, 60
  interactions with Mamardashvili, 2, 3, 57–8, 160
  Moscow Parade, 59
  see also *The Black Monk* (Dykhovichnyi)

Eisenstein, Sergei, 152–3
Erofeev, Venedikt, 92

Faibyshenko, Viktoriia, 15, 84–5
fantastical realism, 106–7
film
  adaptations of novels, 160
  cinema as an exploration of consciousness, 147–8
  cinema's dialectical potential, 152–3
  cinematic generations, 4
  Czechoslovak New Wave, 33
  film analysis by Mamardashvili, 147, 148, 152–3, 155–6, 167–8
  the movie theatre as a conceptual space, 156
  as phenomenological material for Mamardashvili, 40
film, Russian
  film-philosophy affinity, 3, 5, 22–3, 30–1, 161
  journey motifs, 104
  Kazakh New Wave, 80
  literary texts and, 168
  Mamardashvili's generational influence on, 3–5, 160, 172–4
  the "new quiet ones," 79–80
  scholarship on, 3
  winter landscapes, 104

film art
  adaptation and representation, 171
  and the analysis of consciousness, 147–8, 156
  the dialectical image and, 170–1
  and human thought, 152–3, 164, 168
  philosophy and, 40, 168–9
Fokina, Olesia, 23
Forms and Content of Thought, 7, 15, 41
freedom
  Cartesian philosophy of, 17–18
  creative period of the Thaw, 32
  of creativity, 68–9
  and the human condition, 68
  Mamardashvili's intellectual freedom, 10–11, 31–2, 34–5
  Mamardashvili's sartorial freedom, 9–10, 32, 93
  as a possibility, 18
  "Pushkinian freedom" concept, 11, 18
  as topic of Mamardashvili's work, 9
Freud, Sigmund, 42

Gamsakhurdia, Zviad, 78–9, 100
Gasparyan, Diana, 36, 38, 44
Georgia
  civil society in, 11, 83, 86
  elections in, 100
  Georgian language, 83–4
  independence movement, 78, 112
  Mamardashvili's Georgian identity, 12, 84, 86, 87
  need for social engagement of the people, 86–7
Godard, Jean-Luc, 147, 152, 157, 160, 169
goodness, quality of, 65–6
Gorbachev, Mikhail, 33
Grushin, Boris, 14, 32, 33, 35

Hegel, Georg Wilhelm Friedrich, 15, 134–5, 168
Hegelian Marxism school, 14
Heidegger, Martin, 169
Higher Courses for Scriptwriters and Directors, 2, 57, 81, 100, 125
human condition
  as absurd, 108–9, 154–5
  aporia and, 154
  concept of madness and, 69
  Europeanness, concept of, 94–5
  freedom and, 68
  as greater than national identity, 87
  grotesques as metaphors for, 106

human predestination and the eternal
    soul, 111–12
  internal/external relationship, 16, 37–8,
    166
  the "knot" (*uzel*) of, 154–5
  language as attribute of, 89–90
  Mamardashvili's concept of, 164
  movie theatre metaphor for, 156
  as process of becoming, 87
  as transcendental mystery, 110
  two worlds of, 108–9, 111
human thought
  agency of the "I," 18–19
  Cartesian *cogito*, 17, 18, 19, 21, 110,
    156–7
  concept of, 149, 154
  as distinct from ideology, 153
  as distinct from thinking, 149, 150
  film as a form of, 152–3, 164, 168
  "I think, I exist, I can," 21, 156–7
  "I think" (*Ia mysliu*) as a spiritual act,
    19, 112
  immortality through, 150
  Mamardashvili's writing on *The Train
    Stopped* (Abdrashitov and Mindadze),
    148–9, 153
  to think for oneself, 13
  unknowability of, 150–1, 155
  as the voice of consciousness, 43–4, 70,
    149–50
humanism
  anti-humanism in *Another Sky*
    (Mamuliya), 94
  in *Demoted* (Sokurov), 47–8
  Mamardashvili's turn to, 84–5
Husserl, Edmund, 39, 42, 171

Ilenkov, Evald, 8, 14, 15
immortality
  collectivity and, 129
  concept of, 128
  immortality/infinity tensions in
    Tolstoy, 128–30
  Mamardashvili on eternal life, 141–2
  through shared human thought, 150
  see also Target (Zeldovich)
individuality
  in *The Black Monk*, 64–5, 66–7, 71
  and the desire for immortality, 129
  individual/collective being relationship,
    135
  indivisibility of, 64–5, 67, 72
  and the process of thought, 149

indivisibility
  and the conception of mental illness, 66
  of consciousness, 64–5, 67
  of creativity and mental illness, 66, 72
  ethical dimension, 65–6
  of individuality, 64–5, 67, 72
  the sum of life concept, 67–8, 71
infinite
  concept of, 128
  conflation with the eternal, 124
  consciousness as, 134
  finite/infinite relationship, 134–5,
    138–9
  Hegelian concept of, 134–5
  immortality/infinity tensions in
    Tolstoy, 128–30
  Mamardashvili's philosophy of, 133–7
  spurious infinite, 134–5
  the Tolstoyan paradox, 129–30
  understanding of, 124
Iulina, Nina, 35

Kafka, Franz
  The Castle, 103, 106, 107–8, 113, 117
  illusion of choice in, 112–13
  in Mamardashvili's work, 108, 109
  The Metamorphosis, 105–6, 113–14
  style indirect libre, 115
  The Trial, 103
Kant, Immanuel
  concept of mental illness, 69, 74
  consciousness/being relationship, 38
  cosmopolitanism, 87
  infinity and, 134
  Mamardashvili's philosophical roots in,
    16–17, 19–22
  on mental illness, 64
  transcendental, 20, 110
Karst, Roman, 113, 116
Khotinenko, Vladimir, 2, 3
Kierkegaard, Søren, 168
Kovalov, Oleg, 45
Kundera, Milan, 160

language
  absence of in *Another Sky* (Mamuliya),
    80, 90–1, 92, 94
  of consciousness, 87–90, 95
  dialogues of *The Train Stopped*
    (Abdrashitov and Mindadze), 152
  Georgian language, 83–4
  human thought and, 82
  language play of Mamardashvili, 88–9

language (*cont.*)
  Mamardashvili's linguistic skills, 34, 83
  religious language, 111
  sick consciousness as problem of, 90
  silence in *Another Sky* (Mamuliya), 80–1, 82
  as singularly human attribute, 89–90
  the spoken word, 152
  transmission of the authentic word, 51
  the voice of consciousness, 43–5, 88
  word/image relationship, 172–4
literature
  adaptations of novels, 160–1, 171
  consciousness's relationship to the text, 69–70
  literary references in Mamardashvili's work, 40, 58, 84, 147
  literature of the absurd in Balabanov's work, 102, 105–6, 109, 116
  philosophical study of aesthetic texts, 168
  Target (Zeldovich) as cinematic novel, 127–8
  see also Chekhov, Anton; Kafka, Franz; Tolstoy, Leo
Lotman, Yuri, 68, 69
Loveless (Zvyagintsev)
  failures in communication, 165
  the human condition, 166
  narrative, 162
  nature/civilization relationship, 163
  news soundbites, 165

Makharadze, Filipp, 83–4
Malick, Terrence, 169
Mamardashvili, Alena, 8
Mamardashvili, Merab
  civil death of, 95
  death of, 37, 95, 100
  Descartes influence on, 16–19, 21–2
  early 1950s image of, *14*
  early 1970s image, *10*
  in the film *Should the Sighted Lead the Blind?* 85
  Georgian identity, 84, 86, 87
  influence on Russian cinema, 2–3
  intellectual freedom of, 10–11, 31–2, 34–5
  Kant's influence on, 16–17, 19–22
  lecture topics, 6, 9, 17, 41, 63
  lectures as cultural events, 1–2, 6–7, 31, 35
  linguistic skills, 34, 83
  Marxist-Soviet training, 13–14, 15, 37
  Marx's relevance to, 16
  meeting with Mamuliya, 93
  nevyezdnoi classification, 9–10, 32
  1970s work, 15–16, 35
  oratory skills, 6–7, 8
  political trajectory of, 84–6
  political works (1980s), 11–12, 78–9, 87, 100, 155
  published works, 7–8
  sartorial freedom, 9–10, 32, 93
  speech patterns of, 34–5
  status among the Moscow intelligentsia, 1–2
  time in Prague, 33
  transcriptions of his lectures, 8, 10–11
  at VGIK, 30, 31, 35–6, 48, 113
  vision of civic society, 13
  zest for life, 33–4
Mamuliya, Dmitry
  founding of the Moscow School of New Cinema, 81–2
  influence of the Kazakh New Wave on, 80
  interactions with Mamardashvili, 3, 79, 93, 160
  interests in philosophy and prose, 81, 82
  as one of the "new quiet ones," 79–80
  see also Another Sky (Mamuliya)
Mannheim, Karl, 4, 172
mental illness
  in Chekhov's work, 59
  fragility of identity in *The Black Monk*, 64
  hallucinations and agency in *The Black Monk*, 62–3
  the indivisibility of individuality and, 64–5, 66, 72
  Kant's concept of madness, 69, 74
  Kant's taxonomy of, 64
  in Mamardashvili's work, 64
  and personal creativity (*The Black Monk*), 64, 65, 66–7, 68–9
  Pesotsky's gardens and Kovrin's mental state (*The Black Monk*), 70–1
metaphors
  black box metaphor of consciousness, 36
  of consciousness as fleeting, 41
  of the inner garden, 73–4
  Mamardashvili's Socratic metaphor, 7
  Mamardashvili's use of, 12, 18

INDEX

mirror, 40, 83
    of the movie theatre and the human condition, 156
    musical metaphors, 41
    Newtonian metaphor in Tolstoy, 130–1, 133
    for thought and thinking, 149
    of trains in Tolstoy, 138, 141
    zombies and the absurd, 109–10, 155
Mindadze, Alexander, 147
morality
    conflation of the infinite and the eternal, dangers of, 124
    ethical dimension of indivisibility, 65–6
    internal moral codes, 136
    moral nature of consciousness, 4, 12
    the sum of life concept, 67–8, 71
    Tolstoyan lived moral progress, 132–3, 135–6
Moscow Logic Circle, 15
Moscow School of New Cinema, 81–2
Motroshilova, Nelli, 21

Nemirovskaia, Elena, 87
Neugroschel, Joachim, 115
Newton's Law of Universal Gravitation, 130–1, 133
Nodia, Giorgi, 16
Norshtein, Yuri, 2, 3, 160
Nussbaum, Martha, 160–1

Padunov, Vladimir, 148
paradox
    of consciousness, 30, 36, 40–1, 42–3, 44, 64, 108
    dualistic pairs within Mamardashvili's work, 67
    of freedom, 68
    investigation of language and, 89–90
    the "knot" (*uzel*) of the human condition, 154–5
    within Mamardashvili's philosophical method, 64
    in Tolstoy's thought on immortality, 129–30
phenomenology
    approaches to consciousness, 36–7
    film as phenomenological material, 40
    Mamardashvili's appropriation of, 39–40, 171
    Marcel Proust and, 40
    space of consciousness, 42–3
    transcendental phenomenology, 39, 42

philosophy
    access to consciousness through, 43, 88
    contrasted with religion, 112
    film art and, 168–9
    film-philosophy affinity, 3, 5, 22–3, 30–1, 161, 168–70
    Mamardashvili's criticism of Soviet philosophy, 82
    Mamardashvili's philosophy, 4, 9, 12–13, 43, 82, 86
    on Russian curricula, 4–5
    the *shestidesiatniki* generation, 32
    Soviet philosophy, 31, 32, 35
Piatigorsky, Alexander, 8, 30, 41, 42, 87–8, 111
Pippen, Robert, 168
Plato, 65, 82, 87
Platonov, Andrei, 49
poetry
    defamiliarization through, 40
    poetic device in *Another Sky* (Mamuliya), 81
    references to in Mamardashvili's work, 12, 40
Prague, 33
Problems of Peace and Socialism, 33, 34, 35
Proust, Marcel
    expression of consciousness in, 69
    life as effort in time, 171
    literary analysis of, 16, 34
    Mamardashvili's cycle of lectures, 16, 34, 58, 63–4, 84
    Mamardashvili's reading of in Prague, 33
    as phenomenologist, 40
Pushkin, Alexander, 4, 17–18
Putin, Vladimir, 80

Rayfield, Donald, 70–1, 73
Rekhviashvili, Alexander, 91
religion
    Balabanov's spiritual symbolism, 104–5, 107
    contrasted with philosophy, 112
    faith and the absurd, 110–12
    human predestination and the eternal soul, 111–12
    "I think" (*Ia mysliu*) as a spiritual act, 112
    religious language, 111
    Sermon on the Mount, 136
Repentance (Abuladze), 153, 154, 156–7
Riazantseva, Nataliia, 2, 10, 32, 153

Rowlands, Mark, 39
Rubenshtein, Sergei, 37

Savelev, Dmitrii, 46, 48, 50
Scanlan, James, 133, 135–6
Senokosov, Iurii, 10–11
Shchedrovitskii, Georgii, 8, 14
Shilova, Irina, 35
Shklovsky, Viktor, 40
Should the Sighted Lead the Blind? (Bondarev), 85
Shpet, Gustav, 39
Socrates, 6, 7, 9, 41, 88
Sokurov, Alexander
  interactions with Mamardashvili, 2, 3, 6, 160
  The Lonely Voice of Man, 45, 50
  on Mamardashvili's intellectual freedom, 10, 31–2, 35
  at the VGIK, 45
  see also *Demoted* (Sokurov)
Solntseva, Alena, 165, 166
Solovyov, Erik, 15, 128
Solovyov, Sergei, 59
Sorokin, Vladimir, 124, 125, 127
Soviet structural Marxism, 14–15
Soviet Union (USSR)
  creative period of the Thaw, 32
  end of, 100
  liberal values, post-Stalin era, 31–2
  as non-European, 94–5
  sickness of consciousness in, 90–1
  Soviet intelligentsia and Mamardashvili's liberal values and, 31–2, 34
  Stagnation period, 34
Stishova, Elena, 80, 162
Strukov, Vlad, 3, 101, 160
Symbol and Consciousness, 7, 41, 87–8

Target (Zeldovich)
  aesthetics of, 126–7
  Anna's suicide, 138
  broken universal bonds, 138–9
  as cinematic novel, 127–8
  as film of the novel *Anna Karenina*, 124, 125, 127
  immortality in, 126, 133, 137–8, 139
  measurements of good and evil, 140–1
  narrative, 124, 125–6, 137
  narrative roots, 127–8
  normative rupture in, 139–40
  removal of death, 126

  social reading of, 139
  Tolstoyan true life and, 137–8
Tarkovsky, Andrei, 2, 169
Tbilisi State University, 1, 34, 36, 58, 63, 64, 84, 147, 148, 166, 171
thinking
  concept of, 149, 154
  as distinct from thought, 149, 150
  non-thinking, 156, 166–7
"Time and Space," 44
Tolstoy, Leo
  The Death of Ivan Ilych, 130–1, 132–3
  immortality/infinity tensions, 128–30
  Newtonian metaphor in, 130–1, 133
  paradox of infinity and social milieu, 129–30
  The Pathway of Life, 130, 131, 133, 138
  philosophical position on death, 128–9, 130–2, 136–7
  philosophical study of aesthetic texts, 168
Tolstoy–Mamardashvili connection, 128
train metaphors, 138, 141
true, lived life as progress, 132–3, 135–6
War and Peace, 131–2, 135, 136
The Train Stopped (Abdrashitov and Mindadze)
  as example of human thought, 148–9, 153, 167
  human choices and the crash, 151
  narrative, 147–8
  parallels with the Chernobyl disaster, 151
  as a series of dialogues, 152
  unknowability of human thought, 150–1, 155
transcendentalism
  Kantian thought, 20, 110
  and paradox, 20–1, 110
  and unknowability, 20–1, 44
Tuchinskaia, Aleksandra, 46
Türken, Alper, 134–5

unknowability
  consciousness as the greatest unknown, 69, 73, 110
  of human thought, 150–1, 155
  and transcendence, 20–1, 44

VGIK (All-Union State Institute of Cinematography) *see* All-Union State Institute of Cinematography (VGIK)

Vizgin, Viktor, 31
Volkova, Paola, 6, 9, 31, 34, 35, 88–9, 113

Wayne, Mike, 170
Whitehead, Claire, 59, 61
Wittgenstein, Ludwig, 129–30, 168, 169
The World Marxist Review, 33
Wurm, Barbara, 125

Yurchak, Alexei, 4

Zalotukha, Valerii, 31
Zeldovich, Alexander
　career of, 125
　interactions with Mamardashvili, 2, 3, 160
　Moscow, 125
　study under Mamardashvili, 128
　see also Target (Zeldovich)
Zinoviev, Alexander, 8, 14, 15
Zvyagintsev, Andrey
　Banishment, 162
　career of, 161–2
　cinematic style, 162–3
　commonalities across the works of, 163–4, 167
　Elena, 162, 163, 165
　interactions with Mamardashvili, 2
　Leviathan, 162, 165
　references to Mamardashvili, 161, 164, 167
　The Return, 161–2, 165
　technology and failures in communication, 165
　see also Loveless (Zvyagintsev)
Zweerde, Evert van der, 21–2, 149

EU representative:
Easy Access System Europe
Mustamäe tee 50, 10621 Tallinn, Estonia
Gpsr.requests@easproject.com

www.ingramcontent.com/pod-product-compliance
Lightning Source LLC
Chambersburg PA
CBHW051811230426
43672CB00012B/2689